Stratification and Inequality Series
The Center for the Study of Social Stratification and Inequality,
Global COE Program
Tohoku University, Japan
Volume 14

Global Migration and Ethnic Communities

Stratification and Inequality Series

The Center for the Study of Social Stratification and Inequality,
Global COE Program
Tohoku University, Japan

Inequality amid Affluence: Social Stratification in Japan
Junsuke Hara and Kazuo Seiyama

Intentional Social Change: A Rational Choice Theory
Yoshimichi Sato

Constructing Civil Society in Japan: Voices of Environmental Movements
Koichi Hasegawa

Deciphering Stratification and Inequality: Japan and beyond
Yoshimichi Sato

Social Justice in Japan: Concepts, Theories and Paradigms
Ken-ichi Ohbuchi

Gender and Career in Japan
Atsuko Suzuki

Status and Stratification:
Cultural Forms in East and Southeast Asia
Mitsuhiko Shima

Globalization, Minorities and Civil Society:
Perspectives from Asian and Western Cities
Koichi Hasegawa and Naoki Yoshihara

Fluidity of Place: Globalization and the Transformation of Urban Space
Naoki Yoshihara

Japan's New Inequality: Intersection of
Employment Reforms and Welfare Arrangements
Yoshimichi Sato and Jun Imai

Minorities and Diversity
Kunihiro Kimura

Inequality, Discrimination and Conflict in Japan:
Ways to Social Justice and Cooperation
Ken-ichi Ohbuchi and Nobuko Asai

Social Exclusion: Perspectives from France and Japan
Marc Humbert and Yoshimichi Sato

Global Migration and Ethnic Communities:
Studies of Asia and South America
Naoki Yoshihara

Series Editor: Yoshimichi Sato, Tohoku University
Editorial Board: Koichi Hasegawa, Ken-ichi Ohbuchi, Toshiaki Kimura, Kunihiro Kimura,
Yoshimichi Sato, Naoki Yoshihara, Mary C. Brinton, Jeffrey P. Broadbent

Stratification and Inequality Series
The Center for the Study of Social Stratification and Inequality,
Global COE Program
Tohoku University, Japan
Volume 14

Global Migration and Ethnic Communities

Studies of Asia and South America

Edited by

Naoki Yoshihara

First published in 2012 by
Trans Pacific Press, PO Box 164, Balwyn North, Victoria 3104, Australia
Telephone: +61 (0)3 9859 1112 Fax: +61 (0)3 9589 4110
Email: tpp.mail@gmail.com
Web: http://www.transpacificpress.com

Copyright © Trans Pacific Press 2012

Designed and set by Digital Environs, Melbourne, Australia. www.digitalenvirons.com

Printed by BPA Print Group, Burwood, Victoria, Australia

Distributors

Australia and New Zealand
DA Information Services/Central Book Services
648 Whitehorse Road
Mitcham, Victoria 3132
Australia
Telephone: +61-3-9210-7777
Fax: + 61-3-9210-7788
Email: books@dadirect.com
Web: www.dadirect.com

USA and Canada
International Specialized Book Services (ISBS)
920 NE 58th Avenue, Suite 300
Portland, Oregon 97213-3786
USA
Telephone: 1-800-944-6190
Fax: 1-503-280-8832
Email: orders@isbs.com
Web: http://www.isbs.com

Asia and the Pacific
Kinokuniya Company Ltd.

Head office:
3-7-10 Shimomeguro
Meguro-ku
Tokyo 153-8504
Japan
Telephone: +81-3-6910-0531
Fax: +81-3-6420-1362
Email: bkimp@kinokuniya.co.jp
Web: www.kinokuniya.co.jp

Asia-Pacific office:
Kinokuniya Book Stores of Singapore Pte., Ltd.
391B Orchard Road #13-06/07/08
Ngee Ann City Tower B
Singapore 238874
Telephone: +65-6276-5558
Fax: +65-6276-5570
Email: SSO@kinokuniya.co.jp

All rights reserved. No production of any part of this book may take place without the written permission of Trans Pacific Press.

ISBN 978-1-920901-76-9 (Hardback)
ISBN 978-1-920901-94-3 (Paperback)

Contents

List of Figures	vi
List of Photos	vi
List of Tables	vii
List of Contributors and copy editor	ix
Preface *Naoki* Yoshihara	xiii

Part I: Global Migration and Labor

1. Highly Skilled Professionals and International Migration: A Labor Analysis of Indian IT Engineers in Japan *Akiko* Murata ... 3
2. Patients on the Move: The Development of Medical Tourism in Asian Countries *Mika* Toyota ... 24
3. Rain of Gold Overseas, Rain of Stone at Home?: The Unchanging Fortune of Indonesian Migrant Domestic Workers *Raphaella D.* Dwianto ... 39

Part II: Global Migration, Ethnicity and Communities

4. The Rising Number of Muslim Migrants and Global Tourism: The Case of Pemogan Village in Denpasar, Bali *Yukiko* Nagano ... 61
5. Community and Regional Security in the Immigrant District of Bali Island *Kosuke* Hishiyama ... 84
6. Ajeg Bali and Closed-off Town Planning: The Redevelopment of Denpasar's Central Urban Areas *Naoki* Yoshihara ... 106
7. Economics of the Formation and Development of the Okinawan Urban Ethnic Community: From the Perspective of the Accumulation of Self-Employed Business Strategies *Kōichi* Mori ... 122
8. Migration, Economic Adaptation and Mutual Cooperation: Japanese Rotating Savings and Credit Associations in Argentina *Masahiro* Tsujimoto ... 163
9. The Role of Ethnicity in International Migration: The Re-Migration of Latin Americans from Japan to the US *Ayumi* Takenaka ... 176

Part III: Migrant Education and Generations

10. The Development and Use of Resources in Educating Immigrant Children *In ja* Lee ... 195
11. Japanese Immigrants in Brazil and 'Colonia-go': Japanese as an Immigrant Language *Yasue* Nakato ... 211

Notes	232
Bibliography	245
Index	259

List of Figures

1.1:	The path from Brazil to employment in Japan	7
1.2:	The main paths followed by IT engineers from India who work abroad	7
3.1:	Reasons for becoming a migrant worker	45
3.2:	Indonesian migrant workers, 2009	46
3.3:	Use of remittance by Indonesian migrant workers	50
5.1:	PKD's organizational chart (2006)	98
5.2:	Pecalang's organizational chart (2006)	99
6.1:	Location of Gajah Mada Road	108
6.2:	Built environment on Gajah Mada Road	109
7.1:	Map of São Paulo City, Vila Carrão and surrounding districts	125
8.1:	Rotation of money within a ROSCA	164
8.2:	Occupations of the Japanese in the prewar period	167
8.3:	Record of re-migrants from Bolivia to Argentina	170
11.1:	Annual change in the number of Japanese arrivals in Brazil	216

List of Photos

6.1:	Gajah Mada Road in the Dutch colonial era	110
6.2:	Gajah Mada Road in the 1920s	110
6.3:	Tree planting	114
6.4:	Removal of buildings	114
6.5:	Gajah Mada Road after tree planting	116

List of Tables

1.1: One Indian IT company's dispatch of engineers to Japan in 2008   15
1.2: Advertisements for IT programmers by required level of Japanese language proficiency   19
1.3: One Indian engineer's pattern of rotation to Japan   21
3.1: Destination of Indonesian migrant workers, 2009   45
3.2: Remittance data, 2009   47
3.3: Summary of migrant worker's troubles, January 1 to November 1, 2010   48
3.4: Cases of abuse faced by Indonesian migrant domestic workers   51
3.5: Comparison of wages and fees of migrant domestic workers in Malaysia, 2008   51
3.6: Management of Indonesian migrant workers   54
3.6: Continued   55
4.1: Changes in the number of foreign tourists making direct voyages to Bali (persons)   63
4.2: Population changes in Bali (1985–2006)   63
4.3: Changes in land use in Bali (ha)   65
4.4: Changes in population and household numbers in Pemogan village   66
4.5: Changes in the number of applicants for temporary resident ID cards in Pemogan village (persons)   67
4.6: Previous place of residence of KIPEM extension applicants (September 2005)   67
4.7: Population and number of households in Pemogan village in each district (in 2005)   68
4.8: Details of the 375m^3 of solid waste   73
5.1: Population by religion in Tuban and Bali   93
5.2: Religions of registered persons of KIPS and STPPTS at Pesalakan Tuban in 2006   95
5.3: The employment of registered persons of KIPS and STPPTS at Pesalakan Tuban in 2006   95
5.4: Cross tabulation of religion and employment of registered persons of KIPS and STPPTS   96
5.5: Overlapping membership in PKD and Pecalang (2006)   100

6.1:	Bali's urbanisation in terms of population (by regency)	112
7.1:	The relocation and settlement of Okinawan migrants in Vila Carrão (early period)	128
7.2:	Changes in the membership size of the Vila Carrão branch of the Okinawa Association of Brazil	128
7.3:	Okinawa Association members in Vila Carrão by occupation (1984)	130
7.4:	Number of workers in each member family by occupation (2006)	133
7.5:	Changes in the occupational composition of Oroku Tabaru Village Association members	134
7.6:	Major self-employed businesses of Okinawan migrants in Vila Carrão (2006)	135
7.7:	A summary of Okinawan trade organizations in Vila Carrão	156
7.8:	The formation and development of the Okinawan ethnic community in Vila Carrão (an economic perspective)	160
11.1:	The Nikkeijin population in Brazil and population ratios by region (1958 and 1988)	214
11.2:	Ratios of Nikkeijin generations (1958 and 1988)	214
11.3:	Ratios of languages used by the Nikkeijin at home (1958 and 1988)	214
11.4:	Periods of the Japanese immigrant community in Brazil and number of arrivals	216
11.5:	Number and ratio of arrivals by phase and place of origin (1908–1962)	221

List of Contributors

Raphaella D. Dwianto is Senior Lecturer in the Department of Sociology, Universitas Indonesia, as well as the Head of the International Office of the university. Her key area of interest is urban sociology. Selected publications include: 'Unchanging fortunes of Jakarta informal sector workers' (2008, in K. Hasegawa and N. Yoshihara (eds.) *Globalization, Minorities and Civil Society: Perspectives from Asian and Western Cities*, Melbourne: Trans Pacific Press), 'Urban grassroots in Asian society' (in Japanese) (2006, in N. Yoshihara and K. Niitsu (eds.), *Globalization and Asian Societies: The Horizon of Post-colonialism*, Toshindo publishing co. ltd.) and 'Neighborhood association and community building—Chonaikai in two residential areas in Morioka City' (2003, in N. Yoshihara and R.D. Dwianto (eds.), *Grass Roots and the Neighborhood Associations—on Japan's Chonaikai and Indonesia's RT/RW*, Grasindo).

Kosuke Hishiyama is Associate Professor in the Department of Law, Economics and the Humanities at Kagoshima University. His area of research is urban sociology, regional and community studies and local safety and security theory. Publications include: 'Uneasy society in Indonesia: With special attention to the gated community and CCTV in Bali' (2010, *Procedia - Social and Behavioral Sciences*, 2(1): 14–23) and 'Local security in post-Suharto Bali: From inequality to equality of participation' (2008, in M. Shima (ed.), *Status and Stratification: Cultural Forms in East and Southeast Asia*, Trans Pacific Press, 163–79).

In ja Lee is Associate Professor in the Graduate School of Education of Tohoku University. Her main area of research is anthropological studies on migrants in Japan. Selected publications include 'Plurality of representing identity in migrant culture: A case study on tombs of Koreans in Japan' (1996, *Japanese Journal of Cultural Anthropology*, 61(3): 393–422), 'Dependence on and independence of hometown: An anthropological study on early Korean immigrants in Japan' (2007, in Y. Sekine and T. Shintani (eds.), *Haijosuru Shakai, Juyousuru Shakai:*

Gendai Kegare ron, Yoshikawa Kobunkan) and 'Koreans living in Japanese town: A comparative study on newcomers and oldcomers' (2006, in T. Shintani and M. Iwamoto (eds.), *Toshi no Kurashi no Minzokugaku 2: Toshi no Hikari to Yami*, Yoshikawa Kobunkan, 174–208).

Koichi Mori is Professor at the University of São Paulo, Faculty of Philosophy, Letters and Human Sciences. His primary area of research is cultural anthropology and Okinawan studies. Recent publications include: *Imigrantes Japoneses no Brasil-Trajetórias, Imaginários e Memôrias* (2011, Edusp (Editora de Universidade de São Paulo)), *Conflict Studies in the Humanities (Special Issue)—Migration and Identities: Conflict and the New Horizon* (2011, Osaka University Global COE Program), *Contribuições de Imigrantes Japoneses no Brasil Multicultural e Moderno* (2010, (ed.), Paulo's) and *Burajiru Nihon Imin Hyakunen no Kiseki* (2010, Akashi Shoten).

Akiko Murata is Lecturer at the Center for International Education, Kansai University. Her primary area of research is cultural anthropology. Her recent publications include: 'An analysis of the career development of highly skilled foreign workers' (2011, *Intercultural Education*, 33: 81–97), 'International migration of highly skilled workers: Analysis of the temporary migration of Indian IT engineers and contract labor in Japan' (2010, *Migration Policy Review*, 2: 74–89) and 'The meaning of bricolage in pluri-lingual situations: The analysis of two engineering communities' (2009, *Literacies*, 6(2): 1–9).

Yukiko Nagano is Professor in the School of Human Sciences, Senshu University. Her main areas of research are in the fields of rural sociology and comparative family studies. Selected publications include: Ie *and Women in Modern Rural Society: Continuity and Discontinuity in the History of Shōnai District, Yamagata Prefecture* (in Japanese) (2005, Tōsui Shobō) and *Survival Strategies of* Ie *and Marriage: Japan, Asia, Europe* (in Japanese) (2009, (ed.), Tōsui Shobō).

Yasue Nakato is Associate Professor in the Graduate School of Humanities and Social Sciences, Okayama University. Her key area of research is sociolinguistics. Selected publications include: 'Paraguai nikkei shakai ni okeru akusento no keishō to henyō; Paraguai no Hiroshima kenjin kazoku wo taishō ni' (Inheritance and change of Japanese word accent in a Japanese immigrant community in Paraguay: A case of immigrants from Hiroshima Prefecture and their families) (2011, *Shakai Gengo kagaku*, 13(2): 72–87), *Burajiru Nikkei Okinawa-kei imin Shakai ni Okeru Gengo Sesshoku* (Language contact in the communities of Japanese and Okinawan descendants in Brazil) (2009, coedited with M. Kudō et al., Hitsuji Shobō) and 'Burajiru nikkei imin shakai ni okeru gengo seikatsu: Burajiru nikkeijin no gengo nōryoku ishiki to ishiki ni kakawaru shoyōin' (Language Life in Brazilian nikkey community: Language ability and some factors relevant to language ability) (2007, *The 21st Century COE Program Interface Humanities Research Activities 2004–2006, vol. 6 Language Contact and Admixture*, Osaka University, 315–333).

Ayumi Takenaka is Associate Professor at Bryn Mawr College and the Center for the Study of Social Stratification and Inequality, Tohoku University. Her research interests include comparative immigration studies and social inequality. Recent publications include: 'How contexts of reception matter: Comparing Peruvian migrants' economic trajectories in Japan and the U.S.' (forthcoming, co-authored with Karsten Paerregaard, *International Migration*) and 'Peruvian Migration in a Global Context' (2010, co-editor of a special issue, *Latin American Perspectives*, 37(5)).

Mika Toyota is Assistant Professor in the Department of Sociology, National University of Singapore. Her research interests include transnationalism, border, gender, international retirement migration, migration of health care workers and medical tourism. Dr Toyota has published more than 30 academic articles and book chapters in English and Japanese, including: 'Editorial introduction: International marriage, rights and the state in East and Southeast Asia' (2008, *Citizenship Studies*, 12(1): 1–7), 'Ambivalent categories: "Hill tribes" and "illegal migrants" in Thailand' (2007, in P.K. Rajaram and C. Grundy-Warr (eds.), *Borderscapes: Hidden Geographies and Insurrectionary Politics at Territory's Edge*, University of Minnesota Press, 91–116) and 'Bringing the "Left-behind" back into view in Asia: A framework for understanding the "migration-left behind nexus"' (2007, special issue of *Population, Space and Place*, 13(3): 157–161).

Masahiro Tsujimoto is Associate Professor at the Graduate School of Arts and Letters, Tohoku University. His primary area of research is social psychology. Publications include 'Status, selection, and exchange in an Okinawan mutual aid system' (2011, in K. Kimura (ed.) *Minorities and Diversity*, Trans Pacific Press, 100–112).

Naoki Yoshihara is Professor in the School of Social Information Studies, Otsuma Women's University. His key research interests include urban sociology and Asian studies. Selected publications include: *Grass Roots and the Neighborhood Associations—on Japan's Chonaikai and Indonesia's RT/RW* (2003, coedited with R.D. Dwianto, Grasindo), *Globalization, Minorities and Civil Society: Perspectives from Asian and Western Cities* (2008, coedited with K. Hasegawa, Trans Pacific Press) and *Fluidity of Place* (2010, Trans Pacific Press).

List of translators and copy editor

- Preface, Chapters 7 and 11: Minako Sato
- Chapter 1: Ross Mouer
- Chapters 4 and 6: Kikuko Onoda
- Chapter 5: Tomoko Onuki
- Chapter 8: Fumiko Tachibana Boleyn
- Chapter 10: Teresa Castelvetere
- Copy editor: Miriam Riley

Preface
Naoki Yoshihara

The movement of people across national borders is occurring on an unprecedented scale due to the advancement of globalization. At the same time, the movement itself takes a great variety of forms. This situation is of course closely linked to the transfiguration of the modern nation-state. The basis of its existence, national consciousness and national language, which Benedict Anderson cites as important conditions for the formation of the modern nation-state in his *Imagined Communities*, have become very shaky. As far as sociology is concerned, the field of mobility studies is attempting to discuss this phenomenon in a broader context by putting this situation in perspective. It is a branch of globalization studies that has made marked strides in recent years. I would like to discuss below the potential points at issue under the title *Global Migration and Ethnic Communities*, from the viewpoint of mobility studies, to open the discussion in this book.

Firstly, it is possible to point out that borderless movement is becoming multidirectional and multitiered. The movement under colonialism mostly entailed traveling between former suzerain states and their former colonies. Even in the postcolonial period, the main types of migration were chosen for state policy or economic reasons ('state policy migrant' and 'economic migrant'). In these cases, source and host countries were relatively limited. The usual pattern of movement therefore involved male emigrants who moved first, dragging along their society, workplace or state, and their families followed in their wake. Under this pattern, the classical type of migrants could be divided into two groups—non-migrants such as students and expatriate employees, and permanent migrants. As the globalization of economic activities has increased, however, there has been a marked rise in movement unimpeded by boundaries (national borders) and decoupled from the state, and the nature of migrants who are riding this wave can no longer be explained within a single framework.

The key question for the conventional form of migrant was to what extent would they assimilate into the host country, on the assumption that they would settle/permanently reside in that country. In other words, they were destined to become a 'model minority.' This is why the gaps between the 'model minority' stereotype and various diasporas that have been slow to assimilate have been regarded as a problem. Yet, the aforementioned assumption is losing its foothold as the borderless movement of people intensifies amid advancing globalization. Above all, there is the 'reverse flow' of people from former colonies to former suzerain states through the introduction of a foreign migrant workforce. In the case of Japan, for example, it takes the form of 'importation' of foreign labor to supplement its declining workforce due to the dwindling birthrate and aging population, and it obviously does not tie in with the notion of 'model minority.' Conversely, women have joined expatriate male employees in crossing national borders from former suzerain states to former colonies as the globalization of the manufacturing industry progresses. This form of movement is increasing noticeably in the case of Japan in particular, and is driven by non-career women who are disgruntled about gender-based discrimination/the division of labor in the workplace—being marginalized in a male-dominated sphere.

These women try to break out of Japanese-style gender relations by leaving Japan, but in many cases they end up playing the same gender role to a certain extent within the Japanese corporate community in the host country. In that context, they are positioned at the centre of the gender power relationship. Still, they certainly are light-footed women who move repeatedly across boundaries in search of a place of self-actualization. Speaking of light-footedness, it is impossible to ignore the existence of women who leave their native society in droves for international marriages as well as international retirement migrants who temporarily move overseas for 'long-stay.' In any case, various types of migrants who do not fit the classical model have emerged. They are called by such names as 'lifestyle migrants' and 'cultural migrants.' Regardless of their labels, we find two common traits: the increasing 'de-masculinization of migrants' and the extreme blurring of the boundary between non-migrants and migrants.

With regard to the diversification of migrants, it is notable that the second generation born of 'economic migrants' are making use of their knowledge nurtured by two nationalities and cultures in a positive manner, rather than asking themselves 'where did I come from?.' This group is producing some individuals who play the role of connecting different cultures by positioning themselves on the cultural boundaries. With the advancement of globalization and the increasing importance of cultural resources, the existence of such cultural mediators is attracting close attention. They are the people who freely move all over the world whom Cohen calls 'global diasporas' in his book of the same name.

In conjunction with the said diversification of the movement of people and migrants themselves, the transfiguration of ethnic communities is also notable. The ethnic community that has been mentioned in the same breath as the classical image of migrants is a closed uniform/homogeneous community with no contact with the local community. In other words, it is a community that functions as a shelter for the ethnic minority until they assimilate into the host country. However, even this type of community is changing into something more fluid with various relations with the local community, as the classical image of migrants is shattered by lifestyle migrants, cultural migrants, 'global diasporas' and migrant workers. At the same time, these people are forming social and familial ties across national borders and attracting interest as the drivers of the community who have adopted a lifestyle beyond the 'model minority' stereotype and developed an inter-state characteristic.

Nevertheless, these ethnic communities are still in a transitional stage and face impasses that are inevitable in that context. It is possible to say that they collectively represent the difficulties facing a transnational society brought about by globalization. The first thing we must point out is that these migrants are cut off from various kinds of social capital accumulated by their ancestors in the process of becoming a 'model minority' or 'positive minority' in their home country or society, and therefore they encounter all sorts of difficulties when developing a safety net in the host country because they break away from the classical mold of migrants and live in the inter-state space. It is certainly undeniable that permanent residency and the establishment of inter-state communities by these migrants are promoting diversity within the host societies. And it is also a fact that this has led to some change in the narrative of 'modeled ethnicity,' or the pressure to assimilate, in the host society. As they live dispersed, however, there is a risk that they cannot take advantage of the tradition of their common mother tongue and cultural education from the past and consequently fail to develop identity or self-representation that would otherwise be maintained through their connection to the home country or society. In fact, this paradoxical situation manifests most intensively in the case of emigrant workers. They are placed in a situation in which they are complicit in the depletion of labor resources in the native country while they are prevented from permanent residency by institutional barriers in the host society. For this reason, many are unable to establish the kind of lifestyle that is conducive to self-formation.

Conversely, the host society levels a harsh gaze at these emigrant workers. This gaze encompasses a line of sight that may well try to reject not just emigrant workers but all migrants, and possibly plays a part in the formation of monoculturalism. In that case, we cannot say for sure that the nightmare of Europe will not be repeated in Asia or South America. At any rate, it must be said that the scenario based on the tension-filled coexistence of multiculturalism and monoculturalism bringing about a form of dynamism in the transnational society is like treading on thin ice.

From the above discussion, it is clear that the issues lurking under the title *Global Migration and Ethnic Communities* are infinitely broad and wide-ranging. Although I have mentioned only a few of them here, I believe that they will boil down to the relationship between 'nationality and citizenship' in the end. All of the 11 contributed monographs presented in this volume are more or less concerned with this relationship, whether or not they directly refer to it. I shall introduce the contents of each chapter briefly.

The book is divided into three parts. Part I includes three chapters which focus on three forms of existence of emigrant workers in order to highlight the current situation of global migration. They also extract the problematic in the present state of play. Following Part I, the six chapters in Part II reveal various forms of migrants based on the constellation of such factors as safe and secure town planning, redevelopment and *kou* (rotating savings and credit associations) in local communities, in order to clarify various aspects of the transformation of ethnic communities, including the rural and the self-employed. Part III addresses migrant education and migrant language as the issues inherent to such ethnic communities and discusses the conditions and issues for the identity formation and generational succession of minority children who proactively live in a multicultural symbiotic society.

Chapter 1, by Akiko Murata, points out that the Indian IT engineers working in Japan are 'human resources for export' to Japan selected through intensive competition, and that this situation is closely aligned to market strategies and the needs of Japanese customers. It then exposes a gap between the situation in which these Indian engineers are placed and the rhetoric behind the promotion of the immigration policy to secure highly skilled foreign personnel. In the end, Chapter 1 looks at not only the Indian engineers' view that Japan should guarantee comfortable living conditions for them but also examines the overall system of retaining engineers and professionals as contract labor. While it proposes the simplification of the immigration process for ease of residency in order to improve the situation, it sees the absence of surety for a continuous stay as a problem in the first instance.

Chapter 2, by Mika Toyota, reports the Asia-wide development of private sector-led healthcare services based on neoliberalism supported by the urban middle class, then points to the existence of inequalities in access to healthcare between urban and rural areas and between private and public hospitals. It argues that the expansion of the private healthcare sector is causing influxes of professionals such as medical doctors and nurses across national borders into urban private hospitals as well as the shifting of the target market to middle-class patients and customers. Thus, the transnational movement in relation to healthcare services has seen Singapore become a major host country for healthcare professionals and the Philippines a major supplier of healthcare workers. Toyota proposes that the movement of healthcare professionals should be controlled according to a formal agreement between source and host countries, rather than catering for individual needs.

Chapter 3, by Raphaella D. Dwianto, focuses on issues facing transnational emigrant workers with official and legal citizenship status in Indonesia. Dwianto points out that citizenship is not a permanent arrangement; it is constantly rearranged at the state and international levels and reflects a hierarchy of states. Citizenship is in the midst of social, political and economic relations governed by collective conflicts and prone to fluctuation. Dwianto concludes that the 'rain of stone' experienced by Indonesia's emigrant workers overseas and in the home country suggests their unchanging destiny and demonstrates that the Indonesian state is of no help, even for those with official and legal citizenship.

Chapter 4, the first of Part II, by Yukiko Nagano, presents a detailed examination of conflict over the pollution of irrigation channels with factory effluent between Bali-born farmers and batik factory operators, who are primarily Muslim emigrants from Java, as well as tension over unpaid ID card registration fees between the Balinese people and impoverished emigrant workers from Java. Nagano finds that background factors to these issues include rapid urbanization and the transformation of rural land into suburban mixed-use areas, widening economic disparities among the Balinese people caused by tourism development, worsening economic imbalance that has spread across Indonesia since the Asian Currency Crisis and the transformation of post-Suharto decentralization into exclusionary localism triggered by terrorist bombing incidents.

Chapters 5, by Kosuke Hishiyama, and 6, by Naoki Yoshihara, are also set in the field of Bali. Chapter 5 presents a comparative analysis of the use of community policing in the US, Japan, Indonesia and Bali. It finds that the main purpose behind this initiative in Indonesia was to take temporary expedient measures toward the establishment of the public security system, following the collapse of the centralized regime by reorganizing the existing self-defense groups into a unified force. In Bali's Tuban District, however, community policing has become a complex mixture of the global and the local, the traditional and the secular and unity and diversity. This situation is demonstrated by discussing the interplay between the PKD, a traditional organization, and Siskamling, institutionalized in 1980. It concludes that the purpose of community policing is to promote community participation among local residents.

Chapter 6 discusses the case of town planning for the redevelopment of Denpasar's central district. It finds that although the official view touts it as community-led town planning using a local governance approach, the exclusion of Muslim emigrant workers who were drawn from Java with the expansion of tourism and the lack of support from local business-people makes the endeavor a piece of introverted, closed town planning. In reality, this tendency manifested itself when it combined with the Ajeg Bali movement for the revival of Balinese traditions and is highlighted as an example of monoculturalism. At the same time, it is argued that it is highly compatible with neoliberalism-based urban restructuring and that it is inseparable from the concept of 'beautiful cities,' guided by a zero tolerance approach.

In Chapters 7, by Kōichi Mori, and 8, by Masahiro Tsujimoto, the scene moves to South America. Chapter 7 looks at the urban ethnic community of people of Okinawan origin in Sao Paulo City, Brazil. Firstly, it examines in detail the findings of a preceding study by Takashi Maeyama. It then meticulously traces the economics of the formation and development process of the urban ethnic community, together with an analysis of statistical resources in relation to the opportunity structure of the local market, focusing on the cumulative development of self-employed business strategies in Carrão Village.

During the process of analyzing preceding studies on an empirical level, it pays close attention to the decisive role played by local areas in which forefathers immigrated and settled, arguing that these places were suitable locations for subsequent migrants to choose self-employed occupations, engage deeply in immigrant groups and form enclaves.

Chapter 8 discusses rotating savings and credit associations (ROSCAs) in the Japanese-Argentinean community. It vividly describes how the under-resourced people of Japanese descent have raised funds through ROSCAs to run small businesses or to cover expenses in times of crisis such as natural disasters or ill health. It reveals that certain measures such as the careful selection of ROSCA members are taken in order to prevent default. Nevertheless, losses from default are treated as necessary expenses so that the effective operation of ROSCAs is not interrupted by such events. This chapter discusses non-payers of ROSCA installments in parallel with free riders in collective action theory, and signals the prospect of opening up a new theoretical horizon beyond migration/mobility studies.

Chapter 9, by Ayumi Takenaka, closes Part II by discussing the role of ethnicity in global mobility on the basis of arguments presented in the preceding chapters. It addresses the remigration to the US of the Latin Americans accepted by Japan as immigrants with ethnic privileges, and advances its argument by inquiring into their reasons and motivations. While the said remigration can be seen as a phenomenon in which Japan is used as a stepping-stone to gain entry into the US, in this chapter it is discussed as one consequence of the ethnicity-based movement to Japan. It argues that the expansion of the ethnicity-related potential, that is, using the ethnic privileges conferred on themselves as the first step towards remigration to the US, makes the ethnic adaptation of Latin Americans in Japan problematic.

Finally, in Part III, Chapter 10, by In ja Lee, focuses on the state of education for the children of newly arrived Korean immigrants taking up residency in Japan, and describes the way migrants are strengthening the foundation of their daily living in Japan by utilizing the resources they temporarily relinquished—the native language-speaking environment and social capital accumulated in the home country—or somehow recreating the lost resources themselves. It shows that migrants are in fact extending the sphere of their activity and accumulating more resources as they ride on the crest of globalization. Needless to say, education not only serves as a medium to make it possible but also occupies a crucial position in passing available resources onto future generations. This chapter clearly discusses the role/position of education through instantiation.

Conversely, Chapter 11, by Yasue Nakato, returns to the Japanese emigrant community in Brazil and sheds light on the process of the rise and fall of Colonia-go, a hybrid of the Japanese and Portuguese languages. Nakato points out that while the process overlaps with the history of the struggles of the Japanese emigrant community, it was largely defined by Brazil's immigration restriction and assimilation policies—and yet Colonia-go has been used for a long time by the Nikkeijin community, including the descendants of those emigrants who have grown up as Brazilians. Nakato concludes that, nevertheless, Colonia-go is increasingly rejected as a language for Japanese language education and vanishing from the Japanese-Brazilian community. Although it is not directly mentioned, Chapters 10 and 11 implicitly pose the question of generational succession.

Acknowledgements

This book is published as part of the Center for the Study of Social Stratification and Inequality's series. I am very honored to have the chance to publish this volume through a grant offered by the CSSI. This book was initially planned to be co-authored/edited by myself, Ayumi Takenaka and Masahiro Tsujimoto, but I ended up becoming the sole editor for various reasons. I would like to take this opportunity to thank my two colleagues for their understanding. The editing stage of this book was a very difficult one, as I was editing *Ajia Hito no Idō jiten* (The encyclopedia of human mobility—Asia) at the same time, but I was fortunate enough to receive much learned advice in relation to the book's contents from Toshio Iyotani, Shinji Yamashita, Kazuo Yoshihara, Masami Sekine and Shinzō Araragi. Thoughtful attention to detail given by Airin Izumi of the CSSI Secretariat on a daily basis was also indispensable.

Most of all, the publication of this book owes much to the strong encouragement given to me by Professor Yoshio Sugimoto of the School of Social Sciences, La Trobe University and Director of Trans Pacific Press. If not for Sugimoto's initiative and Izumi's dedicated support, this book would not have seen the light of day. I am grateful to Miriam Riley for her excellent editorial assistance.

Naoki Yoshihara
November 2011

Part I:
Global Migration and Labor

1 Highly Skilled Professionals and International Migration: A Labor Analysis of Indian IT Engineers in Japan

Akiko Murata

Introduction

This paper analyzes the project-based labor and international migration of IT engineers from India to Japan. According to government statistics from its registry of foreigners living in Japan for 2009, 22,858 Indians were registered as residing in that country. The actual number is somewhat lower, however, as some on the registry leave without cancelling their registration, and Indian engineers and their families accounted for a good portion of that number (Sawa and Minamino 2003: 334–335). Indian engineers in Japan can be found at a wide range of firms; and, most are working on project-based assignments for US or European based multi-national corporations as well as Japanese companies.

These software engineers employed on a contract basis are highly skilled mobile professionals who earn sizeable incomes and are able to enjoy a good lifestyle while in Japan. However, this study reveals that although these engineers may be well rewarded with competitive wages, they experience similar kinds of anxieties and uncertainties as do their Japanese counterparts also working on a contract basis. The system of work that generates their international mobility requires many of these engineers to flexibly adjust to the uncertainties generated by the capitalist structures, and their project-based labor affects the working conditions listed in their employment contracts, which in turn determine their length of stay in Japan. These highly skilled but flexible professionals form one segment of the foreign professionals employed in Japan, a group inadequately represented in the literature. This chapter reports on findings from a study on Indian IT specialists in Japan, revealing the experiences and anxieties incumbent with being part of a highly skilled but highly insecure internationally mobile labor force.

Policies affecting skilled foreign professionals working in Japan

In advanced economies, the competition to secure the service of highly skilled professionals (such as scientists and engineers) with cutting-edge knowledge and expertise is intensifying. Immigration policies in OECD nations are shifting from approaches designed to limit intakes to those that promote 'selective immigration' in order to attract such professionals and thereby enhance the performance of their national economies (Watabe et al. 2007). In this context, the Japanese government has been maintaining an open immigration policy for selected foreign professions evident since 1988 in the Government's Sixth Basic Plan for Employment (Dairokuji Koyo Taisaku Kihon Keikaku) (Ministry of Labor 1999). Efforts in this regard were further strengthened from around 1999 in the form of the Government's Second Basic Plan for Immigration Control (Dainiji Shutsunyukoku Kanri Kihon Keikaku) (Ministry of Justice 2000).

Until now, discussion on the merits of allowing highly skilled professionals into the country has focused on their economic value as a resource or input facilitating the nation's economic growth. For example, to advance the management of research and technology, the 2003 White Paper on Commerce and Trade (Tsusho Hakusho) stated that the injection of outstanding expertise from overseas was an important means of generating the innovation to drive Japan's economic growth.

Policy discussions have touched on the need to provide an environment that will enhance the willingness of highly skilled professionals from abroad to commit to a medium- or long-term stay in Japan. However, those discussions have not paid serious attention to the workers who have been framed in terms of set periods of time in line with the needs of Japanese firms and the workings of the transnational labor supply system. For example, according to a survey of firms on the first Tokyo stock exchange by the Ministry of Welfare and Labor in 2008 (Kosei Rodo Sho 2008), about half of the firms employed non-Japanese, with only 40% of those firms hiring their foreign workers as *seishain* (regular full-time employees). Also, the Council to Promote the Entry of Highly Skilled Workers into Japan (Kodo Jinzai Ukeiri Suishin Kaigi 2009: 2) stated that 'non-

Japanese had not been adequately utilized as part of the core labor force' (*kikan jinzai*). The report indicated that the problem lay in the inability of Japanese firms to fully utilize such employees and the unattractiveness of Japan as a place to work and live. Employment practices at the firm level were cited as in need of attention. It is now time that a broader discussion be introduced that carefully addresses the issues raised by the way firms hire and employ their labor force. To have that discussion, we need a survey of the way contracted labor is employed along with a full analysis of the mechanisms by which the international movement of such labor occurs.

Contracting highly skilled foreign professionals: Introducing this project

This chapter attempts two things. The first is to consider the institutional context in which Indian engineers come to work in Japan. The second is to analyze the way in which the mechanisms of those institutions impact on their employment experiences and the overall period of their stay in Japan. A significant portion of research on highly skilled professionals has not paid attention to the labor supply system of project-based software professionals. Given that fact, I begin by reviewing some of the research on highly skilled foreign professionals in the labor force, and then examine material on the contracting of foreign workers in Japan and consider how my own research resonates with and expands that corpus.

Tsukazaki (2008) reported on her investigation into highly skilled foreign professionals in Japan. In this study, she attached weight to the idea that foreign professionals did not see Japan as being attractive from a career point of view (2008: 19). Tsukasaki's study indicated that the expectations that Japanese firms placed on their foreign employees with regard to career development were not necessarily in line with those of their employees. By looking into employment status, her findings point to a more generic challenge facing Japanese firms in their engagement with highly skilled professionals rather than reveling the labor context of foreign professionals in a concrete fashion. Tsukasaki's research does not extend to examining the institutional context within which contract labor is generated.

The engineers who participated in my research were all employed by Japanese firms on a contract basis. As the length of their contract was determined in the first instance by the Japanese firms, there is a need to analyze the way in which their employment choices came to be conceived within the confines of the superstructure, or system, which shapes the international flow of this specialized labor force. Kajita, Tanno and Higuchi (2005) have studied the international migration of Japanese-Brazilians who have come to work in Japan, the types of work they are given and their residential patterns while in Japan. Tanno (2007) has reported on the labor market through which such Brazilians find employment in Japan, and on the lifestyle they adopt while living there. These two studies point to the importance of the system for international migration and the nature of that of contract labor as major factors shaping the experience of Japanese-Brazilians working in Japan. Tanno's findings have significantly influenced the design of this research, and it is useful to begin by considering the differences and similarities in how Japanese-Brazilians and Indian IT engineers gain employment in Japan.

Both labor flows are shaped by agents or brokers who form the core of what Kajita, Tanno and Higuchi (2005: 318) refer to as the 'market intervention system of international migration' (*shijo baikai-gata iju shisutemu*). However, as Figures 1.1 and 1.2 indicate, the level of the agents' involvement differs. In the case of the Brazilians, multiple agents are involved. Those wishing to work in Japan to earn income for their families in Brazil (*dekasegi kibosha*) find their way through the auspices of promoters, brokers and travel agents who may collaborate with one another and with other players, such as those who prepare the necessary documentation to allow entry into Japan. Some may go directly to labor contractors, while others enter the Japanese labor force as individuals and find employment on their own.

As Figure 1.2 shows, the path taken by Indian IT engineers is much more straightforward than that in the example discussed above. All enter via the conduit of Indian IT firms and placement agencies that employ them directly. While many of these IT firms have established offshore operations and engage in software development, the latter specialize in the dispatching of engineers. When searching for work in Japan, Japanese-Brazilians turn to intermediaries and contractors to assist them in finding a job with a Japanese employer. However, Indian IT engineers are often working for an Indian firm as a (regular) employee. This presents a significant difference. Many of the large Indian IT companies dispatch their own employees to various locations around the world, with the North American market representing their primary target. Japan is just one of many countries to which Indian IT firms send their employees.

Figure 1.1: The path from Brazil to employment in Japan

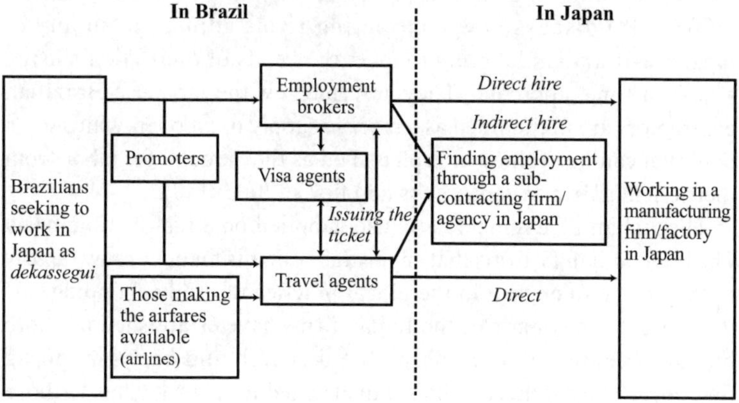

[Figure: flowchart showing path from Brazil to Japan employment]

In Brazil → **In Japan**

Brazilians seeking to work in Japan as *dekassegui* → Promoters / Those making the airfares available (airlines) → Employment brokers ↔ Visa agents ↔ Travel agents (*Issuing the ticket*) → *Direct hire* / *Indirect hire*: Finding employment through a sub-contracting firm/agency in Japan / *Direct* → Working in a manufacturing firm/factory in Japan

Source: Kajita, Tanno and Higuchi (2005: 92).

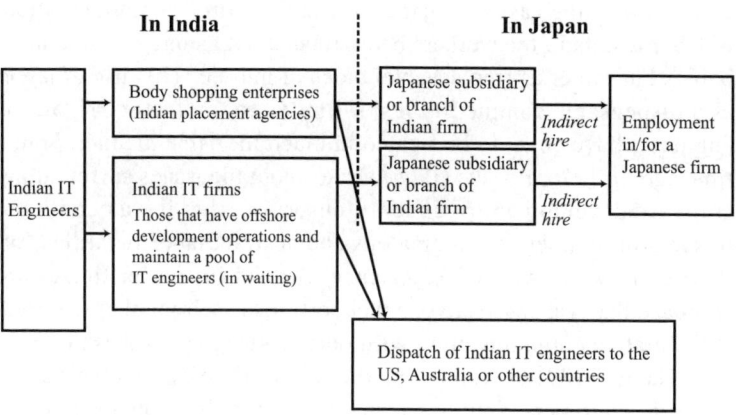

Figure 1.2: The main paths followed by IT engineers from India who work abroad

Source: Compiled by the author.
Note: In addition to the IT engineers interviewed for this study, others are working for Japanese companies that have operations in India. There are also those who come to Japan to work for the Japanese partner of a joint venture that was formed with an Indian company. Still others come to Japan via their employment in a (non-Japanese) MNE.

Despite those differences, both systems feed foreign labor into Japan according to a similar principle. Kajita, Tanno and Higuchi (2005: 148) discuss how contracting firms adjust the supply of Japanese-Brazilian laborers to meet the needs of their clients using a 'just-in-time' approach. They describe how the Japanese-Brazilian contractors are maintained as a reserve supply of labor-in-waiting—a pool that can be drained or replenished as the demand for labor from their client's firm in Japan ebbs and flows (2005: 150).

The Indian IT engineers are also supplied on a just-in-time basis. The large Indian IT firms that supply labor in this manner grew rapidly as they came to engage in the global practice of 'body-shopping.' At the present time, many of the Indian firms have established offshore business centers that combine the dispatch and body-shopping functions. The engineers who are dispatched from such firms to those of their clients are called 'on-site engineers' and 'bridge engineers.' The main function of these workers is not confined to software programming, but also includes facilitating communications between the client and the offshore office. In the practice of body-shopping, the term 'body' implies the labor-intensive nature of programmers' work, and 'shopping' refers to the 'quick and easy purchase' of engineers as project-based contractors (Xiang 2007). Tanno (2007: 6–7) writes about how in the case of Japanese-Brazilians this commodification of labor results in the workers being treated not as integrated human beings but rather as (replaceable) blobs of muscle. This use of labor as a dispensable commodity is not limited to the factory floor; IT engineers have come to be treated in much the same manner. Some time ago, in 1976, Brooks (1995) wrote about the issues surrounding software development in general, observing that it was common to see programmers as automatons and abstract labor regardless of their skills and levels of experience. Brooks further criticizes an approach that was insensitive to that portion of their job that required collaborative communication with other colleagues. Aneesh (2006) and Xiang (2007) describe how the just-in-time system works for software engineers, and how firms are able to draw on a supply of engineers in waiting, workers who have been temporarily 'benched.' This chapter considers how Indian engineers experience the just-in-time aspects of their employment in the Japanese context, paying special attention to how they cope with economic downturns when the demand for their services dips.

A key difference between the Brazilian and Indian workers is in terms of the size of their pay packets. Although both groups come to Japan on short-term contracts, the manual workers engaged in simple repetitive tasks are poorly paid whereas the engineers who are developing and maintaining rather complex IT systems are rather generously remunerated, a matter commented on further below. For those engineers coming from a newly emerging nation, the opportunities to earn high wages abroad in the advanced economies are a welcome bonus. It appears to be a win-win situation for both the Indian IT engineers and for their clients in Japan. However, this 'win-win' situation is criticized by critical labor analysts such as Matloff (1998) as a neoliberal pursuit of multinational corporations sacrificing domestic labor forces in favor of cheaper imported labor. Matloff argues that the US visa system, which offers an H-1B visa for foreign skilled professions, is purposely designed to allow US firms to hire foreign professionals on short-term visas for rates considerably below those paid to US citizens doing similar work. In Japan as well, the importation of foreign IT engineers does not always result in the forward-looking and constructive employment of such labor, as seems to be envisaged in policy documents. As Kurata (2004: 16) notes, foreign professionals are, at times, hired simply because they are cheaper. Ten (2005) found that some Chinese software houses also operate in the same way. Part of the problem here lies in the ambiguity with which the category of work referred to as 'highly skilled professional' is defined. It is in fact a double-edged concept. On the one hand it singles out as exceptional those persons who possess a high level of skills or knowledge. On the other hand it is code for a system that allows the services of such persons to be easily acquired for a nominal fee without any long-term obligation. My research was geared to explore this area with regard to Indian IT engineers and their remuneration.

It is assumed by the Indian IT firms that the labor force they dispatch overseas will reside at their destination on a temporary basis. Once the contracted task is completed and further demand for the company's services cannot be found in the destination country, it is expected that the employee will, without exception, immediately return to India. Temporary migration of skilled professionals from developing countries to OECD nations is not a phenomenon that is exclusive to India. For a long time, observers of the labor flows of professionals saw their movement in negative terms as a brain-drain from the developing to the developed world. However, more recent studies such as those of Johnson and Regets (1998) and Saxenian (2002) have pointed to the increasing trend of such professionals to return to their countries of origin, and have given a much more positive twist to the patterns using the term 'brain circulation.' Nevertheless, it would also seem to be true that the flow back home is often set in motion by an economic downturn in the more advanced country that served for some time as a temporary home for such migrant labor. (In other words, it can be seen as a just-in-time measure on the macro level, or, as the case may be, a matter of 'just-not-in-time.') In the 1990s, many Indian engineers were working in the US or Australia, but when the IT bubble burst they were quickly repatriated (Xiang 2007: 17; Yamada 2009: 478). The H-1B visa becomes invalid once the sponsoring firm no longer employs the holder of that visa, who is requested to return to their home country immediately. As I mention below, similar conditions have colored the experiences of Indian IT engineers in Japan. In looking at the situation of those engineers, one goal underpinning my research is to discover the extent to which they could influence or have discretion over the length of their stay in Japan. The interviews that I conducted indicate that language was a major determinant regarding their length of stay in Japan in ways that were not identified in the research of Aneesh (2006) or Xiang (2007) on Indian IT engineers in English-speaking countries.

Traffic on the circuit connecting India and Japan—according to which Indian IT engineers move back and forth between the two countries—is, in the final analysis, governed by the business cycle in Japan. As indicated above, the mechanism that allows labor into and out of Japan on a 'just-in-time' basis is not new. Kajita, Tanno and Higuchi (2005: 272) referred to Japanese-Brazilians who went home and then returned to Japan as 'repeaters,' while Mori (1999: 3) referred to this circular movement as *kanryu-gata iju* (circular migration). However, Japanese-Brazilians who have been given permanent residence status ultimately have the right to decide whether to stay in Japan or return to Brazil, although their decisions are influenced by economic conditions in both countries. In contrast, Indian IT engineers do not have that choice. The length of their residency depends on the contract that was negotiated on their behalf by their Indian employer. That in turn depends on the market-determined needs of their Japanese clients. Even though their visa might have a longer period granted by the immigration authorities when they arrive, it is expected that they will return home once the contracted task is completed. The exceptions, of course, are the engineers who are employed on regular and long-term bases by an Indian subsidiary in Japan or by a Japanese firm itself. Iguchi (2009) has called for policy changes so that once approved for entry (into Japan) they would have permanent residence and be able to circulate freely between the receiving country and their country of origin. Such a policy would facilitate circular migration. However, such a policy is yet to be adopted, and at the present time the situation is such that Indian engineers will for the foreseeable future be moved about at the whims of their Indian employers and the market forces to which Japanese firms are subjected. In the report that follows, the relationship between residential patterns and the circular flow of engineers will be discussed.

The next section discusses findings regarding the way the dispatch of Indian engineers to Japan is organized, how Indian engineers are assigned to Japanese clients and how the Indian firms maintain their supply of highly skilled workers. It then moves on to examine the effect that the uncertainty regarding their period of residency in Japan has on the engineers and how they go about altering the conditions determining their length of stay in Japan. After analyzing the relationship between language proficiency and the movement of engineers, the findings section concludes by considering a few cases in which Indian engineers have experienced circular mobility into and out of Japan.

Findings

The findings discussed here are based on data collected between March 2008 and September 2009. The main data were collected from interviews with 63 Indian engineers drawn from eight Indian IT companies and from business persons in Indian IT firms and other organizations involved in the IT trade between Japan and India. The interviews were augmented by observations made regarding the activities inside the Japan-based offices of Indian IT companies. Twenty-seven further interviews were conducted in India at IT companies and offshore development centers where I was able to observe the facilities and activities in those settings. The Indian IT companies in question service a range of foreign firms, but the focus of this research was on those engineers that came to be engaged for Japanese clients.

The supply of engineers from Indian IT companies to Japan

As stated above, Indian IT companies largely handle the labor supply of Indian IT engineers through their offshore development centers. The research took into account the full trajectory of the

Indian engineers' experiences, from the recruitment phase to their employment in Japan.

Not all IT engineers working for large Indian IT companies are sent overseas by their employer. Each engineer enters a competitive pool, and only the most capable are selected. Bhatnagar (2006) reported that at the beginning of the 21st century Indian engineering universities were annually producing 2.5 million graduates. These graduates face severe competition just to get into one of the large IT companies. According to one of my interviewees in charge of the recruitment of new graduates, the large firms visit the top 50 universities located in major Indian cities to conduct interviews with prospective employees. In the end, only a small percentage of applicants are employed. New employees are trained for several months before being assigned to a project. I visited one of the offshore development centers focused on doing business with Japanese firms. Roughly 300 engineers were working there, but of which only about 30 would actually be sent to Japan. The competition for a posting to Japan was considerable. Whether or not one is chosen to be a member of the onsite engineering team (on an in-country Japan team) depends on the decision made by their Indian IT firm.

As stated above, the Indian IT companies are oriented primarily toward the North American market. The Indian IT engineers themselves desire to work in an English-speaking location, with a preference for the US where many Indian IT companies have extensive ties. However, the engineers are not always sent to their destination of choice. Nevertheless, the benefits associated with being abroad anywhere are such that many will still take up assignments in a less popular location. I was told that in the past many Indian engineers were reluctant to go to Japan owing to differences in food and language. It seems that the situation is changing. At the offshore development offices I visited, work was centered on Japan, and many of the engineers there were studying basic everyday Japanese knowing that an opportunity to work in Japan might arise.

Such an opportunity occurs whenever a Japanese firm approaches an outlet established in Japan by one of the Indian IT companies and requests that it send them an engineer. Over 50 Indian IT companies maintain such offices in Japan. The next step is for the Japanese branch to consult with the head office back in India. Most of the engineers who achieve an assignment in Japan obtain either a visa to work as a technical specialist or one for employees coming to Japan on an intra-company transfer. Upon arriving in Japan, few pass through their company's local branch; most proceed directly to the Japanese firm where they will be stationed.

The average age of the 65 engineers interviewed for this project was 29, and their average monthly salary was about J¥470 thousand (USD5200 as of January, 2011), a figure nearly six times that which they could expect to earn in India (about J¥80,000). It is not surprising, therefore, that nearly all of the interviewees claimed that economic outcomes were the main reason for working in Japan. Above I cited a criticism of the H-1B visa category in the US on the grounds that it served mainly as a means for American firms to employ skilled foreign workers for below par wages. However, the three parties approached for this study (the Japanese client firms, the Indian IT firms and the 65 Indian engineers themselves) all saw the economics of that arrangement as producing a 'win-win-win outcome,' although the Indian engineers do not cost less than their Japanese counterparts when their relocation costs were taken into consideration. Having said that, it is important to remember that this research dealt mostly with the largest Indian IT firms. The situation may be very different for those employed by India's smaller firms. One must also consider the likelihood that the situation might have changed because of the recent economic downturn in Japan.

From the viewpoint of the Japanese client firms, a major attraction of subcontracting IT work through Indian IT companies is that the employment of the Indian engineers is project based. In other words, the Japanese side is able to avoid the fixed costs that go with regular long-term employment. Even in terms of hiring new graduates from Japanese universities, their lower initial wages are often offset by the cost of training them up from 'zero.' The large Indian IT companies take a 30–60% slice of their engineer's salary in Japan. (Even so, the engineers 'take home' a net income that is still 2.5 to 4 times greater than that which they would receive in India.) These calculations are consistent with the win-win-win assessment noted above. Nevertheless, despite the economic cheer all around, it is the engineers that bear the brunt of an economic downturn. Such are the ways of the just-in-time system as it functions in the global body-market for Indian IT engineers.

Labor supply through the just-in-time system

Aneesh (2006) analyzed how Indian IT companies have deployed just-in-time labor management techniques (derived from the Toyota system for inventory management) in order to moderate the labor supply of IT engineers. Inventory control forms the basis of the just-in-time or *kanban* system. The main function set for the inventory management system is the 'continuous flow' of inputs—having the inputs ready to use only when needed. The goal regarding labor is avoiding under-employment and redundancy. In the case of the IT engineers, the Indian IT companies minimize human resource 'redundancies' by relocating their engineers from places of minimal demand to those of high demand, thereby optimizing their human capital.

As indicated above, as a system to maximize the return to selected individual workers in the larger pool of labor available at a firm's disposal, that which brings Japanese-Brazilians to Japan (as described by Kajita et al. 2005) and that which supplies Indian engineers are functional equivalents. Focusing on the demand for IT specialists in the US, Indian IT companies have rapidly expanded their operations internationally on a grand scale.

The main point here is that the system is fundamentally designed to accommodate the changing demands of client firms. The key to the system's functionality lies in the willingness of the engineers to respond quickly and flexibly to such shifts in demand that their employing firm in India sees fit to satisfy. That is why, upon arriving at Tokyo's Narita International Airport, the engineers proceed with all haste to their work site and endeavor to be on top of the requisite tasks as soon as possible before touching base with their own firm's office in Japan. When replying to a question about the engineers' need for orientation in Japan, one of the human resource managers of a large Indian firm stated that their engineers are billable from day one of their arrival, therefore they should go directly to their clients so that no billable time is lost. (This, of course, is what continuous flow is all about.) I was told about one extreme case where an Indian engineer was dispatched to Japan with such haste that he arrived at the Tokyo-Narita International Airport without knowing the client firm's name or address.

Table 1.1 provides an overview of the situation concerning the comings and goings of engineers through one Indian IT firms' Japan branch.

In line with the just-in-time supply system, the engineers are usually sent back to India within two weeks of completing their work in Japan. In 2008, 5% of the 183 engineers working for the Indian IT company that supplied the data in Table 1.1 finished their work in

Table 1.1: One Indian IT company's dispatch of engineers to Japan in 2008

Number of engineers sent to Japan	183 persons
Average length of stay in Japan	6 months
Number of engineers sent to Japan more than once	5%
Average time between trips to Japan	3.4 months

Japan, returned to India, and then were sent once more to Japan.[1] I asked about whether it might make good sense for the repeaters to simply remain in Japan for the intervening three-month period. I was told, however, that to do so the firm would have to pay the engineers the Japanese rate, whereas their wages revert to the Indian rate once they return to their home-base at the firm's offshore development center on the subcontinent. Aneesh (2006) and Xiang (2007) analyzed the benching system that was used by Indian IT firms in the US and Australia. However, benching in Japan seems to be a rarity, and engineers are sent home to India until a contract is in hand for a project requiring their services at a Japanese location. My research uncovered firms that benched employees in Japan, but often at a reduced salary. Whatever hardships that might result for the engineer would have to be faced by the engineer alone. Of course, 'sitting on the bench' in Japan incurs the risk that business conditions might deteriorate and adversely affect the demand for one's services at a potential client firm. The ultimate risk at that point was redundancy and being stranded unemployed in high-cost Japan (with one's residency status likely to expire). Interviews with several benched IT specialists uncovered additional concerns that their skills would decline or be superseded while they waited for their next assignment (not knowing how long that wait would be).

Although some indicated a preference for a short-term stay in Japan, most engineers wanted to be able to reside in that country for an extended period. In addition to the financial reward, they cited the modern conveniences and simply an affinity for Japanese culture and life. Many expressed a desire to live in Japan for a few years at least, should the opportunity arise. The Indian engineers mentioned that they enjoyed shopping for electric goods and gadgets at Akihabara; buying a Japanese camera, taking photos and sharing them with family and friends; travelling in Japan; skiing; staying at hot springs and the like. For most of the engineers I interviewed, coming to Japan was their first time abroad, and they found that being in a different culture was a stimulating experience. Only one of the interviewees wanted to return home soon. Most did not contemplate being in Japan permanently, but welcomed the possibility of living there for two or three years until their children were old enough to enter school in India. Despite desiring to remain in Japan for a longer period of time, the engineers were fully conscious when they arrived that their stay would be determined by the project load to which they had been assigned and by the budgeting situation at their client firm. They were often unclear as to how long they would be staying in Japan. One large Indian IT firm reported that some of their projects are reviewed by a budgetary committee every quarter, as the client's accountants release to management the most up-to-date information on the firm's performance over the preceding quarter. Until a decision was made about budget allocations for the subsequent quarter, the futures of all projects were up in the air. Thus, there would be little long- or even medium-term certainty regarding the future of an individual IT project. A firm could at its own discretion reduce, completely axe or suddenly increase the budget for such projects. It could without warning contact the Tokyo branch and request that the engineer be sent home.

In most cases when requested to return to India, an engineer is required to leave Japan within two weeks. (A very small number of engineers working in Japan are employed directly by their firm's branch in Japan and do not work under such tight constraints.) During the period when their specific project was under budgetary review, a number of interviewees reported that anxiety and stress levels increased significantly. Some of the engineers could get a sense of how their project was likely to fair from subtle signals or rumors circulating around the office, but many said they had no idea as to the future of their project right up until the time it was deemed to be completed. In some cases engineers were simply floored by the shock of being told on the spot that their project had ended 'then and there.'

Separation: Being cut loose

The just-in-time labor supply system through which Indian engineers come to Japan is quite sensitive to the business cycle. This was noticeably evident in the downturn that resulted from the financial crisis that started in the Northern fall of 2008. A number of the projects on which the Indian engineers I interviewed were working either ceased altogether or were simply postponed. Many of the engineers were promptly sent back home to India. According to staff at the Japanese branches of the Indian firms, the crisis hit not only foreign financial concerns, but work at many of the Japanese clients was halted or otherwise delayed. In the six months leading up to March 2009, the number of projects under way had dropped by about one third. One office had a support team of about 20 persons in April 2008, but had reduced the number to four persons by May 2009. As support staff, the remaining four had to carry the workload of the departed staff members. The result was long periods of consecutive overtime. When I visited one of the engineer's homes on a weekend, my interview was continually interrupted by phone calls from the company he was servicing. At the same time, the number of new projects also declined and that of engineers coming to Japan followed suit. Between May 2008 and May 2009, the number of visas requested from Japan's Immigration Office by one Indian branch fell by about half. As one after another Indian engineers returned home, the fire-sale advertisements for used goods—furniture, white goods, etc.—rose proportionately in the newsletters sent out through the Indian community's mailing list. According to government statistics, applications to enter Japan under the categories for technical specialists or for persons with special knowledge fell by 23.3% (Ministry of Justice 2009).

Hoping to return to Japan, many of the engineers left the country without turning in their alien registration card.[2] They simply went home having the proper documentation to re-enter Japan. This means they are able to return immediately to Japan if things improve, and that gives them some competitive advantage when the next round of employees are being selected to be dispatched to Japan. In their study of the Japanese-Brazilians, Kajita et al. (2005) reported that many changed jobs frequently without reporting their change of address, and consequently were said to have a 'faceless existence' from the point of view of the local civil administration. In that regard the same could be said of the Indian engineers, as it became unclear as to whether they were still in town, elsewhere in the country or back home in India.

Many of the engineers who come to Japan are regular employees with a parent firm in India. (The exception would be those who work for dispatch companies that send them out only as 'temps.') Nevertheless, it is not guaranteed that work will be waiting for them when they return. As the ripples spread globally from the 2008 financial crisis in the US, the Indian IT firms were also badly stung. One after another, the big Indian IT firms such as TCS, Infosys, Satyam and Patni began to lay off workers and to reduce the pay of those who remained. When I visited the offshore development centers of large Indian software firms in March and April 2009, engineers in the firm's cafeteria were pressing each other for the latest information about the firm's employment situation, and the air was rife with rumors. That was a sign that they were unsure about their own job prospects in a very uncertain environment. Informants at offshore development centers intimated that there was no labor union at most such centers. With no one to stand up for their interests, it stands to reason that the level of anxiety was higher than it might otherwise be.

To be sure, some engineers were happy to return to India after just a short stay. However, most of my interviewees indicated a desire to have a longer consolidated stay in Japan. In order for that to happen, however, they would need to be employed as a regular employee or on some form of extended contract with either a Japanese firm or with the local subsidiary of an Indian IT firm. Most wanted more freedom to control or to set the period of their sojourn in Japan. As they were familiar with how the IT industry worked in India, most preferred to work for the Japanese branch or subsidiaries of an Indian IT company. That option, they felt, would also allow them to continue to work with Japanese clients even after returning to India.

Having expressed that wish, most recognized that they would have to gain a rather high level of Japanese language proficiency if they were to shift their job from the parent Indian IT firm to the Japanese subsidiary or branch offices or to another firm in Japan. When I enquired at three Indian branch firms in Japan, one firm stated that they did not really hire Indian engineers locally, while the other two indicated that the number of Indian engineers employed locally was only about one sixth of the total number of Indian engineers they were looking after in Japan. In other words, the Indian subsidiaries and branch firms in Japan would only consider for direct employment those with a very high level of Japanese language proficiency.

Language and mobility

It is not always necessary for an Indian IT engineer to speak Japanese to gain employment in Japan. Even if they cannot speak much Japanese, they are still able to communicate using universally under-

Table 1.2: Advertisements for IT programmers by required level of Japanese language proficiency

	Number of advertisements	%
Native proficiency	55	48.6
Fluent Japanese (Level 1 on the Japanese Language Proficiency Test)	31	27.4
Knowledge of Business Japanese (Level 2 on the Japanese Language Proficiency Test)	18	15.9
Daily conversational Japanese	1	0.8
Minimal Japanese	1	0.8
No Japanese	7	6.1

stood IT vocabulary, diagrams and some degree of broken Japanese (Murata 2009). One can also come across instances where an interpreter is employed as a 'go-between.' However, to be employed directly by a branch of one of the large Indian IT firms, a high level of Japanese language proficiency is often required, as a considerable portion of their work would involve interfacing with Japanese clients. If one looks at sites advertising such jobs, that requirement is clearly stated. For example, on the Daijob.com site (used by many engineers), 115 advertisements were listed on September 25, 2009. Many called for native language proficiency (see Table 1.2).

For this reason, while many Indian engineers would love to apply for one of the permanent positions in Japan, they are deterred by the language requirement. Indian firms are able to rapidly expand their operations in the US using English as one of their main assets. The 'power migrants' from Asia, including Indian engineers, combine a high level of specialization with a high level of English language proficiency as part of the skill set they take to countries like Australia, where they have been able to compete with locals on a level playing field (Ishii, Sekine and Shiohara 2009). In Japan, however, Indian IT engineers are not so easily able to use English as a major playing card.

At the same time, because not many Indian IT engineers have the necessary level of Japanese language proficiency, a solid advantage is achieved when a certain level of competency is attained. Those who reach the required level find it much easier to secure an on-going position in Japan. In fact, there is a certain irony when an Indian IT engineer gains employment in Japan less because of his IT skills and more due to his Japanese language proficiency. One company that dispatches IT engineers to Japan outlined how they recruited new IT graduates and gave them several months of instruction in Japanese before sending them to that country. However, the same company's 'reward' was that most of their employees would work for it for about one year and then be transferred to one of the large Indian IT firms. Although their level of IT knowledge and experience might still be rather limited, by flaunting their Japanese language skills they could easily secure employment in Japan.

One Indian IT engineer in his mid-thirties had quite successfully made that move. He was very aware that his Japanese language abilities had been his major asset in getting ahead, rather than his IT expertise. Upon graduating from an Indian university with a degree in computer engineering, he had an interview with an Indian-Japanese joint venture. Although he knew no Japanese, he lied and said he had some Japanese background and was hired as a result. He was then sent to Japan where he studied Japanese and then transferred to the branch office of an Indian IT firm as a regular employee. At the age of 32, his annual remuneration was about J¥10 million (USD100,000). Because he had gained regular employment in Japan, he was no longer tied to a particular project and was able to switch to another if the one he was working on did not work out. He said that while working tirelessly to lift his level of expertise in IT, he also continued to improve his Japanese to take his proficiency to another level. His view was that in order to obtain a long-term position with a Japanese firm he would of course need to be competent on the IT side of things, but he also believed that his 'soft skills' in being able to communicate in Japanese and develop a good network in dealing with Japanese client firms would be crucial assets.

Circulating labor

The international labor supply system developed by Indian IT firms that supply labor according to the movement of the market and the needs of overseas firms has also given rise to the circular flow of IT engineers between Japan and India. This flow is evident in the movement of some of the Indian engineers mentioned above—the 'repeaters.' Here I report on the experiences of two engineers who had come to Japan on repeat assignments.

One project team leader, Rajiv,[3] aged 26, was on his fourth stay in Japan. Rajiv's level of Japanese proficiency was intermediate, but

Table 1.3: One Indian engineer's pattern of rotation to Japan

Country of employment	Length of stay (months)
Japan	2.0
India	3.5
Japan	5.5
India	3.0
Japan	12.0
India	2.5
Japan	3.5

he was very good at liaising between the Japanese client firm and the Indian offshore development center. He was trusted by the firm's clients in Japan and had come to Japan every few months, as shown in Table 1.3.

Because Rajiv is able to spend time with his parents each time he returns to India, he indicated that he would be happy to continue the current arrangement for another three or four years. At the time of the interview he had saved approximately J¥3 million (USD30,000). It was his plan to purchase a piece of land with his savings. While he was happy with the income side of things, even more important was the chance to work in Japan, to become more familiar with how Japanese businessmen thought and to dive into Japan's business culture. He felt that the education in Japan would serve him well if he settled in Japan and worked for an offshore development center. It was his belief that he would one day be able to get the most out of his experiences in Japan by playing an important role as a bridge between the two economies. In fact, he was seeking a longer, on-going position in Japan and was considering the possibility of obtaining an MBA in that country and finding employment with a company that would allow for a long-term career path. At the same time, however, his parents were suggesting that it was time to get married. Until he had children, however, he felt he could travel in and out of Japan, and was uncertain as to what to do in the future.

Another project manager, Chandra, had been back and forth to Japan so many times that he had lost track of the number. In 1997, he began a three-year stint as a regular employee with the Japanese branch of an Indian IT firm. He returned to India in 2000 and began working for another Indian company that sent him on short trips to Japan a seemingly endless number of times. Then, a few years before our interview he was back in Japan, again directly employed by the same branch of the Indian IT company. His Japanese language proficiency was at a very high level, and he had such good rapport with Japanese clients that he had had opportunities to work as a 'Japan specialist.' Were he to switch to another Indian IT company, it is very likely that they would have located him in Japan.

The important point to be made here is that the two engineers discussed above had added to their IT expertise through their experiences in Japan. By developing a communicative and interactive competency in Japanese, both had been able to secure good on-going employment either in Japan or as a circulating engineer. While many Indian engineers would like to find themselves in a situation similar to that enjoyed by the two introduced just above, the reality is that few are able to attain such outcomes.

Iguchi (2009) has called for an immigration policy that would allow workers to freely circulate into and out of the country. The fact is that such a policy has yet to be adopted, and Indian IT firms have developed their own just-in-time system to allow for 'circular migration.' However, it is a system designed to meet the needs of firms and the market for their services, not one that allows the engineers much self-determination. Of course, some engineers, such as the second one cited above, have been able to use the system to forward their own interests, but they are still having to think carefully before planning the next step that would allow them to settle in Japan on a longer-term basis as regularly employed professionals. At the same time, most continue to be dependent on the changeable needs of the firms that employ them. The burden of moving back and forth to Japan, especially when a family is involved, falls back to the engineers themselves. The burden becomes particularly onerous when elderly parents or children of school age are part of the picture. Accordingly, many of the engineers in such circumstances end up leaving their families in India and working as *tanshin fu-nin* (lone wolves in the field).

Conclusion

The interest that prompted this research grew out of a feeling that the situation of highly skilled professionals who come to Japan as fixed-term contract workers or as dispatched workers had not been adequately studied. This research focused on the movement of Indian IT engineers who came to Japan on a contract basis. It considered ways in which the supply systems for workers from Brazil and for IT specialists from India were designed to regulate the international flow of labor to Japanese firms through functionally equivalent just-in-time systems. In that context, it honed in on the experiences of the Indian IT specialists in terms of (1) the conditions under which they worked when their contracts had been deemed to be completed, (2) the role of language in determining patterns of mobility and (3) the sustained rotation of engineers between Japan and India.

What significance does the research hold for the immigration debate in Japan as it pertains to highly skilled professionals? The engineers who were interviewed for this research had gone through a highly competitive selection process to eventually be chosen as an outstanding 'human resource for export' to Japan. At the same time they were subjected to the wiles of the market and the needs of individual clients in that country. A few of the engineers were able to make it onto the migratory circuit between Japan and India. The research highlighted the gap that exists between the situation of the Indian engineers and the rhetoric behind the push for a more open immigration policy designed to promote the entry of highly prized human capital into Japan from abroad. The debate revolves around the idea that such a resource should be utilized with a medium-term commitment on the part of Japan. The situation described in this chapter, however, does not simply represent the view of Indian engineers as to what Japan ought to be doing to make their lives more pleasant. It is about a larger system that leaves the engineers and other professionals (who are clearly important to the future of Japan) in a compromised situation. The research points to the importance of simplifying the immigration process in order to facilitate the flow of such professionals into Japan. Nevertheless, making it easier for professionals to obtain residency status for an intermediate period of time does not by itself necessarily guarantee that they will continue to come to Japan.

To further the debate on immigration in Japan, the research points to the need to consider a wider range of factors than has been the case thus far. Those factors include the way industries are occupationally structured, labor market mechanisms in Japan, the patterns of international labor supply and the institutional context in which that supply occurs, the demand of Japanese firms for flexible labor and the employment system in Japan. Only then will we be able to have a constructive debate on how to best secure the services of the highly skilled human resources that are emerging abroad.

2 Patients on the Move: The Development of Medical Tourism in Asian Countries

Mika Toyota

Introduction

The movement of patients seeking medical care across international borders is on the rise worldwide. Although established migration theory has long asserted international migration to be a venture of the young and healthy, evident in recent migration trends across Asian countries is the increasing transnational mobility of the 'unhealthy.' People today cross borders for a wider range of reasons than ever before. While traditional motivations such as finding 'work' remain salient, other factors are growing rapidly in number—these include education, marriage, retirement, and, the concern of this paper, finding appropriate medical care.

There are different modes of trade in the health services sphere: firstly, the cross-border movement of foreign patients; and secondly, the migration of healthcare professionals. These two flows are not separate but rather form an integral part of a new development in the trade in healthcare services in Asian countries. Thailand attracts more than 1.4 million foreign patients per year and receives direct foreign investment for medical tourism. Singapore and Malaysia import foreign healthcare workers to meet domestic demand and to provide services to foreign patients. Conversely, the Philippines and Indonesia have an aggressive policy of exporting healthcare workers. By focusing on the movement of patients, the aim of this chapter is to examine transitions in healthcare services in the region that have occurred as a consequence of the broader trend towards the globalization of healthcare.

Medical tourism refers to travel undertaken specifically for biomedical procedures where patients want to take advantage of superior accessibility, expertise, facilities or affordability. Health tourism, on the other hand, signifies a broader range of health treatments including spa, massage, anti-ageing facial treatments and the like, and these customers may be categorized as 'tourists.' As Henderson (2004a: 117) notes, for many patients medical travel 'arises from pain and suffering and carries intimations of human mortality, which are discordant with the hedonism of mainstream tourism.' Although some countries do not distinguish between tourism for health or medical purposes, statistically what I refer to here as 'patients' indicates those who travel specifically for the purpose of obtaining medical treatment.

Over the last ten years the growth of the medical tourism industry in Asia has been spectacular. For example, the number of medical tourists in Singapore rose from 21,014 a year in 1997 to 665,380 by 2009. Underpinning the growth of transnational mobility for healthcare in the region are three broad socioeconomic trends.

First of all, at the broader level, privatization, capital market liberalization and social-sector reforms have led to an increasingly dominant role for the private sector provision of healthcare in the region and have created the conditions that gave rise to the growing trade in medical tourism. The advent of the General Agreement on Trade in Services (GATS) has also contributed to the trade (Chanda 2002). Although it was in the wake of the Asian financial crisis of 1997 that several Asian countries (Thailand, Singapore, Malaysia, India and the Philippines) promulgated national economic policies to promote medical tourism as an alternative means of earning foreign exchange, it is important to note that there were pre-conditions to these policies. The privatization of healthcare and corporatization of public hospitals were implemented well before medical tourism and biomedical industry development policies had taken off in the region. In both Malaysia and Singapore, the healthcare systems have shifted from government-dominated health service provision to greater private sector involvement. For example, in Singapore healthcare reforms were announced in 1981 and the 1983 National Health Plan was designed to indicate the new direction. It stresses that Singapore will not be modeled as a welfare state where healthcare is provided as part of essential welfare services (Asher and Nandy 2006; Chee 2010; Phua 1991; Purcal 1995; Reisman 2006). Healthcare has already been perceived as an industry—a 'profit-making enterprise' in the world market. In this regard the development of the medical tourism industry should be seen as a logical progression from the preceding period of privatization and corporatization.

The second socioeconomic factor is linked to changing demographic social structures in the region, namely a growing middle class. While medical tourism is often perceived as flows of patients from developed countries to the developing world in search of lower cost medical services, this framework by itself is insufficient to explain on-going regional dynamics in the development of medical tourism. Existing empirical research clearly indicates that the majority of patients are from within Asia. In the 1990s an expanding urban middle class demanded high quality healthcare that boosted a booming private sector within the context of the growth of market economies in the region. The Asian financial crisis of 1997–98 hit this new industry and medical tourism policy was forced to appeal to a more diverse market. Nevertheless, the majority of patients in Singapore are still from neighboring countries, for instance, with 50% coming from Indonesia and 11% from Malaysia in 2005.

Recently, Taiwan, Korea and Japan, which are among the most developed economies in Asia, have started promoting medical tourism to stimulate local and national development, and their main target populations are often from less developed Asian countries. The flow consists mainly of better-off individuals who travel abroad to access healthcare services that are either unavailable locally or are perceived to be of better quality overseas. For example, the Japanese government started issuing medical travel visas from January 2011, specifically targeting the middle class population in China. Therefore, it is important to highlight the fact that the growth of a large affluent middle class in the region has created new demands for better medical facilities and specific expertise that may not be available in the home country.

The third factor underpinning the rise of medical tourism is that across the region private health expenditure has been increasing relative to government expenditure, and out-of-pocket payments are also high. However, there are efforts underway to reduce dependence on out-of-pocket payments for healthcare, particularly to benefit the poor. New challenges have emerged with the rising trade in health services in terms of equitable access to healthcare within individual countries. The provision and financing as well as regulatory functions of the public sector need to adapt accordingly to these transformations. The benefits of the liberalization of trade policy in the health sector should not only go to the better off. Balancing domestic demand from the poorer sectors and maintaining equity have become critical issues that must be taken into account when taking advantage of the economic opportunities associated with the trade in health services. In Thailand, for example, the Health

Card and 30-baht Schemes were introduced in order to increase universal access to basic health services, especially for vulnerable and disadvantaged people in rural areas, alongside the development of medical tourism in the larger cities. Conscious efforts have been made in order to reduce the widening disparities between rural/urban areas and public/private sector services.

These new trends urge us to re-think the existing analytical framework of medical tourism development that stresses the globalization of healthcare services and the unequal availability of these between developed and developing countries. I would argue that this oppositional South/North framework is a rather problematic way of investigating the dynamics of recent medical tourism development in Asian countries. ASEAN leaders have identified healthcare as a priority sector for region-wide economic integration as the opening of healthcare markets promises substantial economic gain and increases regional competitive advantage. In this chapter I aim to investigate the active involvement of recipient countries and stress the circulation of patients within the region in order to further our understanding of the globalization of medical services today.

Neoliberal ideology and the privatization of healthcare

During the 1960s and 1970s, the provision of healthcare was considered to be a government responsibility and/or obligation towards its citizens, as was clearly expressed in the 1978 Declaration of Alma-Ata (WHO-UNICEF). By this stage, healthcare entitlement had become a critical component of social citizenship rights (Moran 1991). However, this European view of the state's responsibility is at odds with the concept of the privatization of healthcare. In the UK, for instance, the utilization of the National Health Service (NHS) by foreign patients has been a source of anxiety at official levels (Borman 2004). In contrast, post-colonial developmental states such as Singapore and Malaysia took different directions with their healthcare reform. Pursuit of free-market capitalism based on neo-liberal ideology underpinning their economic development policies extended to healthcare and identified it as a potential service industry. In the 1980s, when the international agenda shifted strongly towards the privatization and commoditization of healthcare provision, these countries swiftly adjusted their healthcare reforms without much concern for social responsibility, as was experienced by European welfare states. Rather, their healthcare reforms were a part of a package of economic policies clearly focused on strategies to facilitate competition in the global economy.

In Singapore, for example, key documents outlining the direction of healthcare reform policy emphasized that this country would not be modeled as a welfare state. The policy was clearly designed to move away from a welfare state framework. Instead, one of its objectives was 'to promote personal responsibility for one's health and avoid over-reliance on state welfare or medical insurance.' Historically, the colonial governments established social security saving schemes in both Singapore and Malaysia. These schemes—called the Employees Provident Fund (EPF) in Malaysia and the Central Provident Fund (CPF) in Singapore—were funded by contributions from employers and employees in fixed proportions and were originally designed to be accessed during retirement. These schemes have undergone many changes, but they essentially remain individual saving plans with no element of cross-subsidization except within families (Chee 2010: 339). For example, in Singapore, a national medical saving account system, *Medisave*, was introduced in 1984. Under this compulsory saving system Singaporean employees contribute 6–8% (depending on age) of their monthly salaries to a personal CPF savings account. Every month, a portion of the CPF savings goes into each individual's *Medisave* account to help Singaporean employees build up their own resources for healthcare purposes. The savings can be withdrawn to pay hospital bills, day surgery and for certain outpatient expenses of the account holder and immediate family members. Since this *Medisave* scheme is not sufficient to cover a catastrophic illness, a supplementary medical insurance scheme, called *MediShield*, was introduced in 1991. A portion of *Medisave* savings can be transferred to pay the premiums of *MediShield*. Both schemes are fundamentally individual-based savings schemes and the amount of savings varies significantly according to the level of income.

Accompanying the healthcare financing reforms, reforms in healthcare provision were also made consonant with neoliberal thinking. Government hospitals were 'restructured,' which essentially entailed the corporatization of healthcare provision. In Malaysia, for example, the private share of Total Health Expenditure (THE) has increased from 24% in 1983 to 56% in 2008. While studies carried out in the 1970s found that healthcare was generally accessible and income was not a significant barrier to the utilization of public healthcare in Malaysia (Heller 1982; Meerman 1979), nonetheless the corporatization of the healthcare sector poses challenges for the equitable access of these services today (Chee and Barraclough 2007), as it contributes to increased fees in public hospitals. In the case of Singapore, the corporatization of government hospitals was launched in 1984 and the National University of Singapore Hospital (NUH) was corporatized in 1985. Singapore's corporatized public healthcare system is, therefore, government owned, but operates according to corporate principles and has private sector participation.

In line with the privatization and corporatization of the healthcare sector, both Malaysian and Singaporean governments have emphasized so called 'Asian family values' in their national economic development policies. This value system essentially aims to establish a social system in which the family, rather than the state, is relied upon to meet social security and welfare needs (including healthcare). As a result of these 'successful' healthcare sector reforms—the privatization of healthcare, the financing and corporatization of hospitals—public healthcare expenditure has declined. Among the countries that provide some form of public healthcare subsidization, total health expenditure (THE) at 4.3% of GDP in Singapore and 3.8% of GDP in Malaysia is remarkably low compared to the USA (14.6%), Canada (9.6%), Japan (7.9%) and the UK (7.7%). Since March 2010, the Singaporean government has allowed *Medisave* funds to be used at specific private hospitals in Malaysia. This has provided a cost saving option benefitting not only individuals but also the state.

Medical tourism as national development strategy

From as early as 1965, the Singaporean government has encouraged private consumption of health services. The private healthcare sector expanded to meet the growing demand from foreign customers from neighboring countries. In 1986 the Singaporean government had already planned to turn Singapore into an international medical centre for patients from around the region (Phua 1991: 6–7). According to Ministry of Health statistics, Singapore had received 14,287 patients (11,464 inpatients and 2823 day surgeries) in 1993, and the number steadily increased to 21,014 (15,247 inpatients and 5767 day surgeries) by 1997. These foreign patients were mostly from Indonesia and Malaysia. However, the number dropped significantly in the wake of the 1997 Asian financial crisis, down to 13,225 (9703 inpatients and 3522 day surgeries). Singapore not only experienced a sharp drop in numbers of foreign patients but also a shift of the local population to public hospitals. As a result the private sector suffered a sharp drop in occupancy rates—from 70% to 55% (Rabobank International Asia Pacific 1999: 26). This compelled the Singaporean government to find new strategies to attract foreign patients from beyond its neighboring countries to places such as the Middle East and Russia.

Upon recovering from the Asian financial crisis, Singapore observed a rapid growth in medical tourism, receiving 150,000 foreign patients in the year 2000 bearing SGD345,000,000. The sector further expanded to reap SGD415,000,000 in 2003, when over 230,000 foreign patients visited that country. Big as it was, this growth was not sufficient to satisfy the ambitions of the Singaporean government. The Health Minister Mr Khaw Boon Wan (2003) made it clear at the Launch of Singapore Medicine that in order to be at the peak of this competitive medical tourism market in the region, Singapore had to reach beyond neighboring countries and develop new strategies to attract foreign patients, while at the same time differentiating itself positively from such regional competitors as Thailand and Malaysia:

> Our dream to make Singapore a regional medical hub is an old one. ... But our dream was much more ambitious. With 500 million people in ASEAN, just 10% alone would be a sizeable volume for our healthcare sector. And now with tens of millions in China and India entering the middle class every year, we can be even more ambitious. ...Ten years ago, Singapore was the undisputed medical hub for this region. We were the clear leader. Indonesians, Malaysians, Bruneians came here for treatment, in large numbers. Today, many foreign patients are still coming here, but competition from the region has increased and foreign patients now have choices...

In collaboration with the Economic Development Board, the Singapore Tourism Board and International Enterprise Singapore, an ambitious 10-year plan called 'Singapore Medicine' was launched in October 2003. Led by the Ministry of Health, the multi-government-industry partnership committed itself to establish Singapore as 'Asia's leading medical hub.' To this end, the Singaporean government will be investing SGD2,000,000 a year for this purpose. Its target is to increase the number of foreign medical tourists to one million per year and to expand the income of the medical tourism industry to SGD300,000,000 (USD2.3 billion) by 2012. If the target is reached, it is forecast that this would create 13,000 new jobs.

Thailand experienced a booming expansion of the private healthcare services sector during the 1990s, and the number of private hospitals increased rapidly over this period. However, when the Asian financial crisis hit that country in 1997 there was a parallel crisis in the private hospital sector, largely because the local Thai middle class shifted to lower cost public hospitals and there were not enough people to take up the slack in luxury private hospital services. The Thai government saw foreign patients as the savior of the distressed private medical industry. In 1998, the 'Long-stay and Health Care Project' was initiated by the tourism and health service industry. The Thai government set up clear economic incentives to promote Thailand as a major medical hub in Asia. This effort was not embarked upon to simply rescue the healthcare sector, but was part of a larger mission to expand and diversify exports. In June 2004, the Thaksin government created a strategic plan aiming to increase the number of medical tourists to two million by 2008. This led to the privatization of many hospitals. The leading players in this new sector of medical tourist centers include Bumrungrad hospital, Bangkok hospital, Thon Buri hospital and Phyathai hospital groups. The Bangkok Dusit Medical Services owns a chain of 14 hospitals belonging to the Bangkok hospital group. As a result, the volume of foreign patients increased from half a million in 2001 to 1.3 million in 2008, generating USD1.3 billion in that year. The Tourism Authority of Thailand intends to further boost medical tourism targeting two million medical tourists in 2010 and 10 million by 2015. The Ministry of Health predicts medical tourism will generate 400 billion baht according to the five-year plan of 2010–2014. For this purpose, the government has launched a plan titled 'Health Beauty Holiday in Thailand.' The plan adds more services in the realms of Thai traditional medicine and alternative medicine. For example, a 'Health Promotion Hospital,' the Kamala Public Health Center, will be built in Phuket and will incorporate traditional Chinese medicine into its array of medical services on offer. This project is being co-funded by the Chinese government. Indicative of its growing success, foreign investors including Dubai Istithmar and Singapore Temasek holdings have started purchasing major shares in private hospitals in Thailand.

Striking the balance between economic opportunities and domestic equity

In his vision of 'Singapore Medicine,' Health Minister Mr Khaw Boon Wan was fully aware of the new challenges in terms of balancing the competing demands of foreign and local patients. At the launch of the plan he explained the strategies behind it—referring to the 'Toyota Way':

> We should draw inspiration from Toyota. Toyota produces Corolla for the masses and Lexus for those who demand more. It also takes part in Formula-1 racing.
>
> To sell Corollas, it pushes "zero defects" and mass production to derive quality at the lowest possible cost. Likewise, for the common medical conditions that the bulk of our patients come to us for treatment, we should also ensure maximum reliability, zero defects and lowest possible cost. These are our Corollas.
>
> That is why I publish on the MOH website the price comparison of the common medical conditions. The public seems to welcome such transparency. It is to push our hospitals and doctors to critically review their operations, to see how they can do more with less, and bring their Corolla production cost to as low as possible, while ensuring good quality control.
>
> This requires us to make sure that we do not over-engineer our Corollas. Of course, there are patients who demand frills, branded implants, just as there will be buyers of Lexus who can afford and want more than Corollas. Our response should be to offer them Lexus, with the wood paneling, full leather upholstery and custom-made Levinson sound system. We should not attempt to fit all these into our Corollas, driving up costs and putting them beyond the reach of the masses.
>
> Separately, we should take part in Formula-1 to show the world that we can hold our own against the best in the world and win. Hence, we do IVF, heart transplants, liver transplants and separation of conjoint twins.
>
> To be a regional medical hub requires us to do well at all three levels. There is actually no money to be made racing in Formula-1. In fact, you lose money. But we need to take part in order to push up our capabilities and to benchmark ourselves against the best in the world.
>
> By mandate, the public hospitals' focus is on Corollas for the masses. But the private hospitals especially should leverage on our Formula-1 reputation, build on the Corolla platform, and enhance it

> with extras to offer their customers the Lexus. Public hospitals have started making our hospital bill size transparent. The private hospitals should also take step [sic] to make their charges transparent so that their patients can select more wisely and be more reassured. (Khaw Boon Wan 2003)

Although the government essentially regards Singapore as a 'non welfare state,' there are some forms of minimum social security provision for needy citizens. An endowment fund, called *Medifund*, was established by the government in 1993. *Medifund* serves as a safety net of last resort for those who are in poverty and unable to afford basic healthcare or those who are mentally ill patients requiring long-term care. Furthermore, in order to meet the needs of the growing number of elderly Singaporeans, a new scheme called *Medifund Silver* was launched in November 2007 to assist particularly needy elderly patients aged 65 years and above. In 2009, almost 90% of *Medifund* assistance went to patients with acute ailments, while the remainder went to those receiving intermediate and long-term care. This portable subsidy scheme allows for greater private sector participation in the provision of subsidized healthcare. In 2009, *Medifund* assistance also subsidized patients in 11 private nursing homes for the first time. Accredited private nursing homes set aside a proportion of their beds for patients eligible for Ministry of Health subsidies.

Unlike Singapore, other Southeast Asian countries have large rural populations, uneven economic development and urban/rural disparities. Across the region there is rural/urban discrepancy in terms of access to healthcare as well as disparities in the availability of healthcare personnel. Retaining nurses and doctors in rural areas has not been an easy task. The Thai government has responded to this problem using mandatory government bonding since the 1970s, and both financial and non-financial incentives have been provided to compensate doctors who take on rural practices. They also recruit local students for hometown placements as nurses and doctors. Through these measures the gap in density of doctors between the poorest northeast region and Bangkok has been reduced from 21 times in 1979 to 9.4 times in 2000 (Kanchanachitra, Wibulpolprasert and Thammarangsi 2007).

The significant growth in the development of medical tourism has raised public concern in Thailand, focusing on the issue of whether medical tourism exacerbates inequalities in access to healthcare between rural and urban areas and between public and private hospitals. As revenue from foreign medical patients has risen (amounting to USD1 billion in 2005–06) there has been a significant drift from the teaching hospitals to the private medical sector, especially among the more highly specialized staff. It was reported that during the same time period (2005–6), more than 300 specialists resigned from the public sector to join private hospitals. This has led to the closure of some provincial public hospitals that have been unable to finance medical services. Despite the introduction of the Health Card and 30-baht schemes supposedly to ensure universal access to basic health services, especially for vulnerable and disadvantaged people in rural localities, there have not been enough healthcare workers to successfully implement the schemes throughout the country. In design the schemes were liberal and innovative, however, in reality they failed to offset the pecuniary attractions of private practice. It has been reported that some 60–70% of public physicians work in private practices outside of office hours for financial reasons.

Furthermore, this internal brain-drain of highly specialized staff from the public to the private sector is arguably having a negative effect on teaching hospitals. In order to maintain the quality of medical training, the outflow of senior specialists from medical schools will have to be curtailed. While the expansion of the private healthcare sector has caused this brain-drain, the role of medical tourism may not really be that significant, as foreign patients actually accounted for less than 1% of the total patients in Thailand (Na Ranong, Na Ranong and Jindarak 2009). Only six to eight hospitals in Thailand are serious about medical tourism. Rather, the rapid growth of private hospitals signifies Thailand's burgeoning middle class, and the equity issue should be regarded principally as a domestic concern.

Foreign patients embarking on medical tourism in Asian countries are often portrayed as 'Westerners' (from the USA or Western Europe) in search of lower medical costs—'first world treatment at third world prices.' Such a description, however, only applies to a small minority. In fact, the majority of Thailand's medical tourists come from Middle Eastern countries. According to the 2009 statistics provided by the Tourism Authority of Thailand, the UAE is the key customer for Thailand's medical tourism (43.6%), followed by Qatar (8.9%), Oman (6.0%), Japan (5.3%), Myanmar (5.0%) and Bangladesh (3.6%). On the other hand, in the case of India, 19% of foreign patients are from neighboring Asian countries—Bangladesh, Nepal and Sri Lanka, followed by Iraq (18%), the Middle East (16%), Africa (9%)

and Afghanistan (9%), whereas in the case of Singapore, in 2005 50% of foreign patients were from Indonesia, followed by 11% from Malaysia. Clearly, the north/south dichotomy is insufficient to explain the dynamic flows of medical patients within the Asian region. The equity issue of medical tourism also needs to be discussed in relation to the growing middle class in the region. Without their new demands for better medical facilities and specific medical expertise, medical tourism would not flourish at its present pace.

Management of healthcare personnel

As seen in the case of the internal brain-drain in Thailand described above, managing the circulation of healthcare professionals has become a new challenge in the face of the rapid growth of the international trade in health services. The circulation of healthcare workers may go beyond a shift from public to private sector. There is now also an increasing international circulation of healthcare workers within the region and beyond.

In Singapore, statistical data suggests a high density of healthcare workers at a rate of 5.9 (measured by the number of doctors, nurses and midwives per 1000 population). Singapore, however, is a major importer of doctors and nurses from neighboring countries. Since Singapore is targeting one million medical tourists by 2012, Health Minister Mr Khaw Boon Wan foresees a worsening medical staff shortage. The ministry allocated SGD1.9 billion to be spent in the five years from 2008 to 2012 to increase wages and to employ additional staff. In 2007, Singapore registered 668 new doctors, consisting of 230 fresh graduates from the National University of Singapore and 438 overseas-trained doctors. In 2008, out of 1248 doctors registered, 739 were foreigners. A recruitment target of 1000 foreign trained doctors was set in 2009. Currently, two out of three doctors in Singapore are 'foreign-trained' (The Temasek Review 2010). Scholarships for training allied healthcare workers such as physiotherapists or speech therapists are also to be doubled. An estimated 30% of all nurses working in Singapore are non-Singaporean, mostly coming from the Philippines, China, India, Malaysia and Myanmar.

Conversely, the Philippines has become a major exporter of healthcare workers in the global healthcare trade. In terms of annual nurse production per 100,000 persons, the Philippines has a very high output compared to other Southeast Asian countries, amounting to 78 in 2007 compared to Singapore's rate of 32 (in 2010), Malaysia 34 (in 2008), Indonesia 15 (in 2008) and Thailand of 12 (in 2009). In the 1950s it used to be state universities that dominated nursing education and training. In the 1990s, however, nurses became an important export commodity for the Philippines, leading to the rapid expansion of nursing schools as export-driven businesses established to meet global demands. As a result, currently more than 80% of nursing schools in the Philippines are private, market driven businesses. During 2005–2007 an average of 55,000 nurses per year were produced, more than seven times the number during 2000–2004. The sudden increase of enrolled nursing students outpaced the capacity of training staff and clinical training sites. As a result, in 2009 an estimated 400,000 licensed nurses in the Philippines were unable to find employment in the nursing profession because of the gap that has opened up between production capacity and actual market demand. Indonesia also exports nurses, despite the fact that at a national level that country falls below the minimum threshold of 2.28 doctors, nurses and midwives per 1000 population as defined by the World Health Organisation. It is reported that only half of the nurses who graduate in Indonesia find employment upon graduation (Pachanee and Wibulpolprasert 2007).

The recruitment patterns of healthcare professionals have shifted from individual applications to formal bilateral agreements between source and destination governments. The UK-Philippines agreement was signed in 2002. Canada and Japan then entered into agreements with the Philippines and Indonesia for the import of certified nurses and care workers. The recruitment drive organized by Singapore, however, went furthest to recruit healthcare workers. Singapore has signed mutual agreements with China and Myanmar to provide scholarships for students from these countries to be trained as nurses at nursing schools in Singapore for three years, on the condition that they work for six years at hospitals in Singapore after graduation. At the regional level, ASEAN members signed an agreement in 2006 to begin negotiating mutual recognition of qualifications and professional licenses across ASEAN countries to facilitate flows of nurses, followed by an agreement for medical practitioners in 2008. However, due to the disparity between countries in terms of quality of education and training, licensing requirements, and diverse languages and other cultural dimensions of daily medical practice, it has proved rather difficult to make actual progress in its implementation. Singapore's strategy of in-house training scholarship schemes seemed to work better to overcome inconsistencies in the quality of educational training.

Development of global healthcare standards

In order to attract patients from abroad, recognized high quality (meeting international standards) medical services need to be guaranteed. This has led to the adoption of international hospital accreditation schemes such as that afforded by the Joint Commission International (JCI), using external procedures accepted worldwide for the recognition of quality. To be competitive in the medical tourism industry, possession of such 'Accredited' standards as the JCI became critical. Currently (as of January 2011), 16 hospitals in Singapore, 11 in Thailand, six in Malaysia and three in the Philippines have been accredited. Adopting such international standards contributes to the rapid expansion of high-end, technology-intensive healthcare and improvements in quality control.

Although the JCI is considered as an international universal standard, it is actually a US qualification and is expensive to achieve. It is said that a three-year accreditation from JCI in the Philippines costs close to USD46,000. Since the cost of acquiring the JCI is rather prohibitive, alternative hospital accreditation programs are emerging within Asia. The National Accreditation Board for Hospitals (NABH) is managed by the Quality Council of India. This accreditation system is now gaining wider recognition, and hospitals in the Philippines will be seeking NABH accreditation in 2010. NABH accreditation is an attractive alternative as it costs a little over half that of the JCI. NABH plans to extend its market into Bangladesh, Nepal, Sri Lanka and Dubai as well as to African countries such as Kenya and Nigeria by establishing a separate division to look after its overseas operations. Medical tourism development in India does not only include healthcare facilities designed to attract foreign patients but is now also exporting its accreditation system to become a global player in the healthcare industry. The emergence of such new practices in medical tourism development help us catch a glimpse of the transformation of Asian regional dynamics in the face of the globalized trade in healthcare today.

As the medical tourism market becomes more competitive, each country has to devise distinctive strategies to attract new potential patients and customers. Top hospital groups in India (Fortis Hospitals,

Apollo Hospitals and Columbia Asia Hospitals) are now targeting Africa as a prime market for customers. Conversely, Singapore's healthcare companies are focusing on the growing Russian middle class. Russia's first private hospital was built in Vladivostok and another is set be built in Tatarstan (Toyota 2011). Medical tourists from Russia do not necessarily have to come to Singapore to receive treatment; they can obtain high technology medical treatment of Singaporean standard in Russia. This is aimed at encouraging medical tourists from neighboring countries around Russia to attend Singaporean-owned hospitals located in Russia. The globalization of trade in healthcare not only stimulates the transnational mobility of patients and healthcare workers—it has also led to the hospital accreditation quality assurance system as well as investment in medical technologies and facilities on a transnational level.

3 Rain of Gold Overseas, Rain of Stone at Home?: The Unchanging Fortune of Indonesian Migrant Domestic Workers

Raphaella D. Dwianto

Introduction

'Rain of gold overseas, rain of stone at home' is an old Indonesian saying that might best apply to the situation of Indonesian transnational migrant workers.[1] For many around the world, moving away from one's hometown or village can provide better opportunities to improve life chances. Sometimes migration offers the only path to chances for a more prosperous future. In terms of migration in search of employment, even though the journey to the destination country almost always entails sacrifices and uncertainty, millions are still willing to incur costs and face risks in order to improve their family's living standards.[2]

Transnational migrant workers from Indonesia are not a new phenomenon. Even as early as the late 1970s, newspapers in Malaysia were reporting an approximate number of 100,000 illegal migrant workers from Indonesia and the Philippines in plantations in Johor and Sabah (as quoted in Chin 1997: 359). Due to geographical and cultural proximity, neighboring Malaysia has been and is likely to remain a destination country for Indonesian migrant workers. Apart from Malaysia, another key destination country for these workers is Saudi Arabia. This is a preferred destination due to its proximity to Mecca, the holiest city for Moslems. The trend has not changed much over the years. The number of Indonesian migrant workers has continued to increase, particularly following the 1997–1998 Asian financial crisis when Indonesia was strongly advised to implement a policy encouraging people to travel abroad to work in order to reduce the government's job-creation burden.

In 2009, the majority of migrant workers from Indonesia (43.7%) were placed in Saudi Arabia by private placement agencies;[3] whereas 19.60% were sent to Malaysia, 9.39% to Taiwan, 6.39% to the United

Arab Emirates, 5.23% to Singapore, 5.13% to Hong Kong and the rest to Middle Eastern countries such as Kuwait, Jordan, Qatar, Oman or others, from a total number of 632,172 workers. However, the majority of these migrants end up working in the informal sector, such as working as a laborer on farms/plantations or in construction, or as a domestic worker if the person is female.[4]

The reason these Indonesians leave their families behind and go to work in other countries as far away as the Middle East is economically based. The most often mentioned motivation cited by migrant workers is the search for a better income. Other commonly noted reasons include accumulating capital to open a business, supplementing a spouse's income or difficulties finding employment at home. The remittance money sent from these migrant workers to their families is generally used to cover the costs of daily life back home in Indonesia, building/renovating a house or paying the school tuition fees of children/siblings.[5] Looking at the amount of remittance, according to 2009 World Bank data, a total of USD6793 million reached Indonesia, representing 1.3% of the country's total GDP. This placed Indonesia at 16th in the world in terms of the percentage of remittance from the total GDP, and the fifth in Asia, after India, China, the Philippines and Bangladesh.

According to the macro-data on remittance a bright future seems to be waiting for Indonesian migrant workers, however, the day-to-day experience of these workers paints a gloomier picture. This chapter highlights the challenges faced by transnational migrant workers who hold formal and legal citizenship status in Indonesia through their experiences at home as well as abroad. Starting with the real-life stories of three workers, and supported by macro-level data, this chapter follows the argument of Stasiulis and Bakan (1997) that citizenship is not a fixed form but is rather endlessly negotiated, on national and international levels, revealing a hierarchy of states.

Stories of Indonesian migrant women domestic workers: Rain of gold abroad?

It was almost midnight in London in the year 2000. A young PhD student from Indonesia was sitting in the compartment of a London underground train on his way home after doing some part-time work at the Indonesian embassy. He was surprised when a 20-something-year-old woman of Malay appearance approached him and asked whether he was from Malaysia. He was even more surprised when the woman suddenly burst into tears after learning that he was Indonesian. It turned out that the woman—let us call her Minah—was a migrant domestic worker from Indonesia, who had run away earlier that day from her Middle Eastern employer who had repeatedly physically assaulted her. Minah had left her employer's house in London (the employer had moved from Saudi Arabia to England, bringing Minah with them). On the day of her escape, Minah was supposed to go to a park near an underground station to meet another domestic worker from Indonesia, whom she had befriended in London. However, very unluckily for Minah, she could not remember the exact name of the park, therefore she did not know which underground station would be her destination. That day she had left her employer's house very early in the morning at six am, and had spent the whole day on London underground trains, trying to figure out which station she was supposed to get to. She was very relieved when she met the Indonesian PhD student.

The student helped find a temporary place for Minah to stay. He immediately called the Indonesian embassy, yet, since it was almost midnight, no one answered. The student then called a staff member at the embassy he knew, to ask whether Minah could stay overnight at Wisma Indonesia (an embassy guesthouse). The student was surprised when the staff member gave a negative answer and only advised him to call the supervisor of the guesthouse. The student then called the supervisor to ask permission for Minah to stay, even though she was not an official guest of the embassy, because it was already past midnight by then, and also because Minah was unable to speak English and had no relatives in London. But first of all, he made the request because she was Indonesian by citizenship and in a crisis situation. Yet, the supervisor's answer was also in the negative. The student had never expected such a response, because he had been imagining that official representatives of the Indonesian government in that country would at least provide a shelter for the beaten Indonesian domestic worker. The one and only thing that the supervisor at the embassy offered to the student was his advice, which went—more or less—as follows: 'Let us think from the perspective of humanity; why don't you take her home and let her stay temporarily at your place.' Upon being given the advice, the student dropped his jaw in astonishment, not because his rented-room was too small to accommodate another additional person, but more due to the response of an official representative of his country towards an Indonesian citizen in a critical situation in a foreign country.

To cut the story short, the student brought Minah to his rented-room. The following day, the student found other Indonesians who could provide temporary refuge to Minah. From the network of Indonesians in London, Minah was able to find new employers and continue working as a domestic foreign worker in London under much better conditions. Minah's story was never made public, but she can be considered a rather lucky person in light of her encounter with another Indonesian who was ready to help her achieve a positive outcome.[6]

Almost a decade has passed since the events in Minah's story. In November 2010, Indonesia was shocked when the case of an Indonesian migrant domestic worker in Saudi Arabia emerged. Sumiati binti Salan Mustapa, a 23-year-old woman from Dompu in the Province of West Nusa Tenggara in Indonesia, was hospitalized in the King Fahd Hospital in Madinna, Saudi Arabia, due to injuries she received in a brutal physical assault at the hands of her employer, during which she was bruised and her mouth was cut with scissors. Sumiati's case was widely made public. Her suffering from the physical ill-treatment of her employer had not been known of until she was admitted to hospital with severe injuries. Based on that, the President of Indonesia appointed his Minister of Women's Empowerment and Child Protection to go to Saudi Arabia. Yet, a week after the appointment, the minister was unable to depart to the country as she was still waiting for visa approval by the Saudi Arabian embassy in Indonesia, at the time on a long holiday due to a national religious celebration.[7] Even a high-ranking official envoy of the President of Indonesia could not get permission in this instance to enter a foreign country to deal with a critical situation faced by an Indonesian citizen.

Although Sumiati cannot be considered lucky, the story of another migrant domestic worker called Kikim involved far more tragic events. Kikim Komalasari binti Uko Marta (aged 39), had left Indonesia in June 2009 through PT Bantal Perkasa Sejahtera, one of many private agencies for the placement of Indonesian migrant workers, and was placed to work as a domestic servant in a family in the city of Abha, Saudi Arabia. Kikim left behind a 46-year-old husband and three children aged 18, 10 and five. She had wanted to earn some money to fund her eldest child's university studies. According to the Indonesian embassy, Kikim's lifeless body was dumped in a garbage bin. From the bruises on her body, it was beyond question that she died from injuries incurred during rape and other forms of sexual and physical abuse. Kikim's case was publicly announced only a few days after the case of Sumiati was revealed.[8]

Transnational migrant workers

Migrant workers and global trends

In 2009, the UNDP produced a Human Development Report (HDR) focusing on the theme of migration. Since its first publication in 1990, this was the first HDR report to highlight the significance of migration in the 21st century and apply a human development approach to the issue.[9] Through such an approach, the 2009 HDR begins with an attempt to understand the reasons underpinning migration. Though the word 'migration' itself is widely understood as the movement of people from one country to another, the report shows that the number of people who move internally (within a country) is four times greater than that of those who relocate to another country, reaching a figure of 740 million. For those who indeed move to another country, contrary to the general assumption that international migration mostly occurs from developing to developed countries, only one-third from a total of 200 million international migrants migrate in this direction. Most international migrants are travelling from one developing country to another, or from a developed country to another.

The reasons these people choose to leave their place of origin are as mentioned in the introduction: for higher income, better access to education and healthcare services, better prospects for their children and so forth. Although most migrants move by choice, for some number of people it is the only option they have. Places that are unstable and involved in armed conflict displace people. Another group of migrants in a vulnerable position are the victims of trafficking, who in most cases are young women or children.

Rather in contrast to the hope of better access to social services, many migrants who are temporary or irregular workers face systemic disadvantages in their country of destination, making it difficult and sometimes impossible to access local services on equal terms with local people. Despite problems at the destination country, people of low income in developing countries continue to migrate, since it can present a vital opportunity for their household and family to diversify and improve their livelihoods.

Indonesian migrant workers: In hope of 'rain of gold'

The aim of improving livelihoods is often espoused by Indonesian migrant workers. In 2008, the central bank of Indonesia conducted a national survey of remittance patterns among Indonesian migrant workers. One of the findings from the survey shows that nearly 90% of migrant workers from Indonesia go abroad in search of a greater income (see Figure 3.1), while an insufficiency of spousal income is reflected by 30% of migrant workers. They also mention that the lack of job opportunities at home pushes them to seek employment in other places, including overseas. A more optimistic reason given for migration is the plan of accumulating capital to establish a micro-scale business. Another point to be highlighted in the flow of migrant workers from Indonesia is a form of chain migration, revealed in the fact that many become migrant workers because they follow relatives in that situation abroad (19%).

Important to note at this point is that although transnational migrant workers' reasons for finding employment abroad are often seen as personal choices, they are actually structurally determined.[10]

Although in the 1980s and 1990s Malaysia had been the destination country for most Indonesian migrant workers, mainly in the informal sector due to the increasing demand for blue-collar labor and decreasing local labor supply in Malaysia and also due to geographical and cultural proximity to Indonesia, the year 2009 recorded that Saudi Arabia had overtaken Malaysia as the primary country of destination for this group of migrants. As many as 276,633 workers, or 43.7% of the total migrant worker population, headed to the Middle East in that year (see Table 3.1). Malaysia continues to occupy second place, with 19.6% of total migrant workers from Indonesia finding employment in their neighboring country. Other Asian destinations include Taiwan, Singapore and Hong Kong, receiving a total of 19.75%, and other Middle Eastern destination countries include the UEA, Kuwait, Jordan, Qatar and Oman. Together with Saudi Arabia, these Middle Eastern countries receive nearly two thirds of all Indonesian migrant workers annually.

In their destination country, more than 80% of migrant workers from Indonesia work in the informal sector, while only 16% enter formal employment (see Figure 3.2), reflecting the nature of unskilled labor from Indonesia. The informal sector covered by Indonesian migrant workers includes work in plantations, construction and domestic work.

Figure 3.1: Reasons for becoming a migrant worker

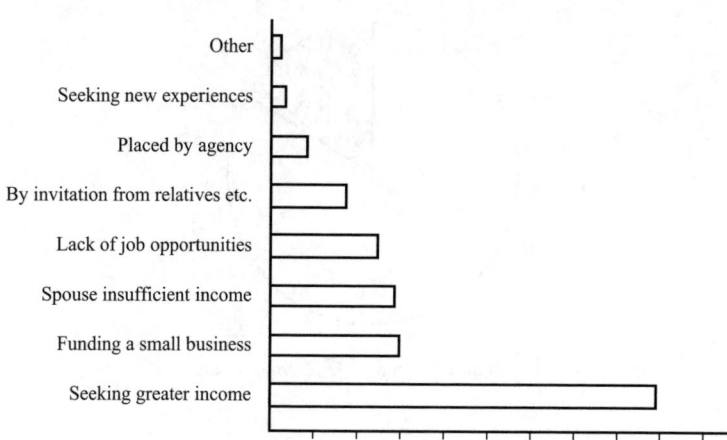

Source: *National Survey of Remittance Patterns*, Central Bank, 2008 (as quoted in *Kompas* November 26, 2010: 46).

Table 3.1: Destination of Indonesian migrant workers, 2009

		Migrant Workers	**%**
1.	Saudi Arabia	276,633	43.76
2.	Malaysia	123,886	19.6
3.	Taiwan	59,335	9.39
4.	UEA	40,391	6.39
5.	Singapore	33,077	5.23
6.	Hong Kong	32,417	5.13
7.	Kuwait	23,041	3.64
8.	Jordan	10,932	1.73
9.	Qatar	10,010	1.58
10.	Oman	9,700	1.53
11.	Other	12,750	2.02
	Total	632,172	100.00

Source: *Kompas*'s research and development (2010).

Despite the large number of Indonesians engaged in the informal sector abroad, when looking at 2009 remittance data from the World Bank, payments from Indonesian migrant workers reached USD6,793 million in total, placing it 16th in the world in terms of the

Figure 3.2: Indonesian migrant workers, 2009

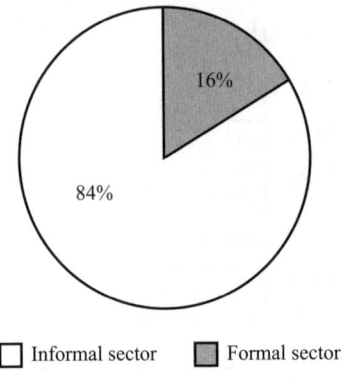

Source: *Kompas* (November 26, 2010: 46).

amount of remittance received, or 2nd in Southeast Asia following the Philippines (see Table 3.2).

The money is then used to cover the daily living expenses of families in Indonesia, to build or renovate their houses, to pay for their children's or sibling's schooling and other costs. Sometimes the money is also used to pay back that borrowed from other people or from the agency that sent them abroad. This could be to cover the departure fee they had been required to pay prior to going to their destination country. Apart from using the money for daily necessities or repaying debts, the families of migrant workers or migrant workers themselves also allocate money for investment purposes, such as purchasing land or rice fields or cattle, and for the initial capital to start their own micro-scale business. Although small in number, some workers also put money in their savings. The various uses of remittance by Indonesian migrant workers can be seen below in Figure 3.3.

Along with the growing number of Indonesian transnational migrant workers and the increasing significance of the amount of remittance being sent home, the number of concerning situations faced by these workers is also becoming a serious challenge. In 2009, a total of 7,709 incidents were reported to have occurred. During that year, most troubles occurred in Asian countries rather than in the Middle East. Yet, during the following year of 2010 the opposite was the case, with 78% of the total incidents reported occurring in Middle Eastern countries. Looking at the content of cases emerging in 2010

Table 3.2: Remittance data, 2009

Rank	Country	Remittance (in million USD)	Percentage of GNP
1	India	49,256	3.9
2	China	48,729	1
3	Mexico	22,153	2.5
4	Philippines	19,766	11.7
5	France	15,551	0.6
6	Germany	10,879	0.3
7	Bangladesh	10,523	11.8
8	Belgium	10,360	2.2
9	Spain	9,904	0.7
10	Nigeria	9,585	5.6
11	Poland	8,816	2
12	Pakistan	8,720	6
13	Lebanon	7,558	22.4
14	Egypt	7,150	4
15	UK	6,847	0.3
16	Indonesia	6,793	1.3
17	Vietnam	6,626	7
18	Morocco	6,271	6.6
19	Serbia	5,406	12.6
20	Russia	5,359	0.5

Source: World Bank (2010), as summarized in *Kompas* (November 26, 2010: 46).

(see Table 3.3), the range extends from being laid-off without advance consultation (the most often-cited case) or having to perform tasks other than those mentioned in the working contract, to experiencing physical (the third most often mentioned reason) or sexual abuse (fourth on the list).

Migrant domestic workers from Indonesia: No 'rain of gold' abroad

Physical and sexual abuse are the most often forms of harm experienced by women migrant workers from Indonesia. The majority of Indonesian women who are working abroad in the informal sector are employed as domestic workers. In 2009, the number of cases of abuse experienced by Indonesian women migrant domestic workers that surfaced reached 7,709. Among these cases, there are still a number that are ongoing. Most cases that surfaced in that year occurred in Asia Pacific countries. Even though the number of cases in the Middle East was much lower, there has been indication that this figure might

Table 3.3: Summary of migrant worker's troubles, January 1 to November 1, 2010

	1	2	3	4	5	6	7	8	9	10	11	12	13	14	15	Other	Total
Asia Pacific																	
Brunei	2	7	3	7	3	2	9	–	–	25	4	2	2	1	80	9	156
Hong Kong	32	24	5	23	52	5	92	5	5	117	18	32	5	–	831	147	1,437
Japan	–	–	2	–	–	–	–	–	–	–	–	–	1	–	1	–	4
Korea	–	1	–	–	–	–	1	–	–	–	–	–	–	–	1	–	3
Macao	–	2	3	5	1	–	4	–	–	4	–	1	–	–	45	2	68
Malaysia	41	26	61	83	60	16	47	4	4	289	56	22	12	10	713	192	1,636
Singapore	63	60	69	98	173	44	167	25	25	345	40	43	3	–	1,549	89	2,619
Taiwan	193	75	23	52	90	51	154	32	32	494	75	173	10	2	1,473	234	3,216
Total	331	195	166	268	379	118	474	66	66	1,274	193	273	33	13	4,962	673	9,339
Middle East & Other																	
Bahrain	4	4	41	8	48	57	32	3	9	156	39	1	6	–	171	22	601
Jordan	8	2	77	23	118	49	52	4	31	241	28	23	11	2	302	42	1,013
Kuwait	23	21	235	46	301	104	247	3	31	317	17	15	7	20	779	88	2,254
Libya	–	–	3	1	–	–	1	–	–	5	–	–	1	–	9	–	20
Oman	31	25	98	31	117	114	120	9	29	421	49	7	19	5	702	58	1,835
Qatar	26	34	117	45	211	115	159	8	28	391	105	5	18	5	994	55	2,317
Saudi Arabia	363	318	1,475	976	2,114	1,709	1,626	159	450	7,197	837	191	213	71	8,581	916	27,196
Syria	2	1	17	27	31	7	10	1	2	66	16	6	3	–	60	5	254
UEA	84	79	287	224	471	210	381	11	71	940	137	23	60	10	2,511	187	5,686

																Other	
Other	5	5	30	22	44	15	27	7	4	126	19	3	6	1	208	6	529
Yemen	–	1	2	2	1	1	1	–	–	7	1	–	1	–	14	–	31
Total	546	490	2,382	1,405	3,456	2,382	2,658	205	655	9,867	1,248	275	345	114	14,331	1,379	41,736
Grand total	877	685	2,548	1,673	3,835	2,500	3,130	396	721	11,141	1,441	548	378	127	19,203	2,052	51,075

Source: BNP2TKI as quoted in *Kompas* (November 26, 2010: 46).

Notes.

1. Job does not match with contract. 2. Unable to work. 3. Salary has not been paid. 4. Insufficient documents. 5. Physical abuse. 6. Sexual abuse. 7. Problems from employer's side. 8. Unable to communicate. 9. Accident during working. 10. Sick due to work. 11. Existing sickness. 12. Employer passed away. 13. Pregnant. 14. Having child. 15. Cut-off contract one-sidedly.

Figure 3.3: Use of remittance by Indonesian migrant workers

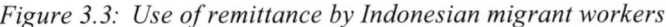

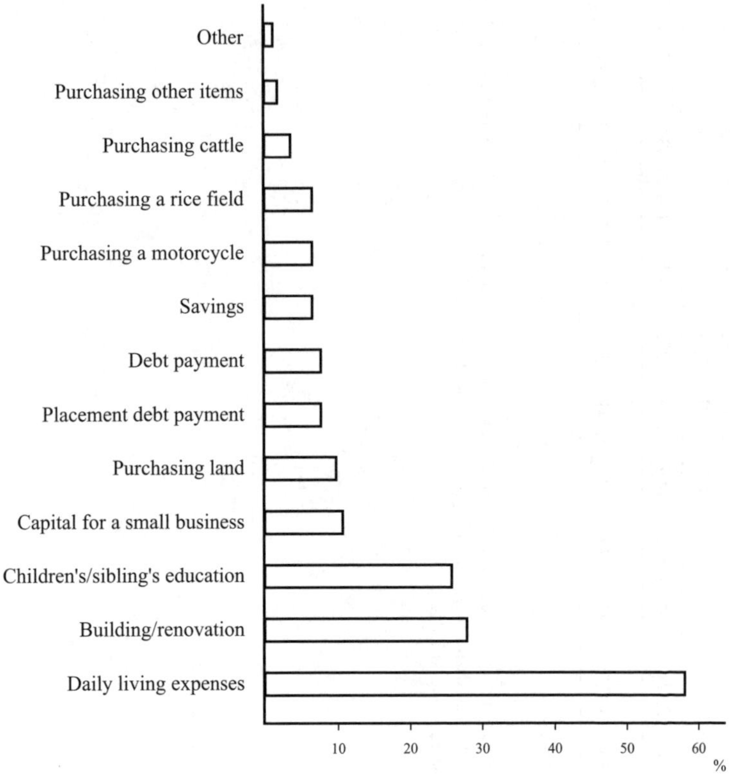

Category	%
Other	~1
Purchasing other items	~1
Purchasing cattle	~3
Purchasing a rice field	~6
Purchasing a motorcycle	~6
Savings	~6
Debt payment	~8
Placement debt payment	~8
Purchasing land	~10
Capital for a small business	~11
Children's/sibling's education	~25
Building/renovation	~28
Daily living expenses	~58

Source: *National Survey of Remittance Patterns*, Central Bank, 2008 (as quoted in *Kompas* November 26, 2010: 46).

actually be higher in reality, as instances involving domestic workers that occur in the private realm often stay hidden. Looking at the number of cases being handled in 2010, those that occurred in Middle Eastern countries in fact out-numbered cases in the Asia Pacific (see Table 3.4).

Apart from facing the possibility of being subject to physical and sexual abuse during their stay in host countries, Indonesian migrant domestic workers also experience gaps in their salary compared to domestic workers from other countries. Wage data from migrant domestic workers in Malaysia provides evidence of this fact (see Table 3.5). The salary of Indonesian domestic workers is approximately half that earned by domestic workers from the Philippines. Compared to

Table 3.4: Cases of abuse faced by Indonesian migrant domestic workers

	2009			2010		
	Middle East	Asia Pacific	Total	Middle East	Asia Pacific	Total
Closed	505	5,869	6,374 (82.6)	165	96	261 (18.75)
In process	1,129	206	1,335 (17.3)	924	207	1,131 (81.25)
Total	1,634	6,075	7,709 (100)	1,089	303	1,392 (100)

Source: *BNP2TKI*, as quoted by *Kompas* (November 26, 2010: 46).

Table 3.5: Comparison of wages and fees of migrant domestic workers in Malaysia, 2008

	Monthly salary		Cost of placement	Domestic workers (%)
	Lowest (in USD)	Highest (in USD)		
Indonesia	125	175	6 x monthly salary	85
Cambodia	150	200	5 x monthly salary	8
Philippines	200	450	1 x monthly salary	6
	400	–		
Sri Lanka	130	150	4 x monthly salary	< 1
Thailand	130	150	4 x monthly salary	< 1

Source: The Institute for Ecosoc Rights/atache of the Philippines, as quoted in *Kompas* (November 26, 2010: 46).

workers from other Asian countries such as Cambodia, Thailand and Sri Lanka, Indonesian workers receive less. Among domestic migrant workers, those from Indonesia achieve the lowest monthly salary. If salary is considered to be commensurate with the skill of the worker, then it can be said that domestic workers from Indonesia are perceived to be the least skilled, as 'stupid but obedient' (Lan 2006).[11] The perception of 'unskilled but obedient' is intentionally produced primarily by the training agencies for domestic workers in Indonesia. Based on qualitative research, Rudnyckyj (2003) found that training agencies implement audits, evaluations and timetables and administer forms of verbal address and bodily discipline to aspiring migrant domestic workers in the training process, resulting in displayed docility. Such perceptions put Indonesian migrant domestic workers into more vulnerable positions.

In addition to the above conditions, these Indonesian workers pay the highest fees to enable them to become domestic workers in Malaysia. They have to pay an average of six times their monthly salary for their placement.

Despite experiencing wage disparity when compared to fellow workers from other countries, Indonesian women continue to migrate as domestic workers. This reflects the way the division of labor has been changing internationally and how such conditions encourage flows of women workers—not only from Indonesia, but also from other countries such as the Philippines, Sri Lanka and the Caribbean—from developing to more developed countries, including emerging economies. The rapid industrialization of countries in Asia in the late 20th century such as Singapore, Malaysia and Taiwan resulted in the increase of employment opportunities for working class women, heightening their job expectations (Chin 1997; Lan 2006). These women formed the new middle class, and became first generation career women in their families. Their status as middle class and career women also led these women to be the first generation to hire live-in domestic workers. Chin sees the trend of having a housemaid among Taiwanese career women as a way of 'outsourcing part of their spousal and maternal duties' (1997: 357). Among middle class Malaysian Malay, Chinese and Indian women, hiring a live-in servant is a part of a lifestyle, part of the rules of admission into the middle class of Malaysia. Having a live-in domestic worker is one of the indicators of belonging to the middle class (Chin 1997: 372).[12] The need or demand from these middle-class women encourages further waves of migrant domestic workers.

Migrant domestic workers: No 'rain of gold' at home

In contrast to the increasing demand for migrant workers, the management of migrant workers in Indonesia, including domestic workers, is still insufficient to assure protection for them during pre-departure, while at work abroad and even upon their return to Indonesia. Table 3.6 below on the management of migrant workers from Indonesia shows the details.

Let alone for those who migrate illegally, people who seek jobs abroad and depart legally as migrant workers from Indonesia are not supported by an accountable and transparent system at home that would facilitate access to protection as an Indonesian citizen. In the standard procedures of becoming migrant workers, at least two important entities are (or should be) working together with a clear division of authority. One is the government and the other is the non-government entity, which in the case of Indonesian migrant workers would be the private agencies that recruit, train and send the workers abroad.[13]

Looking first at the role of the government, law no. 39/2004 delegates all protection matters in relation to migrant workers to private agencies. In fact, not only is protection the responsibility of private agencies, in the recruitment and training of migrant workers prior to their departure government involvement is limited to a minimum. Recruitment of migrant workers from their villages is usually conducted directly by a private agency or indirectly through networks of workers that have returned home. Such channels of recruitment are not coupled with sufficient information on migrant workers' issues. This insufficiency of information results in a low degree of understanding regarding the importance of issues concerning migrant workers in general, which in the end, prevents people from taking part in protecting those who are being recruited as future migrant workers. Even though the government is monitoring the process of recruitment by private agencies, there are still a significant number of un-monitored private agencies. Apart from the recruitment process, the government is also involved in pre-departure training. Yet, there has been no standardization of the content of training with very little emphasis on the rights of the workers, nor standardized procedures applied to private agencies by the government. The above conditions show the dependency of the government on private agencies, and behind this condition lurks the limited budget allocated for issues affecting migrant workers.

When looking at the conditions of migrant workers once they are abroad, despite the frequency of problems occurring, the number of attaché assigned to deal with such issues is very limited. This results in the inability of the government to deal with the abundant concerns and provide protection to migrant workers, although some new measures are being implemented. Apart from this, the responsibility-sharing mechanism among agencies, employers, the government and workers themselves is yet to be established. The absence of this system results in the absence of institutional support for the workers abroad, and the workers themselves have to be responsible for anything that happens to them.

The conditions for migrant workers upon return to Indonesia are not much different when it comes to institutional support from the

Table 3.6: Management of Indonesian migrant workers

Pre-departure	
Imigration law & regulation	No. 39/2004 law delegates all protection matters of migrant worker to private agencies for overseas Indonesian workers. Lack of transparency from private agencies. Insufficient budget allocation. Lack of involvement from third party.
Authority in administration	Administration dominated by dependent-relation between government and private agencies.
Information on migrant worker issues	Insufficient information to the people in general, resulting in lack of knowledge of migrant workers' issues, and a low degree of understanding regarding the importance of taking part in protecting future migrant workers.
Monitoring of recruitment by private agencies	Have been conducted, however, still a high number of private agencies are un-monitored, mainly at the level of villages, where they usually recruit future migrant workers. Punishment for private agencies is limited to administrative reprimand.
Costs paid by the migrant workers	Lack of standard for cost to be paid by future migrant workers. High cost to be paid by the migrant workers.
Pre-departure training & standardized content of training	Have been conducted, but with very little emphasis on workers' rights. Lack of standard of cost & institution who conducts the training.
Specified procedures for ending of working contract	In general, the workers do not make any legal working contract.
Authority of government to cancel working contract that does not meet minimum standard	In general, working contracts for migrant workers have not been highlighted, nor developed.
Accuracy of information on opportunity of work	Government body has begun developing accurate information, however they do not yet control the implementation of working conditions for migrant workers.
During working abroad as migrant worker	
Atache of labor issue	Insufficient number of attaché assigned to deal with migrant worker issues.
Service of protection and empowerment at embassies/consulates	Began to take place, but still insufficient compared to number of existing migrant workers.

Table 3.6: Continued

Treatment towards non-document holder migrant workers	Migrant workers without legal documents are being refused when they approach embassies/consulates to obtain their legal documents.
Access to legal-formal system/procedures for conflict resolution	Non-existent. Only on the level of discourses of 'cultural diplomacy' mediation support for migrant workers.
Responsibility sharing among agency-employer-government-worker	Migrant workers become victims since nobody will take responsibility in case of trouble; this is the result of insufficient government control over agencies.
Support in the form of independent lawyer	Embassies/consulates have appointed independent lawyers, yet the number of cases is actually much higher compared to those who surface and seek support or protection from embassies.
Upon return to Indonesia	
Networks for returned migrant workers	Non existent. Non-government organizations have not initiated such networks.
Training, business & capital consultation for returned migrant workers	Some local governments have begun such training and consultancy, but insufficient compared to number of returned migrant workers.
Collaboration with society for protection & empowerment of migrant workers	Insufficient civil society for partnership in protection & empowerment of migrant workers.

Source: The Institute for Ecosoc Rights/Migrant Care, as quoted in *Kompas* (November 26, 2010: 47).

government and private agencies. The insufficiency of civil society's role in establishing partnership between government and agencies for networks of returned migrants, and for the protection and empowerment of returned migrant workers, also puts the workers in the position of having to fend for themselves.

Looking at the management issues concerning migrant workers from Indonesia and at the statistical facts of migrant domestic workers, the point to be highlighted is that rights as migrant workers to access various support services, including rights to protection, are being denied, at home when they are preparing to depart, abroad when they are working and again at home when they return.

Unchanging fortune: Negotiated citizenship

The rights secured by the state for its people to allow their freedom yet still assure their welfare points to rights afforded through citizenship.[14] When rights are being denied, such as in the case of Indonesian migrant domestic workers, does this mean the concept of citizenship itself has disappeared due to the effects of neoliberalism, under which, instead of citizens there are only those who happen to live in a certain country? And since the inhabitants are not citizens, the government can applied a 'laissez faire' attitude and let them take care of themselves at the behest of the free market. Having joined the market, is it the individual's sole responsibility to become rich, educated and successful, or alternatively, become poor, uneducated and unfortunate (Wibowo 2003).

Before going further to connect citizenship and neoliberalism, it should be noted that the most common perception of citizenship looks at it as an ideal type, which is basically a historically constructed feature of modern state ideology.[15] Citizenship is perceived as a static relationship between an individual and a state, or as an object-like legal status granted to 'deserving' individuals on the basis of achievement, natural attributes or accident of birth. Therefore, the state should be a neutral and fair arbiter of rights based upon objective criteria, while the individual is perceived to be subject to fair and equal conditions of access to rights afforded by citizenship. As mentioned above, this conceptualization is a historically constructed feature of modern state ideology that reflects real consequences. However, Stasiulis and Bakan point out that in reality, women, slaves, colonial subjects, immigrants, religious, racial and ethnic minorities and conquered indigenous peoples were excluded historically from the ideal image of the citizen, and often from the rights accorded to such citizens (1997: 115).

Beginning from the concept of citizenship as ideal-type, Stasiulis and Bakan (1997: 113) argue that rather than looking at citizenship as a largely juridical relationship between an individual and a single nation-state, it should be re-conceptualized as a negotiated relationship. As a negotiated one, citizenship is subject to change, acted upon collectively or among individuals, which exist within social, political and economic relations of collective conflict. The process of negotiation takes place within a context which is shaped by gendered, racial and class structures and ideologies; and it involves international hierarchies among states.

Following the argument of Stasiulis and Bakan, the 'rain of stone' being experienced by Indonesian migrant domestic workers at home as well as abroad, revealing their unchanging (miss)fortune, clearly represents the fact that the capacity of the state of Indonesia as the home nation of the workers is ineffective in terms of acting on their behalf, despite their formal and legal Indonesian citizenship. The case of Indonesian migrant domestic workers is one of citizenship being negotiated on international as well as national levels.

Part II:
Global Migration, Ethnicity and Communities

4 The Rising Number of Muslim Migrants and Global Tourism: The Case of Pemogan Village in Denpasar, Bali

Yukiko Nagano

Introduction

Known as the 'Island of the Gods' or the 'Last Paradise,' the island of Bali in Indonesia is one of the world's most famous tourist resorts. The growing number of foreign tourists and the burgeoning tourism industry have brought about significant changes to Balinese society. A leading shift among them is the increase in the number of migrants arriving from outside the island in search of employment. The majority of these work-driven migrants are not from outside Indonesia but from other parts of the country. In this multiethnic nation, an increase in the number of internal migrants means growth for the ethnic groups with different religions and languages from the Balinese people, the majority of whom practice Hinduism.

This increase in migrants has added tension to the rapid changes in Balinese society brought about by tourism and increased the effects of the slump in the tourism industry in the wake of the terrorist bomb incidents of 2002 and 2005. These changes are particularly evident in Denpasar, the capital of Bali province. This chapter discusses the case of Pemogan village (Desa Pemogan) in the suburbs of Denpasar, in an attempt to shed light on the changes occurring in Balinese rural communities affected by the increased number of internal migrants.

Changes in Balinese society as a result of global tourism

Increased number of foreign tourists

In Bali, the development of tourism went into full swing in the 1980s. After 1985, the number of foreign tourists increased rapidly, from 211,222 persons in 1985 to 1,412,839 persons in 2000, a nearly seven-fold rise in 15 years (Table 4.1). The year 1998 was the only year during this period that saw a decrease in the number of tourists, due to the collapse of the Suharto regime triggered by the Asian currency crisis. After peaking in 2000, the number of tourists remained lower, with a decrease following the September 11, 2001 terrorist attacks in New York and a dramatic drop after the Bali terrorist bombing of October 2002. The island saw the return of tourists in 2004, only to see another decrease in the wake of the second wave of bombings in December 2005.

Population growth

The development of tourism increased employment opportunities and resulted in population growth. Bali's population rose from 2,558,479 persons in 1985 to 3,247,772 in 2005, a 27% increase over two decades (Table 4.2). The population of the province's capital Denpasar increased even more rapidly, from 364,419 persons in 1995 to 463,915 in 2005, a 27% increase over a single decade.

We must not overlook the fact that, even after the year 2000, the population of Bali has continued to rise at an even more rapid rate than before. This means that, despite the stagnant tourism industry and decreasing employment opportunities, the number of migrants coming to Bali in search of employment is still growing.

Increased number of migrants and KIPEM

We must be aware that the increase in population as evident in the above statistics considerably under-represents the actual population growth. This is because the figures only depict the number of people who became residents of Bali through the government prescribed change-of-residence procedures, which include a change of the address stated on each person's Indonesian ID card, called KTP (Kartu Tanda Penduduk). In addition to these new residents, Bali houses migrant workers called KIPEM. KIPEM is an acronym of the Indonesian term 'Kartu Identitas Penduduk Musiman,' which refers to the seasonal resident ID card. In Bali, migrant workers who come from other parts of the country in search of employment are called KIPEM, because they hold this temporary resident ID card.[1] These migrant workers are not counted as residents in statistical terms. However, Bali has a huge number of migrant workers from Java and Lombok. Considering these circumstances, the population of Bali is estimated to be far larger than that represented in the official data.

Table 4.1: Changes in the number of foreign tourists making direct voyages to Bali (persons)

Year	Number	Year	Number
1985	211,222	1996	1,138,895
1986	243,354	1997	1,230,316
1987	309,292	1998	1,187,153
1988	360,413	1999	1,355,799
1989	436,358	2000	1,412,839
1990	489,710	2001	1,356,774
1991	554,975	2002	1,285,842
1992	735,777	2003	993,185
1993	884,206	2004	1,457,565
1994	1,030,944	2005	1,386,448
1995	1,014,085	2006	1,260,270

Source: Statistik Bali, Bali Dalam Angka.

Table 4.2: Population changes in Bali (1985–2006)

Year	Bali	Denpasar
1985	2,558,479	–
1990	2,656,649	–
1995	2,828,026	364,419
2000	2,998,770	398,932
2001	3,048,317	–
2002	3,090,497	–
2003	3,139,022	–
2004	3,179,918	446,226
2005	3,247,772	463,915
2006	3,263,296	458,337

Source: Statistik Bali, Bali Dalam Angka.

The terrorist bombing of 2002 triggered tighter control of migrants without this temporary resident ID card. Specifically, it became a strict requirement that all Indonesian nationals whose address as stated on their ID card is not in Bali province and who intend to work in this province for three months or longer obtain a seasonal resident ID card. However, few migrants to Bali bother to apply for a temporary resident ID card. It is thus impossible even today to count the precise number of migrants coming from other provinces of Indonesia in search of employment.

Changes in land use: Decreasing paddy fields and increasing suburbia

Tourism has resulted in significant land-use changes in Bali. Table 4.3 shows a decrease in the area of wet paddy fields and an increase in that of residential land. The area under wet paddy fields fell from 98,830 hectares in 1985 to 81,207 hectares in 2005, that is, a 17,623-hectare decrease in two decades. At the same time, the area of residential land increased from 27,761 hectares in 1985 to 46,317 hectares in 2005, that is, a growth of 18,556 hectares over the same two decades. This indicates that over these two decades, the area of wet paddy fields decreased by about the same size as the increase in residential land. This change in land use came about as landowners sold farmlands, signifying that some agricultural land was converted into land for residential, commercial or industrial purposes such as roads, housing sites, factories, hotels, restaurants and souvenir shops.

Changes in Pemogan village

Desa Pemogan is a rural village in the suburbs of Denpasar. The village exhibits typical changes in Balinese society brought by global tourism. Below I use this village as an example to describe tensions between original inhabitants and migrants and discuss the background to these frictions.

Population growth and decrease in paddy fields in Pemogan village

Pemogan village is located in the south of Denpasar at a distance of seven kilometers from the city's central district. It is within commuting distance from the central zone, which houses a concentration of government buildings and private enterprises. The village is also close to Kuta and Sanur, two of Bali's most popular tourist hotspots. A bypass connecting the airport and the tourist areas cuts across the southern part of the village.

Due to its location as described above, Pemogan village has experienced rapid population growth in recent years. In 2005, it had a population of 19,424 persons and 3,990 households. The fact that it had a population of just 10,273 and 1,748 households in 1995 means that both its population and number of households doubled in a single decade (Table 4.4).

Pemogan village was a once a suburban/rural community. In former days, the majority of its residents were farmers. In recent years,

Table 4.3: Changes in land use in Bali (ha)

	Wet paddy field	Field	Crop estate	House & surrounding yard	State forest & woodland	Other	Total
1985	98,830 (17.5)	147,185 (26.1)	105,880 (18.8)	27,761 (4.9)	136,331 (24.2)	47,299 (8.4)	563,286 (100)
1990	93,291 (16.6)	125,915 (22.4)	130,852 (23.2)	33,266 (5.9)	136,791 (24.3)	43,171 (7.6)	563,286 (100)
1995	89,116 (15.8)	125,922 (22.4)	129,234 (22.9)	39,314 (7.0)	138,779 (24.7)	40,921 (7.2)	563,286 (100)
2000	85,777 (15.2)	127,429 (22.6)	127,164 (22.6)	43,550 (7.7)	138,611 (24.6)	41,136 (7.2)	563,667 (100)
2005	81,207 (14.4)	133,547 (23.7)	126,657 (22.5)	46,317 (8.2)	134,533 (23.8)	41,405 (7.4)	563,666 (100)

Source: Based on Bali Dalam Angka.
Note: Figures in parenthese indicate percent of total.

Table 4.4: Changes in population and household numbers in Pemogan village

Year	Population	Households
1995	10,273	1,748
2005	19,424	3,990

Source: Based on documents maintained at Pemogan village office.

the village's paddy fields have been diminishing day by day to make way for roads, residential land such as boarding houses and blocks of flats and commercial and industrial sites such as shops, restaurants and batik or furniture workshops. As a result, residents' occupations have diversified to include civil servants, company employees, military personnel, taxi or minibus drivers, hotel or restaurant employees, owners and employees of independent businesses such as retail shops, restaurants, pottery, batik or furniture workshops and stallholders.

Increase in the number of KIPEM

Pemogan village has also experienced a rapid increase in the number of temporary residents called KIPEM, as well as that of new permanent residents. Table 4.5 shows that this village of a little less than 20,000 residents received over 2,000 applications for new temporary resident ID cards from migrants in one year. A temporary resident ID card is only valid for three months, but can be extended an unlimited number of times subject only to payment of the required fee. More migrants apply for an extension than for a new card. This implies that most low-wage workers with a temporary resident ID card are not really 'temporary' residents, but actually live and work in Bali by extending their temporary resident ID cards many times. In addition, only a portion of migrants in this category actually apply for a temporary resident ID card, because the application involves registration fees. Therefore, the number of migrants in Pemogan village is much larger than is represented by statistical figures.

An overwhelming proportion of KIPEM holders are former Javanese residents from Java, an island adjacent to Bali (Table 4.6). A particularly large number are from Banyuwangi or Jember in East Java, a province close to Bali Island. Most of the migrants from Central Java province are from Pekalongan, a town with a thriving

Table 4.5: Changes in the number of applicants for temporary resident ID cards in Pemogan village (persons)

Year	Application for new card	Application for extension
2004	1,965	–
2005	2,284	6,155

Source: Based on documents maintained at Pemogan village office.

Table 4.6: Previous place of residence of KIPEM extension applicants (September 2005)

	East Java	Central Java	West Java	Lombok	Other[a]	Total
Number (persons)	230	34	5	27	54	350

Source: Based on documents maintained at Pemogan village office.
Note. a = Includes applicants whose previous place of residence is unknown.

batik (Javanese print cotton) industry. The second largest source of migrants is Lombok, another island adjacent to Bali. The Sasak (people from Lombok), like the majority of Javanese, are Muslim. Therefore, most of the KIPEM who have come to Bali to work are Muslims. Both Lombok and East Java have been a large source of migrants who go to foreign countries to work as laborers.[2] KIPEM in Pemogan village are primarily impoverished people from East Java and Lombok who have come to a neighboring island instead of travelling to a foreign country in search of employment.

Communities in Pemogan village

Districts

Let us turn our eye to the districts inhabited by Pemogan villagers. The village houses 16 districts, of which 15 are inhabited by Hindu Balinese and are thus referred to as *banjar* (areas (1) through (5) and (7) through (16) in Table 4.7), with the remaining *kampung* inhabited by Muslim Balinese (area (6), Kampung Islam Kepaon, in Table 4.7).[3] While the Kampung residents of Pemogan are Muslim,[4] they are not recently arrived migrants drawn by the tourism sector but are said

Table 4.7: Population and number of households in Pemogan village in each district (in 2005)

District (BJ = Banjar)	Population	Households
1. BJ Pemogan Kaja	649	168
2. BJ Panti Sari	422	106
3. BJ Panti Gede	551	105
4. BJ Dalem	283	72
5. BJ Dalem Kesumasari	456	94
6. Kampung Islam Kepaon	2,275	265
7. BJ Jaba Tengah	464	95
8. BJ Jabajati	777	140
9. BJ Duku Tangkas	1,393	344
10. BJ Taruna Bhinneka	1,319	293
11. BJ Praja Rakcaka	1,969	438
12. BJ Sakah	2,147	479
13. BJ Rangkan Sari	1,184	158
14. BJ Kajeng	1,898	379
15. BJ Gelegor Carik	1,867	474
16. BJ Gunung	1,770	380
Total	19,424	3,390

Source: Based on documents maintained at Pemogan village office.

to be descendents of Madurese migrants who came from Madura Island in the 17th century. After residing in Bali for generations, these Balinese-speaking Kampung residents in Pemogan maintain a different lifestyle to that of the Madurese. In terms of their own identity, they consider themselves Muslim Balinese.

Hindu original inhabitants versus Muslim original inhabitants

While residents of the 15 *banjar* and the Kampung are the same Balinese people, a gap caused by differences in religion and lifestyle exists between them. One example that highlights this division can be identified in an incident that occurred during the village chief election campaign of 2002. Of the three candidates for village chief, two were elected from Hindu *banjar* and one from the Muslim Kampung. Before voting took place, one of the two candidates from the Hindu *banjar* resigned from the race. As a result, the village chief election was fought between the remaining Hindu candidate and the one Muslim candidate. Backed by a larger number of residents, the Hindu candidate won and became the village chief.

This course of events suggests a sense of rivalry between Hindu and Muslim residents. Specifically, this incident reveals that Hindu residents' collective support for their candidate overcame the small differences and conflicts at play in village life to unite them in a common cause. In contrast to the above description, the dissonance between Hindu and Muslim original inhabitants is not particularly significant. Despite religious difference, both groups are formed by Balinese-speaking local Balinese residents whose families have lived in Pemogan village for generations. They have a long history of coexistence, with Hindu inhabitants living in the *banjar* and Muslim inhabitants in the Kampung,[5] and there is no significant source of friction between the two beyond a sense of rivalry.

Friction between original inhabitants and migrants

Farmers and batik workshops

Today, tensions are mounting between original inhabitants and recent migrants to Bali in search of employment alongside the advancement of tourism. Frictions are more intense between Hindu original inhabitants and Muslim migrants than those between Muslim original inhabitants and Muslim migrants.

For instance, I would like to point to the tension evident between local farmers and batik workshop owners. Despite the decrease in the area of paddy fields, the village still has approximately 200 hectares of farmland and houses 300 to 400 farmers. Following the expansion of tourism in the late 1980s, Pemogan began to see an increase in the number of batik workshops. Originally, batik was not produced on Bali Island. As its tourism industry flourished, however, many batik workshop owners and craftsmen moved to Bali from Pekalongan, Central Java, one of the famous batik-producing areas, and began to produce batik for tourists and export purposes. Batik workshops built in residential areas have caused noise issues creating friction with neighbors. In addition, wastewater containing chemical dyes has been discharged from batik workshops into rivers and has polluted irrigation water, giving rise to a serious source of conflict between workshop owners and rice farmers. These problems that are characteristic of mixed residential areas are complicated by the fact that the majority of farmers are Hindu Balinese and migrants are generally Muslim non-Balinese.

Registration fees involved in the KIPEM application

The most prominent concern among residents of Desa Pemogan is evident in the relationship between Hindu original inhabitants and Muslim temporary residents, referred to as KIPEM after the ID card as discussed above. The procedures to apply for a temporary resident ID card must be undertaken through the relevant *banjar* or *kampung* office. These involve a registration fee of 100,000 rupiahs for a new application or 30,000 rupiahs for an extension, before the applicant is registered with the village office. These fees are burdensome for temporary residents who have come such a distance in search of employment. Twenty-five percent of the fee is retained by the village office for its services, with the balance being distributed to the *banjar* or *kampung* through which the application was filed. Today, for villages with a large number of temporary residents, registration fees collected from KIPEM applicants have become a valuable source of income, the second largest source after subsidies from the province and the city. Quite a number of migrants actually fail to complete the application process, seeking to avoid the registration fees and complicated procedures. After the first terrorist bombing in 2002, local neighborhood watch groups began to conduct more frequent no-notice inspections to identify these illegal workers, creating tension between migrants and original inhabitants.

Types of Pemogan residents

As a result of the rapid population growth and the quick succession from a rural/suburban community to a mixed residential area under the influence of global tourism, Pemogan village is now experiencing a concentration of conflicts and problems. Pemogan residents can be roughly divided into four categories:
1. original Hindu Balinese inhabitants;
2. original Muslim Balinese inhabitants;
3. Hindu Balinese residents from other parts of Bali province; and
4. Muslim non-Balinese migrants from outside Bali province.

Migrants described in (4) above can be further divided into: (i) independent business owners, and (ii) impoverished people in unstable employment. My discussion thus far has identified that the most visible friction is that between (1) original Hindu inhabitants and (4) Muslim migrants. Below I analyze the background of this conflict by discussing some specific examples of type (1) and type (4) residents.[6]

Cases of Hindu original inhabitants: Farmers belonging to an irrigation organization (*subak*)

First, let me introduce the lives of type (1) residents, that is, original Hindu residents who have lived in Pemogan for generations. I do this by describing the results of interviews with farmers who belong to a local irrigation organization (*subak*).[7]

Unemployment problems of tenant farmers

Mr. Wayan (aged 43), a member of Subak Kepaon, heads a full-time farming household running a total of 1.21 hectares of paddy fields, including 0.21 hectares of his own land and one hectare of tenant land. The family used to run three hectares of tenant land, two hectares of which have been converted into residential land. Due to rising land prices, conversion of paddy fields to suburbs provides landowners with opportunities to obtain large sums of cash. It also allows landowners to run or lease boarding houses, commercial premises, restaurants or general shops. For tenant farmers, however, who constitute the majority of this sector, the conversion of paddy fields to residential land means losing their jobs. Unemployment is a particularly serious problem for tenant farmers without their own land. Mr. Kade (aged 57), a tenant farmer, used to run two hectares of tenant land which has now gradually been converted to housing land, with only 0.4 hectares remaining for him to cultivate.

Water pollution and batik workshops

At the end of the 1980s, farmers in Pemogan began to be troubled by the colored wastewater being discharged from batik workshops. Dyes used to color batik cloth were released straight into irrigation canals, polluting irrigation water and affecting rice growth. Colored wastewater caused a series of impacts, including rashes on farmers' feet, blighted rice and defective rice seedlings. Through the village chief, the *subak* chiefs asked batik workshop owners several times to stop discharging wastewater into the irrigation canals. The amount of wastewater would typically decrease temporarily soon after a complaint was made. However, this problem continues, and has escalated to the extent that some workshop owners have been discharging wastewater secretly at night. As this wastewater contains chemicals, farmers fear that not only their plants but also their livestock, including ducks and cattle, may be adversely affected.

The problem of dumped waste

Wastewater from batik workshops is not the only issue facing Pemogan farmers; they are also concerned about plastic waste accumulating in the irrigation canals. While the irrigation organizations clean the canals several times each month, this endeavor has been unable to contend with the ever-rising piles of plastic bottles and bags. Non-burnable waste has raised the canal beds and has choked the flow of irrigation water into paddy fields.

Pemogan village was the target of an awareness program against the dumping of household waste sponsored by the Mangrove Information Center (MIC), which was established in the city of Denpasar with the support of the Japan International Cooperation Agency (JICA). Every day the mangrove forests of the MIC saw a large amount of garbage drifting about, which could be traced back to Pemogan village. In Bali, household waste was traditionally either dumped into rivers or irrigation canals or buried in soil. This form of waste disposal caused no significant problems up to a certain point in time. However, the situation totally changed when Balinese people changed their consumption patterns in line with broader trends and began to produce a lot of plastic waste, which does not decompose spontaneously, and when independent businesses, such as batik and furniture workshops, were established and began to dump manufacturing waste into rivers.

At a workshop sponsored by the MIC, participants representing different districts initially shifted the blame for this problem onto the shoulders of Muslim migrants. In fact, colored wastewater containing dyes from batik workshops had been seen flowing through the mangrove forests. However, the 375m^3 solid waste collected by the MIC during its three-month-long clean-up campaign included: (1) plastics, such as plastic bottles, bags and sacks (50% of total); (2) ceremony materials (15%); (3) woody waste, such as banana tree trunks and coconut shells and twigs (10%); (4) shells, which represent

Table 4.8: Details of the 375m³ of solid waste

Type of waste	%
1. Plastics	50
2. Ceremony equipment	15
3. Woody waste	10
4. Shells	8
5. Household waste	5
6. Carcasses	5
7. Clothes	2
8. Tin cans	2
9. Mattresses	2
10. Papers	1
Total	100

Source: MIC (2002–3).

waste from aquaculture feed (8%); (5) household waste, such as vegetable and sanitary waste (5%); (6) carcasses, including chickens, pigs and dogs (5%); (7) clothing (2%); (8) tin cans (2%); (9) mattresses (2%); and (10) paper (1%) (see Table 4.8).[8] The fact that this waste included a significant amount of ceremony materials used in Hindu rites as well as the carcasses of pigs, regarded as unclean and never consumed by Muslims, reveals that this problem cannot be attributed solely to Muslim migrants. In discussing the problem of waste, we cannot ignore changes in Balinese people's lifestyles such as the fact that their drinking water now comes in plastic bottles, they now use plastic bags for shopping and their ceremonial offerings are now held in plastic containers instead of banana leaves.

Case study on Muslim migrants (1): Batik workshop owners and employees

Let us now turn our attention to the migrants themselves. First, let me discuss several cases of batik workshop owners and employees in conflict with local farmers over the issue of wastewater.

Batik workshop A

Mr. Sodikin (aged 51), a batik workshop owner, is from Pekalongan, where he worked and learned batik manufacture at his father's workshop. In 1992, he came to Bali with his wife's brothers and was employed in a batik workshop. Around 1999, he set up his own business and established his current workshop. Subsequently, he brought his wife and children to Bali to live with him. Mr. Sodikin started his own business with 23 employees. The number of employees dropped to six following the terrorist bombings in Bali, which resulted in a dramatic decrease in the number of tourists and thus demand for batik products. Mr. Sodikin is not truly an independent business owner, since he borrowed funds from the owner of a garment company in Kuta, from whom he still purchases raw materials (cloth and chemicals) and takes orders. He cannot even pay wages to his employees. Mr. Sodikin wishes to return to Pekalongan someday. Despite his desire, however, he cannot do so until he pays off his debts from the profits from his batik workshop.

Mr. Nurrohman (aged 25) has worked at this workshop since its establishment and is the longest serving of the six current employees. He is a cousin of Mr. Sodikin's wife and is the most skilled employee. At the time of my study (2006) Mr. Nurrohman was engaged to Mr. Sodikin's eldest daughter (aged 18), and they were married in 2007. The five other employees are all from the same village in Pekalongan and are distant relatives of the workshop owner. Their dream is to acquire skills on the job and save enough money to establish their own businesses.

Batik workshop B

The workshop of Mr. Mukhlisin (aged 37) had 25 employees and achieved annual sales totaling 50,000,000 rupiahs at the height of its prosperity in 1995. The number of employees has now dropped to six, with annual sales down to 20,000,000 rupiahs, due to the rising cost of raw materials in the wake of the currency crisis and to a dramatic decrease in orders from overseas customers following the September 11, 2001 terrorist attacks on the World Trade Center Building.

Of the six current employees of Mr. Mukhlisin's workshop, the longest serving is Mr. Huda (aged 35), from Malang, East Java. Mr. Huda's job history after migrating to Bali in 1990 includes making and selling souvenir sandals at tourist hotspots and repairing motorcycles at a used motorcycle shop. He began to work at this business five years ago. As there is sometimes no work for him, at night he makes leather bags at a leather-craft workshop on a part-time basis. The five other employees are all from the same village, and most are younger relatives of Mr. Huda. In addition to the six employees, two freelancers from Banyuwangi, East Java, currently work at the same batik workshop. As the workshop does not always have orders large enough to need additional workers, it is more convenient to use freelancers who are employed on a contract basis when a large order has been received. The freelancers have employment at another workshop and are made available only when Mr. Mukhlisin's workshop has large orders to be filled. His employees work at a wage of 40,000 to 60,000 rupiahs per day, depending on their skill and performance, and live in the staff accommodations (consisting of two rooms) located on the workshop premises. Accommodation and meals are provided free of charge. In its early days, the workshop employed workers from Pekalongan. However, in order to deal with rising prices and wages in Bali, the workshop has now switched to East Javanese employees. Around 1995, the workshop was able to keep costs down thanks to cheap raw materials, and received many orders. As mentioned above, costs have now increased and orders decreased. It is becoming more and more difficult to produce batik in that location, as the surrounding areas are becoming densely populated housing quarters.

The batik workshop owners' association

Currently, batik workshop owners at Pemogan belong to an association of workshop owners called Purnama (meaning 'full moon'). The association was formed in 2003 on the advice of the village head who was attempting to mediate conflicts between farmers and batik workshop owners over the wastewater issue.[9] After the establishment of this association, batik workshop owners and *subak* heads agreed, in the presence of the village head, that batik workshops must filter their wastewater before discharging it into the river, and that offenders of this rule will be fined. According to Mr. Mukhlisin, who represents the association, filtering wastewater does not require considerable capital investment, such as clarification facilities, or a significant amount of time or effort. He notes, however, that the association has no control over lackadaisical, stubborn owners who continue to allow their workshop to discharge wastewater straight into the river.

Although the association started out with 60 members, three to five members left each year due to business failure. Today it has approximately 50 members. A number of batik workshops failed due to a combination of factors: the slump in the export industry;

a dramatic decrease in orders received due to declining tourist numbers in the wake of the terrorist bombings; and the rising cost of raw materials such as cloth and dyes. Another significant factor is the rise in land rent due to increasing land value in Pemogan. Under these circumstances, the number of batik workshop owners who go under and leave the association is expected to increase in the future. Today, the friction over wastewater between *subak* farmers, who are original inhabitants, and batik workshop owners, who are migrants, is not as serious as before. However, this is simply because an increasing number of workshop owners have become bankrupt, resulting in a smaller number of batik workshops. The problem has thus not been completely solved.

For financing and other reasons, batik workshop owners are not temporary residents but are instead new permanent residents who have completed the official procedures to change their address and have been granted an ID card stating their address in Bali. However, most of their businesses are only nominally independent; they are practically subcontractors who take orders from dressmakers who have received the orders as original contractors. Even the few workshops that take orders directly from customers are, as part of the export industry, exposed to competition with Chinese capital and cheap batik from foreign manufacturers. Under these circumstances, payment of wages to employees tends to be delayed. Employees staying for three months or longer are all KIPEM or temporary resident ID card holders. Despite their fairly lengthy stays in Bali, these employees have repeated the procedures to extend their temporary resident status every three months. Since batik is craftwork, workshops originally provided employees with a place of training for prospective craftsmen seeking experience and skills with the intention to establish their own business in the future. Today, however, batik workshops in Pemogan village have become a place of unstable, low-wage daily employment, unrelated to the apprenticeship model of training.

Case study of Muslim migrants (2): Low-wage workers temporarily in Bali (KIPEM)

Below, I discuss those people called KIPEM, low-wage workers temporarily residing in Bali. KIPEM are engaged in various occupations, including working as employees of independent businesses such as batik or furniture workshops, brickyards or potteries, working as farmhands or day laborers employed by construction or public-works projects, as street vendors and restaurant employees at tourist spots, and as street stall vendors called '*kaki lima*' or working as souvenir manufacturers.

Case 1: 'Blue Lombok'—brickyard employees

First, let me discuss low-wage workers from Lombok. In Bali, low-wage workers from that island are called 'blue Lombok.' This is because most migrant workers from Lombok were originally farmers and are engaged in manual labor shunned by Balinese people, working as plasterers, bricklayers and carpenters. In fact, most blue-collar workers employed at construction or public works sites in Bali are from Lombok.

A brickyard in Pemogan employs several migrant workers from Lombok. Mr. Abas (aged 42) is the longest-serving employee and has worked at this brickyard for 10 years. He is actually something more than an employee; with his job covering accounting and placement of orders for materials, he acts as the owner's right-hand man. Back in Lombok, Mr. Abas was an independent farmer, running a 1.5 hectare paddy field. However, with his land being unproductive, he could not make enough money to support himself. He began to work in Bali in 1987. The following year he returned to Lombok, got married, and since then the couple has worked together in Bali in such jobs as brickmakers and carpenters. Mr. and Mrs. Abas work on a piece-rate basis, 120 rupiahs per brick, and receive approximately 40,000 rupiahs per day amounting to 1,000,000 rupiahs per month on average. They send 500,000 rupiahs per month to their eldest son, who lives in Lombok with Mr. Abas's older sister. They also send 30,000 to 50,000 rupiahs per month to Mrs. Abas's parents. Their second son attends a kindergarten in Kampung Islam Kepaon. Mr. Abas says that in Lombok, independent farmers like him often work away from home because they can 'make barely enough money to live, but not enough to buy clothes or send children to kindergarten or school.'

Mr. Fauze (aged 35), a younger brother of Mrs. Abas, got a job at the brickyard through Mr. Abas and has worked there for seven years. Mr. Fauze worked as a tenant farmer in Lombok after finishing junior high school. In 1996, he went to Malaysia to work on a coconut estate and was arrested for working illegally. He worked in Malaysia for approximately three years before coming to Bali. Since his marriage in 2000, both he and his wife have worked at the brickyard. Their five-year-old son lives in Lombok with the wife's parents, to whom they send 100,000 rupiahs per month. The couple saves 300,000 rupiahs per month with the aim of building a house in Lombok.

In addition to Mr. and Mrs. Abas and Mr. and Mrs. Fauze, Mr. Fauze's brothers and brothers-in-law work as employees at the same brickyard. As well as Bali, Malaysia is another key destination for migrant workers from Lombok or East Java, employed in such jobs as housemaids and foreign laborers on estates. While they are rarely arrested, most Indonesian workers in Malaysia are doing do illegally after illegal entry with the help of a contractor.

Case 2: Farm laborers from East Java—rice harvesting teams living in tent villages

Next, I would like to introduce the case of farm laborers from East Java engaged in rice harvesting. March, August and November represent the rice harvest seasons in Denpasar City and Badung Regency. During these times, tent villages appear near paddy fields housing workers harvesting the rice. Signaling another rice harvest season in the suburbs of Denpasar, these tent villages are inhabited by farmhands from Banyuwangi, East Java, who engage in seasonal harvest work in Bali.

Mr. Ayis (aged 50) and his wife live in one of the 15 tents in Badung Regency. They came to harvest rice with their two sons (aged 25 and 18), who live in the tent next door. Mr. Ayis is a farmhand back in Banyuwangi, engaged in cultivating and tilling soil and seasonal rice harvesting. Although his family stays in Bali for no more than 15 days or so at any one time, they spend more time in Bali than in Banyuwangi in terms of annual total length of stay, as they frequently travel between the two islands. They are paid 120,000 rupiahs per ton of rice, which is the same as their piece-rate for rice harvesting in Java. In Java, however, job opportunities as rice harvesters are limited, while in Bali they can find a job throughout the year in one area or another. Rice harvesting is physically the most strenuous of all types of farm work; carrying a heavy load of rice on the back gives one backache. The family has to prepare their own tents and pay their own travel expenses between Banyuwangi and Bali, including ferry and bus fares. As each stay is short, the family members do not apply for temporary resident ID cards. However, they have to pay 15,000 rupiahs per tent to the *pecalang* (a traditional neighborhood watch group in a Balinese village). All dwellers of the 15 tents are from the same neighborhood in the same village and are on 'hello' terms with one another.

Bali and Java islands are very close—the strait between them is said to be a little less than three kilometers wide. Located on the east coast of Java Island, Banyuwangi is just a stone's throw—separated only by the strait—from the west coast of Bali Island, where the ferry landing is located. Partly due to this geographical proximity, many Javanese come from Banyuwangi, East Java, to Bali to work.

Case 3: Javanese vegetable farmers

Not all migrants from Java are low-wage employees. Even though they live in shabby shacks and are called KIPEM by Balinese, some of these migrants rent land in Bali to grow vegetables, successfully enough to save some money and/or send remittances to their family members living apart from them. Mr. Umar (aged 47) has borrowed 0.2 hectares of paddy field in Pemogan village and uses this land as a market vegetable garden. He is from Banyuwangi, East Java, and came to Bali four years ago. Currently, he lives with his wife in a shack built at one corner of his vegetable garden. The farmland has been rented on an annual contract basis and produces leaf vegetables that Mr. Umar plants, tends and ships every day. Sales of his vegetables earn roughly 90,000 to 100,000 rupiahs per day. Before coming to Bali, Mr. Umar lived on his mother-in-law's estate, on which her residence was also located, and worked as an independent farmer running his mother-in-law's 1.25 hectare paddy field. The family's paddy field was only large enough to produce a small amount of rice for sale, in addition to that for in-house consumption. The family could thus not afford to send their children to school.

While it takes three months before rice is ready for harvest, vegetables can be harvested in 20 days to one month. Considering the slumping rice prices and high cost of rice cultivation, no Javanese person would dare to grow rice in Bali. Although he had never grown vegetables before, after much trial and error Mr. Umar became successful at growing marketable produce. Each month he sends 1,000,000 rupiahs to his parents in Java. The main purpose of this monthly remittance is to cover school expenses for his eldest daughter, aged 15, who is in year three at an Islamic private boarding middle school. Mr. Umar repeats that the purpose of his working in Bali is to send his daughter to school so that she will have a good education. While his two sons began to work after finishing junior high school, he wants his daughter to go on to attend university. This is what her older brothers wish for her as well.

All the migrant workers from East Java or Lombok who I met had come to Bali by relying on their siblings, relatives or friends from their hometown or other people with whom they had a social connection who had come to Bali earlier as migrant workers. In Bali, those types of migrants described in cases (1) through (3) above are referred to collectively as KIPEM. To be precise, however, not all of these workers need a temporary resident ID card; only those who intend to live in Bali for three months or longer are required to have one. The rice harvesting farmhands described in Case (2) above do not need a temporary resident ID card, as they repeat a cycle of less than three months' stay in Bali. In addition, a considerable proportion of the employees of the batik workshops and the brickyard had only recently left their hometown and had worked in Bali for less than three months and did not know if they would decide to settle there.

Those migrant workers who work together with their spouse for an extended period of time in Bali, such as the brickyard employees and the vegetable farmers described in Case (1) and Case (3), respectively, have obtained a Bali resident ID card, instead of a temporary resident ID card, by completing the official change of address procedures. This is because they have local sponsors and because it is cheaper and less troublesome to be registered as a local resident than having to pay fees and complete the procedures to extend their temporary resident ID card every three months. However, these migrant workers form the minority. Despite their long period of employment in Bali, most migrant workers I encountered had applied for a temporary resident ID card and renewed it every three months.

The word 'KIPEM' refers to low-wage laborers who come to Bali to work from outside the province. The batik workshop employees, brick-makers, farmhands and tenant farmers described above, all of whom are migrant workers from Java or Lombok, can be regarded as belonging to an impoverished group, living in a shack or basic staff accommodations. Some of these people worked diligently, despite the severe working conditions, and reduced their living expenses to save money to build a house, stall or shop or to send money to their family members to cover their children's school expenses, etc.

Background of conflicts

While the friction between batik workshop owners and *subak* farmers has emerged as a contention between Hindu original inhabitants and Muslim migrants, it also stemmed from the fact that the suburban rural communities were urbanized and transformed into mixed residential areas in a short period of time. The reason why the problem is less serious between Muslim original inhabitants and batik workshop owners than between Hindu original inhabitants and batik workshop owners is because the Kampung has scarcely no farmers and most of its residents are engaged in commerce or tourism. With respect to the problem of noise from batik workshops, complaints were also heard from Muslim original inhabitants. Therefore, the problem with batik workshops is more an issue in the mixed residential areas, where residential, farming and commercial/industrial districts coexist, than a problem with Muslim migrants.

The friction between migrants and original inhabitants over the application fees for a temporary resident ID card is a little different in nature to that between the Kampung, where the original inhabitants are Muslim, and the *banjar*, where original inhabitants are Hindu. On the mosque premises in Kampung Islam, they have established an office handling the procedures to obtain a temporary resident ID card, and have posted a banner saying, 'Remember KIPP (temporary resident ID card) Every Sunday.' These measures are intended to improve the awareness of migrant workers coming from outside Bali province in order to prevent them from suffering any disadvantage as a result of their failure to apply for a temporary resident ID card. As a matter of fact, if a no-notice inspection reveals that a migrant has not applied for, and thus does not possess, a temporary resident ID card, then he/she is required to pay a penalty of 200,000 rupiahs, in addition to an application fee of 100,000 rupiahs for a new card. Furthermore, Islamic public schools in the Kampung accept children of migrant workers with a temporary resident ID card, as well as original inhabitants of Pemogan village. In Denpasar city, the number of children of Muslim migrants has continued to increase, such that in recent years some schools have had to conduct selective examinations due to excessive numbers of applicants.

The Bali bombing incident and Ajeg Bali

A crackdown on Muslim migrants without temporary resident ID cards was initiated in the wake of the 2002 Bali terrorist bombing incident. This was intended to maintain the peace and public order in Bali as a tourist resort. This might have been inevitable, considering that the perpetrator of the terrorist bombing was a Javanese Muslim, and that he is said to have hidden in the Kampung in Denpasar before carrying out the bombing. In fact, for any Muslim coming from outside Bali, the Kampung is the easiest place to slip in relatively unnoticed. However, I cannot help feeling awkward about the government's crackdown on its nationals that appears to be as strict as that on illegal foreign workers.

This tightening of conditions coincided with the spread of the 'Ajeg Bali' movement advocated by the local paper, *Bali Post*.[10] Ajeg Bali is a cultural movement urging the Balinese people to maintain and protect their Balinese nature and tradition from any negative external influences. It was originally a slogan designed to warn local people against being carried away by the tourism boom and selling their hereditary farmland to developers of hotels and restaurants. After the Bali bombing incident, however, the movement was integrated into the maintenance of Hindu culture and began to spread with an increasingly exclusive nature, as seen with the introduction of Hindu-Balinese traditional events and ethnic costumes into school education. This movement is problematic, partly due to the fact that not all inhabitants of Bali Island who have lived there for generations are Hindu.[11]

'The migrant sells beef balls to buy land, while the Balinese sells land to buy beef balls' is a saying that spread in Bali after the terrorist bombing.[12] This is a warning against a situation where migrants from Java work diligently as street stall vendors, selling the Indonesian's favorite snack food—beef balls—and become economically successful enough to buy land in Bali, while lazy Balinese enjoy moments of luxury with the money obtained from selling off their hereditary land bit by bit, until finally losing all of their precious land and family wealth. Here, it is the diligence of the Javanese that rouses Balinese antagonism and inspires fear. By contrast, migrants from Lombok are not regarded suspiciously by Balinese people. Behind Balinese antagonism towards the Javanese is not just a sense of rivalry but also a fear of losing land to Javanese people's hard work.

Conclusion

The tension in Bali between Muslim migrants and Hindu original inhabitants that arose in the wake of the terrorist bombings, as discussed in this chapter, is not so serious as to likely develop into a violent conflict. However, against the backdrop of the stagnant tourism industry and the deteriorating public order following the terrorist bombings, the psychological rift between Muslim migrant workers from Java and Hindu original inhabitants is widening.

The factors behind the frictions between these two groups in Pemogan village include the following.

1. Under the influence of global tourism, rapid urbanization and the shift from suburban rural communities in mixed residential areas has caused concerns.
2. The widening economic gap among Balinese people that has come with the development of tourism cannot be ignored. Tourism increased the rift between landowners and non-landowners. It also brought about a disparity between winners and losers in commerce or tourism.
3. The widening economic disparity, which has been seen all over Indonesia since the Asian currency crisis between stable salary earners and those in unstable employment as well as between those with high education and those with low education, must be noted.
4. The reinforcement of local self-government under the post-Suharto regime has further contributed to exclusive localism triggered by the terrorist bombings. Amid the stagnant tourism industry after the terrorist bombing, there is growing social anxiety in Bali.

Acknowledgements

This work was written based on a report presented by the author at the Ninth Conference of the Asia Pacific Sociological Association held at Kuta in Bali, Indonesia on June 14, 2009, with substantial additions and modifications. This research was supported by a grant from the Asahi Glass Scholarship Foundation (fiscal year 2009).

5 Community and Regional Security in the Immigrant District of Bali Island

Kosuke Hishiyama

Introduction

The island of Bali has long been referred to as the 'island of gods' in tourists' discourse (Picard 1996; Vickers 1989). However, today, the island is facing a significant challenge in terms of locating such an image in light of concerns for the safety of tourists and the security of the regional community (Daring 2003; Suryawan 2005; Vickers 2003). Under the centralized regime, the National Army had a large influence, and the police force was established under the army. As the termini of these institutions, self-defense groups were stationed nationwide (Barker 1999). Unfortunately, the National Army often resorted to violence when enforcing local security. Self-defense groups played the role of local mutual surveillance, and sometimes employed violence in their enforcement tactics. However, with the democratization process, their influence quickly eroded and it became clear that there was a need for both the central and regional governments to work on reconstructing the regional security system. The two terrorist bombing incidents in Bali of 2002 and 2005 dramatically highlighted the issue of security, but this was not just a concern for the tourist district. The growth of the immigrant population was at the same time raising concerns in the residential areas (Nordholt 2005). Given these circumstances, the police set out to increase their presence by implementing countermeasures against terrorism, crime and other illegal activities. Conversely, regional communities were also now trying to foster a community image they hoped to create to enhance the security and safety of the region. Community policing in Bali as a method of achieving local security was indeed a theme that connected these two hot issues.

Community policing movements occurring around the globe provide opportunities for local people to participate in public security activities, emphasizing the notion of equality in participation.

Alternatively, activities of this nature can be seen as a trend toward exclusion that promotes inequality. Giddens (1998) noted that there are two key forms of exclusion. The first is the lack of employment opportunities, medical benefits and access to welfare services experienced by people at the lower end of society, and the second is termed the 'revolt of the elite,' in other words, the voluntary exclusion of the upper class. If the role of community policing is to promote participation from various social classes, it may contribute towards rectifying the current inequality as seen in the above two forms of exclusion.

Another issue to be considered is the public space crises. According to Ericson and Haggerty (1997), community policing is not only a system but also a discourse. *Discours* (after Foucault 1966) includes the struggle, negotiation, exclusion, suppression and network of power regarding subjectivation and identities. So, the community is never free from the possibility of being remotely directed by the police and other authorities (Yarwood 2007). If the inhabitants adopt an attitude of indifference to the contents of community policing, such a tendency will increase. Likewise, the current trend that seeks stronger risk management and surveillance in societies has the potential to undermine the foundation of civil society and public space[1] (Davis 1990: chapter 4; Young 1999).

This discussion becomes even more complex in multicultural societies where immigrants with permits to reside and work live alongside locals. There was a time in the US when some immigrants formed ghettos where exclusive zonings were implemented in the suburbs and division lines based on ethnicity and social class were clearly evident (Mckenzie 1994). At that time, the nation-state solidified its authority by managing the movement of immigrants, issuing permits and conducting regular screenings. However, as people's fluidity increased over the years, many of these divisions have lost or reconstructed their meaning (Bauman 2000; Urry 2000; Young 1999). Thus, finding solutions as to how to coexist with a diverse range of people and how to reconstitute public space within a community constitute issues that communities need to work on, in addition to addressing security concerns.

In order to proceed further, we first need to analyze some real cases of community policing. The main purpose of this chapter is to discuss and elucidate community policing in Bali, Indonesia through a number of case studies from multi-cultural regions. The chapter is structured as follows. First, in order to clarify the character of community policing as *Discours*, the concepts behind community policing in the US,

Japan, Indonesia and Bali will be compared. Through examining the situation of community policing in Bali, we will confirm that its main purpose is to provide a stop-gap measure for the official public security system created when the centralized government system collapsed, and to integrate the existing self-defense groups into one unified cohort. Then, we focus on the characteristics of one of Bali's traditional self-defense groups, Pecalang, that was reactivated during the rise of the nationalism movement. We discuss the activities of two local security organizations in the multi-cultural district of Tuban, which houses a high ratio of non-native residents. The first organization of the two is called PKD and was formed in 2001, with Pecalang as its predecessor. The second is the new Siskamling, a public security system originally institutionalized in 1980 as a central government organization that has been then reformed since 1998 by selectively adopting formats that contributed to the participation of many non-native residents in the area. Further, to better understand the new Siskamling, we will refer to an interview with a former neighborhood group leader who orchestrated the movement and has now become a member of congress. Finally, the possibilities and challenges faced by community policing in Bali will be discussed, based on the cases presented.

Community policing in the US and Japan

The fundamental philosophy underpinning community policing is the synergy between the citizens and the police. In this sense, it can be seen as a transmutation from the modern, specialized and centralized system where police alone monopolize the power of domestic security enforcement. The constellation of such new public security systems varies from country to region. In the US, neighborhood organizations are relatively active, independent and democratic. Hence, forms of community policing tend to reflect the various issues facing the local community.

Community policing must necessarily take a variety of forms, since individual communities or even districts within cities will emphasize different elements to reflect discrete local needs, traditions and values. Regardless of how it is implemented, however, community policing requires the restoration of public order and the involvement of police in maintaining that order (Kelling and Coles 1996: 158).

Furthermore, participants in community policing are granted the authority to restrict police discretion. According to Kelling and

Coles (1996: 175), 'Community crime prevention and business groups organize and apply pressure on police to modify their priorities or tactics.' For example, let us look at the case of the City of New York in the US where police tried to restore order in the subway system. In the 1980s, panhandling was endemic throughout the system (Kelling and Coles 1996: 117) and the New York City Transit Authority (NYCTA) and police moved in to take action. However, the New York Civil Liberties Union in conjunction with advocates for the homeless proffered two stipulations, that 'the homeless could establish shelters and the right to panhandle' (Kelling and Coles 1996: 125). NYCTA and police were required to coordinate and reach mutual understanding with unions, supporters of the homeless, subway passengers and the judicial and government sectors, which proved to be a long and challenging path. However, through the relationships that were built by this process, the police's initial strategy and priorities were modified and this endeavor eventually paved the way to facilitate the application of community policing in New York's public spaces.

Despite the efforts of various organizations, community policing in the US has not been able to resolve community divisions by exclusive zoning. In addition, the US is facing new challenges such as dysfunctional communities (Putnam 2000) and an increase in the number of gated communities (Blakery and Snyder 1997).

Let us now turn to the situation in Japan. In the Japanese community-policing context, it is considered desirable for each local community to follow a common ideal (Crime Control Policy Council of Japan 2003). Traditional community features such as local festivities and cooperative work within the community, intimate communication, *natural* greetings and conversation are considered as models for crime prevention. In other words, the crime rate is expected to drop by restoring such traditional forms of community. Below is a passage that expresses such a view.

> In the olden days, communities in Japan had such frequent opportunities for cooperative work at seasonal festivals and neighborhood group gatherings that communication between members inevitably became intimate. It was natural for people to approach unfamiliar faces in the neighborhood and adults to teach children right from wrong, and the community environment effectively served as a crime and juvenile delinquency prevention system. It is necessary for us to regain deter-

rence by strengthening the regional and family ties that we lost in the process of urbanization and family nuclearization. (Crime Control Policy Council of Japan 2003)

This model entails several issues. The first is a tendency to exclude non-natives and strangers. Also, whether it is productive to restore a sociocultural element that has naturally changed or deteriorated in a top-down manner is another topic for debate. In comparison to the US, the Japanese model is showing an inclination towards a homogenous society.

Community policing in Indonesia

Let us move on to discuss community policing in Indonesia, starting with 'A notice from the head of the national police' (Kepolisian Negara Republik Indonesia 2005):

> The regional communities and citizens are seen as subjects to whom the police provide service and bear responsibility ... and the residents are positioned as equal partners. ... Such concept was formulated in the process of adopting and expanding the existing security system in order to remodel community policing in a way that reflects the social characteristics and the needs of the Indonesian community. ... The features of community policing are not something to be imported from overseas but to be molded in a way that meets the values of the social life of the Indonesian citizens. ... [In the sociocultural context of Indonesian communities] social values are respected more than individual values and the cultural value of each region and ethnic group plays an influence in solving social problems in regional communities. The religious community in Indonesia is also known for its culture of respect and forgiveness. The "customary law judge" that once existed is another aspect of such culture. These circumstances may become features of a model in which community policing plays an effective role.

This article was established in relation to the policy 'Strategy of Social Police' (Strategi Perpolisian Masyarakat), implemented by the National Police in July 2005 to achieve democratic management of the policing system and cooperation with regional communities. What should be noted of the series of articles produced in the strategy is that it shares a similar concept underpinning community policing in the US and Japan, as discussed above, where citizens are regarded as being in partnership with the police. More important, however, is a unique approach in that it seeks 'Bhinneka Tunggal Ika' (lit. unity in diversity), promoting unity amongst the nation's diversity. In other words, the point for discussion is that the Indonesian system, while maintaining a nationwide consistency, was created based on a diversity of communities and cultures. Until 1998, while under the rule of the centralized regime, social diversity was only permitted within the limit of government approval and individuals were buried in the government's collectivized system. Given such historical background, the development of Indonesia's community policing system may be used as a way for the nation-state to reclaim its power, which it lost after the collapse of the centralized regime.

The situation in Bali was the same, in that the police, while taking unique local factors into consideration, adopted community policing as a means to reconstruct the security system. This was implemented under the 'help for the security of the community' (Bantuan Keamanan Desa: BANKAMDES) project in 2005. Through this project, the Denpasar City Police[2] tried to integrate the various self-defense groups as at times they had disregarded common law and resorted to violent behavior to achieve regional security. An escalation of the groups' violent behavior, including lynching, sometimes resulted in the *accidental* deaths of criminals. Self-defense groups were also involved in conducting forced immigration registration checks, which by rights falls into the government's jurisdiction, leading to extortion of what they called 'tax' or even arson in some cases where the immigrants refused to comply. The gaps in regional security systems, caused by the weakening of the central government following democratization in 1998, gave way to the rise of numerous self-defense groups. In order to construct a modern policing system, it was necessary for the police to keep them under control under the name of 'community policing.'

According to the Denpasar City Police 'Establishment of community policing project (BANKAMDES) as an obvious manifestation of the role of community':

> Regional police are organized within each province, regency, city and district. ... However, currently, there is no organization at the town and village level that has a department that deals with public order [since the collapse of the centralized regime]. This gap needs to be filled by implementing a public security system at the town

and village level. ... There is potential danger [when an organization related to public security] deviates from its basic duties... if the regional government, police and community are to learn the duties, roles and functions of each sector and agree on a common ground in the framework... various duties related to the public security and order of the regional community may be carried out effectively, efficiently and continuously. (Kepolisian Negara Republik Indonesia Daerah Bali Kota Besar Denpasar 2006)

We can see here that, in this regulation, the police do not regard self-defense groups as the bearers of regional security, but more as targets for integration. At the same time, the above statement also emphasizes the need for an alternative official regional security organization. Community policing, as per Denpasar City, is a policing system that provides a consistent and comprehensive security network throughout the community.

The traditional policing force, Pecalang

These self-defense groups, which Indonesian police seek to control, can be roughly categorized into three types. The first includes the likes of gangsters, competing with each other for employment opportunities as guards at hotels, shops and sometimes districts in tourist locations. The second type is the voluntary neighborhood organizations that perform various tasks meeting the needs and addressing the concerns of local communities. But here, we would like to focus on a third group, the traditional policing force known by the name 'Pecalang' who, dressed in traditional Bali Hindu attire, perform the role of guards at religious festivals. Pecalang, in general, refers to guardsmen in charge of traffic control at religious festivals. They dress in traditional Bali attire of a checkered black and white hip cloth (*saput poleng*) with daggers (*keris*) at their sides. The name 'Pecalang' means 'those who watch over, those who supervise' in Balinese. Its members are selected from Banjar Adat (customary neighborhood organizations), and their activities are carried out in Desa Adat (customary village) units. According to Widnyani and Widia (2002), Pecalang was originally formed when Hinduism first arrived to Bali in order to support people's social lives. However, by the end of the 19th century, during the era of kingdoms, its role was restricted to guarding temples, then to guarding the merchants under the colonial government and to traffic control during rituals under the Suharto regime. The scale and number of Pecalang were reduced and their roles or organizational format kept changing over the years, but what led them to reactivate in recent years was their appointment as guards for the Balinese campaign of the Indonesian Democratic Party of Struggle (Partai Demokrasi Indonesia-Perjuangan), led by the former President Megawati in 1998.

In 2001, a new provision was added to the Bali Province Regulation stipulating that Pecalang was to play a part in regional security measures to protect Bali's traditional aspects (Propinsi Bali 2001). Furthermore, in 2002, Satria Naradha, the leader of the local newspaper, *Bali Post* Group, bolstered the Ajeg Bali campaign that secured Pecalang's status as the vanguard and symbol of protecting Balinese traditions and community. Ajeg Bali was a nationalistic movement that actively promoted the consistency and identity of Bali, struggling amidst waves of globalization. In other words, it was an expression of Bali's 'need for self-defense' (Nordholt 2005: xvii) and the desire to 'protect [its] identity, place and culture' (Naradha 2004: ii.) Ajeg Bali, making full use of its loose slogan, justified the exclusion of immigrants and set out to unify Balinese by reinforcing 'the ethnic and exclusive profiling of culture and religion' (Nordholt 2005: xxiii). Pecalang, through this movement, also intensified.

According to an article in *Bali Post* dated June 16, 2000, Tabanan Regency in the Midwest of Bali introduced a special traditional policing unit (*pecalang khusus*) as a spontaneous security system (*system pengamanan swakarsa*). The article reported its central role in regional security systems and noted that it anticipated future collaboration with the police and armed forces. The same paper on April 18, 2001 reported that Besakih Temple, the headquarters of Bali Hindu, organized a traditional guards' group (*pecalang*) to crack down on the peddlers targeting tourists on the approach to the temple and maintain the sacred area.

Seeing Pecalang's excessive activities, Bali's provincial government revised the Bali Province Regulation in 2004 to reduce Pecalang's power, once again restricting its role to security duties at religious festivals, but Pecalang continued its involvement in various other activities. *Bali Post* reported on June 13, 2005 that Pecalang groups were mobilized to ensure security at local elections and on June 27, 2006 that they had embarked on coastal defense activities against illegal fishing and environmental destruction. Pecalang's activities to exclude the informal sectors from participation in the economy were also apparent in various regions of Bali (Vickers

2003; Soethama 2004; Suryawan 2005). These movements led the Denpasar City Police to consider Pecalang as a target of control in their BANKAMDES Project that was being developed according to a community-policing model.

Bali of the immigrants

Let us now review the trend of domestic immigrants in Bali. In the mid-1990s, Cukir and Wall (1994) conducted a survey on informal sector workers in the coastal tourist district of Sanur in southeastern Bali. According to this survey, 83% of these workers were non-natives of Bali, of which 68% were Javanese. As for demographics, 97% were below 30 years old and 90% identified as being single. Sixty-seven percent cited 'sufficient income from peddling' as motives for commencing work (multiple answers allowed), followed by 'no other better options' (57%) and 'easy work' (20%). Other frequent answers included 'for experience' and 'to get a foothold for other work.' Peddling in Bali requires authorization and license from the government, but few seemed to pay attention to the regulations or possess the actual license.

According to Yoshihara (2010: chapter 8), non-natives are now separated from Balinese local residents in that they have to carry KIPEM (Kartu Penduduk Musiman, or seasonal resident's identity card), and stricter regulations have been implemented through a top-down policy. Furthermore, as neighborhood organizations banned non-natives from peddling on the street in Sanur in 2000, informal sector workers have now almost vanished from the area.[3] As an alternative, the Tuban district, which we will discuss below, emerged as a residential quarter for non-natives.

As far as the strengthening of regulations goes, Badung Regency, in which Tuban is located, was no exception (Kabpaten Badung 2001, 2003). Badung Regency introduced KIPS (Kartu Identitas Penduduk Sementara, or temporary resident's identity card) in place of KIPEM in 2001 and mandated that non-native residents were to carry it. A fee of 50,000 rupia was charged for the card initially, with a renewal cost of 5,000 rupia to be paid every six months. However, Tuban's appeal, being in the backyard of globally renowned tourist locations such as Seminyak, Legian and Kuta and having low-cost housing within easy commuting distance to tourist destinations, was enough to attract workers from outside the island, despite such tight regulations. For example, Table 5.1 displays the change of population with attention

Table 5.1: Population by religion in Tuban and Bali

	Tuban		Bali	
	2000	2007	2000	2006
Muslim	3712 (26.1)	5184 (37.9)	180,401 (6.0)	198,933 (6.1)
Protestant	437 (3.1)	615 (4.5)	24,652 (0.8)	48,799 (1.5)
Catholic	328 (2.3)	– –	20,299 (0.7)	22,258 (0.7)
Buddhist	25 (0.2)	28 (0.2)	21,287 (0.7)	20,925 (0.6)
Hindu	9,723 (68.4)	7,867 (57.4)	2,752,131 (91.8)	2,956,875 (91.0)
Total	14,225	13,694	2,998,770	3,247,790

Source: *Kelurahan Tuban* (2000, 2007); *BPSB* (2000, 2006).
Note: Figures in brackets represent percentages.

to the religion practiced in Tuban district and across Bali. In Bali, Hindus (Bali natives) comprise more than 90% of the population, and this rate remained steady until 2006. However, in Tuban district, the rate of Hindus is relatively low and was 10 points down in 2007. Accounting for this shift, the rate of Muslim (non-native) residents increased more than 10 points in that year.

From an administrative perspective, the official segmentation of Tuban district is Tuban Town (Kelurahan Tuban), Kuta County, Badung Regency, Bali Province and is mostly occupied by residential areas. There are two customary villages in the district on each side of the international airport, Desa Adat Tuban to the north and Desa Adat Kelan to the south, and these two villages bear the responsibility of carrying out the traditional customs in Bali. Both have two neighborhood organizations within each village, Banjar Tuban Geria and Banjar Tuban Pesalakan in the former, and Banjar Kelan Desa and Banjar Kelan Abian in the latter. As of 2007, the Tuban district as a whole was populated by 3,198 households and 13,694 people in an area of 2.68km^2.

Most workers in Tuban district commute to neighboring Seminyak, Legian and Kuta (the three districts known as Samigita), one of the top tourist resorts in the nation. Work on offer includes hospitality labor dealing directly with customers such as bicycle and motorbike rentals, work at restaurants and hotels as well as souvenir handicraft production, building construction in Samigita and services targeting workers that commute to Samigita from other regions such as food stalls, basic restaurants (*warung*) and push-cart food stalls (*kakilima*).

In this chapter, we focus on Banjar Tuban Geria and Banjar Tuban Pesalakan in Desa Adat Tuban, the north side of the airport, as an example of a region with a large non-native population. There is a significant gap between the number of households registered for Banjar Adat and Banjar Dinas. Households in the former organization comprise natives who are the bearers of Bali's traditions and customs. The latter organization is simply a population register for non-natives. In Banjar Tuban Geria, the registered households for Banjar Adat and Banjar Dinas are 246 and 1,776, and in Banjar Tuban Pesalakan 259 and 2,117, respectively. In both regions, Dinas has eight times more registrations than does Adat.[4]

Tables 5.2 and 5.3 display the religions and occupations of applicants for short term stays in Banjar Tuban Pesalakan. The overwhelming majority of those seeking work are Muslims, in other words, immigrants from outside Bali Island, and we can see from the tables that this area is accepting a higher rate of immigrants than the rest of Tuban district (see also Table 5.1). Table 5.4 shows the list of occupations according to religion. Muslims comprise a high percentage of manual laborers such as construction and factory workers as well as merchants, whereas Hindus, Bali natives, form the majority of employees and self-employed workers. Workers in the former occupations achieve relatively low wages, and those in the merchant category include informal sector laborers such as peddlers and food stall laborers that support the foundation of the tourism industry. The tables also indicate that Balinese, conversely, are mainly employed in souvenir shops in management or other roles and that there is a clear division of labor between Balinese and others.

As we have seen, Tuban district, where many immigrant workers labor and live, is bordered by the airport and the popular Samigita district, essentially functioning as a backyard for the glittery tourist area (*Denpost*, January 3). It is a dark blight packed with small houses that fulfill the needs of workers on relatively low wages. The area is in dire need of an upgrade of its aging infrastructure and suffers from floods caused by the massive amount of sewage discharged from the Samigita district and noise pollution from the neighboring airport, which has been tormenting the residents for many years.

Table 5.2: *Religions of registered persons of KIPS and STPPTS at Pesalakan Tuban in 2006*

	Persons	%
Muslim	932	79.5
Protestant	43	3.7
Catholic	30	2.6
Hindu	148	12.6
Buddhist	11	0.9
Other	9	0.8
Total	1,173	100.0

Source: Created by the author from *Lingkungan Pesalakan Tuban* (2006).

Table 5.3: *The employment of registered persons of KIPS and STPPTS at Pesalakan Tuban in 2006*

	Persons	%
Employee	292	24.9
Merchant	187	15.9
Self-employed	129	11.0
Housewife	127	10.8
Construction Worker	111	9.5
Factory Worker	102	8.7
Service & Entertainment	58	4.9
Other	167	14.2
Total	1,173	100.0

Source: Created by the author from *Lingkungan Pesalakan Tuban* (2006).

In the past, Tuban district was also known for some serious public security incidents.[5] In 1998, on Nupi, Hindu New Year's Day, there was an incident involving a pile of souvenirs being burnt down on the street. These souvenirs were produced or purchased by immigrants from outside Bali Island and were stocked on the street to be sold in Samigita district. The arson was perpetrated simply because 'the pile was obstructing the traffic,' but the incident was clearly influenced by rising Balinese nationalism.

Table 5.4: Cross tabulation of religion and employment of registered persons of KIPS and STPPTS at Pesalakan Tuban in 2006

	Employee	Service and entertainment	Merchant	Self-employed	Construction worker	Factory worker	Housewife	Other	Total
Muslim	192	49	166	101	107	82	107	128	932
	(20.6)	(5.3)	(17.8)	(10.8)	(11.5)	(8.8)	(11.5)	(13.7)	(100.0)
Protestant	10	2	6	5	0	4	8	8	43
	(23.3)	(4.7)	(14.0)	(11.6)	(0.0)	(9.3)	(18.6)	(18.6)	(100.0)
Catholic	10	1	2	1	0	6	3	7	30
	(33.3)	(3.3)	(6.7)	(3.3)	(0.0)	(20.0)	(10.0)	(23.3)	(100.0)
Hindu	74	6	9	21	4	10	8	16	148
	(50.0)	(4.1)	(6.1)	(14.2)	(2.7)	(6.8)	(5.4)	(10.8)	(100.0)
Buddhist	5	0	3	1	0	0	0	2	11
	(45.5)	(0.0)	(27.3)	(9.1)	(0.0)	(0.0)	(0.0)	(18.2)	(100.0)
Total	–	–	–	–	–	–	–	–	1,164

Source: Created by the author from *Lingkungan Pesalakan Tuban* (2006).
Note: Figures in parentheses are percentages of total.

Tuban district's local security 1: PKD

As in other regions, the rising nationalism in Tuban made way for the activation of Pecalang. Pecalang's duties expanded to include escorting the local VIPs to and from the airport. However, the 2001 Bali Province Regulation that gave authority to the Pecalang presented an opportunity to reconsider Pecalang's activities in Tuban. Thus, the Tuban administrative government reconstructed a part of Pecalang as a new organization, a regional security team that went by the name of PKD.[6] PKD stands for Petugas Keamanan Desa, and translates as Desa's Security Team.

At its initial phase, PKD consisted of almost the exact same members as Pecalang. In fact, this development actually allowed Pecalang to expand their influence as they could now patrol Muslim and other religious events under PKD's authority, which was something that Hindu-based Pecalang previously could not do. Furthermore, Pecalang's traditional and customary authorities were adopted without establishing written articles or a constitution based on common law, and incidents of violence were not rare, raising serious concerns among the broader community.

In 2004, Pecalang's power was severely restricted through the amendment of the Bali Province Regulation, and PKD's authority also began to be restricted. The Regulation stated that PKD was to be governed by the Regulation and *awig-awig* (body of customary laws of the Balinese traditional community), and also that PKD needed to strengthen its connections with related organizations (Desa Adat Tuban 2004). The interesting point to note here is the fact that the Regulation stipulated that PKD base itself on *awig-awig*, the set of rules outlining that Bali's traditions and customs include maintaining its traditional neighborhood organization. The PKD at this stage was indeed Pecalang in disguise, wearing a partially fresh and secular mask.

Such circumstances finally changed after PKD was incorporated into BANKAMDES (community policing project by the police) in 2005, and again during its organizational reform in 2006. Figures 5.1 and 5.2 represent PKD and Pecalang's organizational charts, respectively. Table 5.5 shows the overlapping memberships of both organizations. Both have the head of the Desa Adat as chief and two other members as their advisors, and in this sense, the division between PKD and Pecalang is still vague at the top of the team. PKD organized itself into four groups according to districts, following

Figure 5.1: PKD's organizational chart (2006)

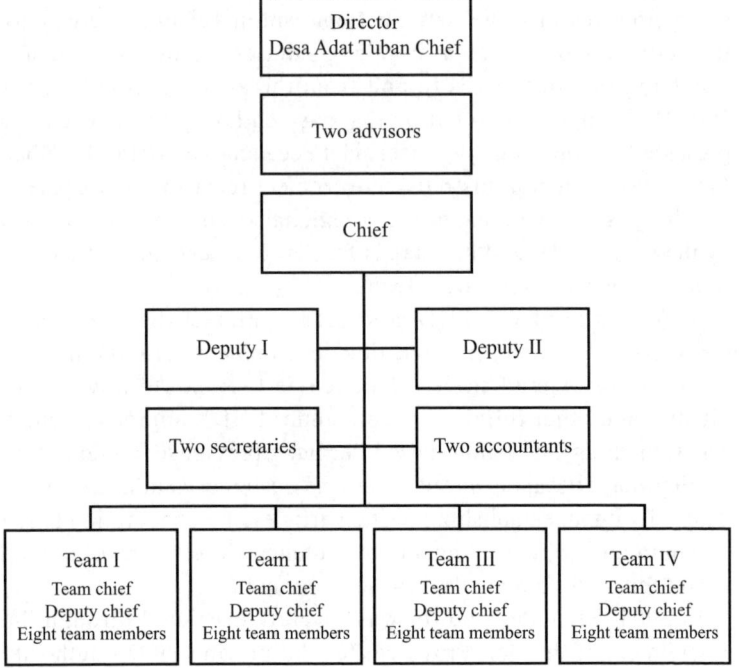

Source: Kelurahan Tuban (2006).

Pecalang's style of recruitment by area. However, at the bottom of the team, among the members of the patrol, there are very few who actually belong to both organizations. It is also noteworthy that PKD has appointed at least one non-native member to each team.

Also, during the 2006 reform, PKD implemented police training and established the route of report between PKD and the police following the incorporation to BANKAMDES, confirmed patrol courses on maps and began using walkie-talkies to enable communication between members. They also altered their patrol routes to pass by the stations of self-defense group Siskamling (see following sections) in the Tuban district to allow exchange of information. Here, we can see the original character of the self-defense group PKD, which is rationalized and maintains communication with grassroots local group Siskamling, even if the base of PKD is formed by Pecalang. We now turn to local self-defense group, Siskamling, to continue the discussion.

Figure 5.2: Pecalang's organizational chart (2006)

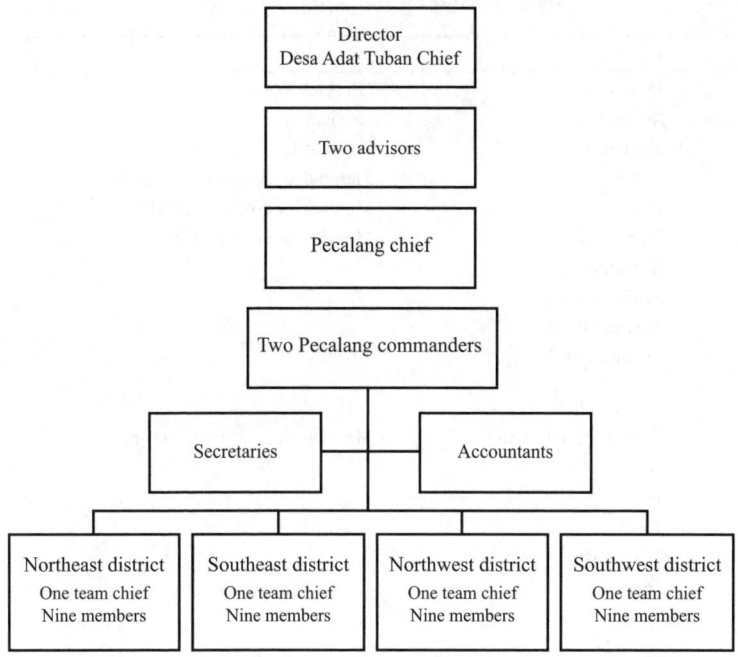

Source: Desa Pakraman Tuban (2006).

Tuban district's local security 2: A local leader's attempt

In 1998, a project entirely distinct from PDK was also in progress. Mr. M (not real name), the then head of Banjar Dinas Pesalakan (neighborhood organization in charge of the administrative aspect of Pesalakan in the district of Tuban), had the idea of maintaining regional public security and unity by reactivating an existing self-defense organization, Siskamling.[7] Prior to 1998, Desa Adat Tuban, the area north of Tuban's airport, had two Siskamling groups conducting night watch duties, each with a small station. From 1998 to 2001, Mr. M abolished the two existing Siskamling groups and ventured to establish new organizations and stations. As a result, Siskamling groups numbered 28 at its peak in April 2003, each with its own station. In Bali, it is common to see only one night watch Siskamling group per neighborhood organization. Also, as Siskamling is basically a voluntary activity, it is becoming increasingly difficult to

Table 5.5: Overlapping membership in PKD and Pecalang at Desa Adat Tuban (2006)

PKD	Pecalang
Director	Director
Advisor A	Advisor A
Advisor B	Advisor B
Chief	Member of southeast district
Deputy I	Member of northwest district
Deputy II	Member of northeast district
Secretary A	
Secretary B	
Accountant A	
Accountant B	
Team I Chief	
Team I Deputy chief	Member of southeast district
Team I-1	
Team I-2	
Team I-3[a]	
Team I-4	
Team I-5	
Team I-6	
Team I-7	
Team I-8	
Team II Chief	
Team II Deputy chief	
Team II-1	
Team II-2	
Team II-3	
Team II-4[a]	
Team II-5[a]	
Team II-6	
Team II-7	
Team II-8	
Team III Chief	
Team III Deputy Chief	Member of northwest district
Team III-1	
Team III-2	
Team III-3	
Team III-4[a]	
Team III-5	
Team III-6	
Team III-7	

Table 5.5: Continued

Team III-8	Member of northeast district
Team IV Chief	
Team IV Deputy chief	
Team IV-1	
Team IV-2	
Team IV-3	
Team IV-4	
Team IV-5	
Team IV-6	
Team IV-7[a]	
Team IV-8	

Source: Created by the author from *Desa Pakraman Tuban* (2006a, 2006b).
Note. a = Non-native member.

secure enough participants in urban areas. Considering these factors and Tuban's urban characteristics with its many immigrants, we can see the significance of having 28 groups in an area where there is only two neighborhood organizations.

Let us now attempt to explore the essence of Mr. M's leadership by reviewing his biography. Mr. M was born in 1961 and completed his education from primary school to university in Bali. He began vocational training in 1974 at Bali Beach Hotel, a historical hotel in the tourist town of Sanur, while still attending vocational school, and continued his training in a Hotel in Kuta, where he was employed until 1977. Then, he worked as a guardsman at another hotel in Kuta from 1980 to 1982, a part-time Indonesian and English teacher at a junior high school in Badung Regency from 1982 to 1989 and as a part-time English teacher at a high school in Kuta from 1986 to 1989. In 1992, he became an English instructor at the Bali Province Hotel and Tourism Education Center. In the meantime, he graduated from a private university in Denpasar, the capital city of Bali Province, in 1986 with a degree in English. From 1988, he also worked as an English tour guide, where he had the opportunity to work directly with tourists. Looking back on his career, Mr. M remembers that it was through his work as a tour guide that he realized that regional security was also in the tourist's interests. He became the head of the neighborhood organization in Pesalakan in 1997, and from the following year began to pay attention to the security of the region.

In recent years, Mr. M ran for the Congress of Badung District for the Democratic Party (Partai Demokrat: PD)[8] and won a seat in April, 2009. PD gained 3,378 votes in the Kuta electorate, which includes Tuban. Tuban won 2,165 votes of which 1,829 were cast for Mr. M (*Denpost*, April 13). Through this election, PD became the third largest party, gaining a key role in the battle for majority in the Badung Congress, which used to be dominated by two major powers: PDIP, a central player in the democratization process since 1998 and led by the former President Megawati, and GOLKAR, a conservative party headed by former President Suharto.[9] The circumstances surrounding the rise of Mr. M may be seen as an indication of the citizen's trust towards his efforts in terms of Tuban's regional security.

Mr. M's philosophy can be summarized in the following words, 'Bali has become Bali because of the people in Bali. Bali is Bali for that reason.' Therefore, it is important for all people residing in Bali, not just the Balinese, to stop excluding all external factors in an obsessive pursuit of 'Bali-ness,' and to try and coexist using such external factors in a positive way in order to activate 'Bali' without excessive 'Ajeg Bali.'

Tuban district's local security 2: The reality of Siskamling

Mr. M's philosophy was reflected in the formation of Siskamling in his local district of Pesalakan. It was not his intention to simply increase the number of Siskamling and their stations. He made sure to include many non-native residents as members, while also taking into account the need to keep an even balance in terms of birthplace so that no one group formed the majority. In fact, several Siskamling groups were entirely comprised of non-native members. Mr M also made sure that the system included the characteristics of both Java and Bali. The stations were run in a Balinese style where people sat directly on a raised-floor and communicated with each other using a special wooden bell, *kuru-kuru*. Patrolling, conversely, was conducted in a Javanese style where people used a small wooden bell called *kentongan*. The majority of the rules were based on what was previously set out by the nation-state and were written down clearly in handbooks carried by each Siskamling leader.

While establishing common ground by having some unified rules, each Siskamling had the freedom to decide on how they appointed their members. For example, one Siskamling had a roster system that took into account the population of each patrol area. The actual patrol was conducted by a group of seven members who took turns every day. The heads of the seven alleys in the district each selected one member, and the nominated seven were then free to decide on their roles, including appointing a leader, *kentongan* holder, torch holder and walkie-talkie operator before they set out on patrol. In another Siskamling, the leader, with a five-year term, was selected in an election, and it was the leader's role to assign members to actual patrol duties according to a weekly roster. Each day, eight members on the roster set out for patrol in four pairs. Meanwhile, the second most popular person in the election became the deputy, and the third became the person in charge of the religious sector. The latter was a demanding position where the responsible person was required to make decisions on public security tasks for various religious events based on consultation with the committee members of each event.

Mr. M believed that while groups were free to choose their own methods or styles, it was essential that their activities were based on a common national set of regulations that various immigrant groups could recognize as common grounds. Bali's traditional guards, Pecalang, adhered to such a very small number of regulations based on their traditions and customs that there was a potential danger that the rules would be stretched or ignored altogether. The PKD faced a similar situation, with the influence of Bali nationalism, as Pecalang was its predecessor and it had a tendency to adopt the latter's excessively authoritarian style. There were, in fact, reports of some former PKD members resorting to arrogant and aggressive behaviors.

For this reason, Mr. M emphasized the importance of a balanced power-sharing arrangement between the control of the authority and the practices at the grassroots level. Siskamling was indeed a system that supported the centralized regime from the very bottom. However, applying the system to contemporary society did not make its groups constituents of the government or police. It is important to remember that Siskamling was originally formed as a comprehensive self-defense organization with a history extending even beyond the foundation of Indonesia. Having said that, it is also true that Bali has seen some excessive grassroots movements in the form of self-defense organizations in its recent history, including the post-1998 reactivation of Pecalang and the 'Ajeg Bali' (Bali-ness) campaign. It is important that these self-defense organizations work from the grassroots level and seek to generate their own position and structure within the current reconstruction of regional security by the government and police.

Mr. M further added that Siskamling should not today be a system that forces citizens to scrutinize each other. Instead, its capacity for vigilance should be passed on and shared with other self-defense organizations, and Siskamling should concentrate on building a system to mutually monitor the functions and authorities granted to such organizations and remain alert for deviant behaviors such as arrogance and violence. Mr M argues that the process would prompt the many immigrants to realize that they too are a part of Bali, allowing them to have a stake in the prevention of the exploitation of the country. In this system, even police would become a target for monitoring. Mr. M cited the following example. Let's say, we have a thief. If the police are the only responsible body, the thief may get away by bribing the police as has been done in the past. After all, the policing system in Bali only began to function in the wake of democratization.[10] Conversely, if the thief is left in the hands of self-defense organizations, they may be beaten to death by lynching. Therefore, a system of coordination is necessary in which, for example, Siskamling groups report on each other and to PKD, PKD arrests the suspect based on its authority and reports to the police, handing the thief over.

Conclusion

Let us now review what we have learned so far. First, in our comparison of community policing, the various examples discussed were affected by the principles that were extracted from the social system and the circumstances imposed by the authorities. In the case of Japan and Indonesia, such community policing was directed to supplement the social system regardless of each local situation. In concrete, we found that in the US, the autonomy of the neighborhood organization was emphasized, whereas in Japan, historical homogeneity was accentuated. In Indonesia, community policing was discussed within the framework of reorganizing regional communities into the national vision of 'unity in diversity.' In Bali, community policing was interpreted as providing a comprehensive and consistent security system. In the case of Bali Island in particular, it was discussed in the context of the response to the traditional self-defense organization, Pecalang, which became increasingly active with the rise of Bali nationalism since the collapse of the centralized regime.

Under such circumstances, two regional security organizations were formed in Tuban district, which was experiencing an increase in the number of immigrants and rising social problems. The first organization, PKD, was developed out of Pecalang. In its early days, PKD faced similar issues as did Pecalang, but it gradually reformed itself by accepting non-native residents into its membership and implementing police training to become a responsible body for the security and communication of a wider region. The other regional security organization was Siskamling. Siskamling had become a household name in Indonesia, but the organization was given a new look as its regional operations were stationed throughout the Tuban district and immigrants were included in its activities. Siskamling focused on getting people involved in the security of the region rather than policing and controlling the community. It was, in essence, an attempt to promote community participation through the process of building a policing system. Here, non-natives were not considered as targets of surveillance but rather as partners in maintaining regional security. From these examples, unlike those implemented by the authorities, we can see the possibility of a new challenge facing Indonesia, a form of community policing that leads to equal participation.

There are, however, questions yet to be addressed. It is unclear how these regional security movements would affect Tuban's position as the backyard of Samigita district. The author believes that Tuban needs to ensure that the enhanced regional security promotes the development of further diverse activities and creates a safety net for residents rather than exposing itself to foreign currency, as in the Samigita district. It is also necessary to raise awareness and to invite the participation of a wider spectrum of residents. These discussions may also be extended and connected to those on urban governance and sustainable cities. At the same time, it should be noted that Siskamling is not the only solution to exterminating the gray zone (bribery and unfair registration) in immigrant registration and informal violence in regional communities. At a more comprehensive level of regional security, further considerations on a more formal checking system, more transparent procedures and further publications are required in the arena of regional security and immigrant administration, which would, without doubt, include Siskamling, PKD and the methods of community policing.

6 Ajeg Bali and Closed-off Town Planning: The Redevelopment of Denpasar's Central Urban Areas

Naoki Yoshihara

Introduction

Quite some time has passed since local governance became a common topic of discussion. At the same time, the term 'governance' has come to be frequently heard not only at the policy level but also in the practice of town planning. Based on this recognition, questioning the ways in which governance is embedded in a community assumes particular importance when discussing the formation and maturity of civil society in that community. However, as far as I know, governance does not seem to have materialized at the local community level; I actually have the impression that governance has remained superficial. The task at hand is to identify, at this point, what constitutes the basis for the formulation of governance, in light of the fact that governance is originally an idea based on institutional design. To begin with, let me outline three observations regarding this point.

First, focus has been placed on the mechanism of 'articulation' that cannot be incorporated into either top-down 'control' by traditional government, or 'coordination' by privatized market relations. Second, attempts have been made to materialize this 'articulation' within desynthesizing, non-compulsory collective practices that arise surrounding the dynamic relations between various actors constituting the community, who struggle and negotiate based on recognition of their different stakes. Third, in order to enable us to set our sights on this collective practice, a perspective has been introduced that keeps pace with the wavering process of understanding it. Needless to say, these observations are extremely ideological in nature.

However, these ideological matters seem to be seldom considered in actual discussions on governance. Assuming that this represents a bottleneck in governance theory, we can identify three main concerns: (1) specialization in techniques without 'principles' or 'spirit'; (2) confusion of forms and effects; and (3) the limitations of linear thinking. This resonates with Harvey's statement regarding the inseparability of neoliberalism and governance (2005).[1] While I refrain from going into details here, it is certain that stronger emphasis on governance is, in practice, more likely to be associated with neoliberalism. These circumstances indicate that governance as an ideology in institutional design has, in a sense, reached a dead end. In any case, it now seems necessary to return to the starting point to question the constitution of governance.

To facilitate the discussion on governance, this chapter focuses on what is actually called 'local initiative-based urban redevelopment.' Specifically, the 'form' of governance emerging from closed-off town planning will be elucidated by reviewing trends in the Denpasar central urban area redevelopment project that sympathize with Ajeg Bali, the 'Balinese tradition' revival movement. I also suggest possibilities and problems inherent to that form.

Setting the scene

Location

Jalan Gajah Mada (Gajah Mada Road), the area in question, is located roughly at the centre of the West Denpasar district of Denpasar, the capital of Bali Province, the Republic of Indonesia (Figure 6.1). To be more geographically precise, the area is located between 8° 18' 52" and 8° 37' 50" south latitude and between 115° 5' 29" and 115° 22' 23" east longitude, and is a total of 726 meters in length. The road is adjacent to the Puputan Square and houses many city government buildings and banks lined up on the east side, with the Badung Market, one of the largest markets in Bali, located roughly at its centre. Jalan Gajah Mada is also known for its historic townscape, with many Dutch colonial buildings remaining here and there along the road (Photo 6.1). The sections of the road lying east and west of Tukad Badung River are called New Gajah Mada and Old Gajah Mada, respectively (Figure 6.2). Two villages (*desa*) lie along Jalan Gajah Mada: Desa Pemecutan Kaja and Desa Dauh Puri Kaja. The road constitutes a typical downtown locale (Dinas Tata Kota Pemerintah Kota Denpasar 2006).

Through the ages, Gajah Mada Road was densely inhabited by Indian Muslim cloth and textile retailers and formed an urban

Figure 6.1: Location of Gajah Mada Road

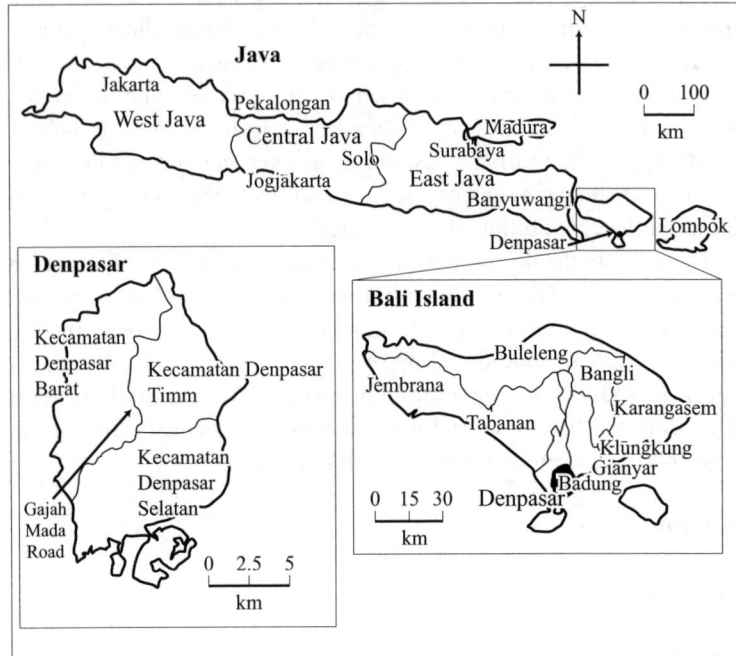

area (Photo 6.2 shows Gajah Mada Road in 1920). For a long time, Denpasar residents have bought the commodities necessary for securing food, clothing and shelter on Gajah Mada Road.[2] According to the June 2006 survey conducted by a joint team from Gajah Mada University and the Denpasar Urban Planning Bureau, there are 111 shop owners along Gajah Mada Road. Of these, 42 reported the year they opened their business: one indicated 'before 1960,' six 'during the 1960s,' 15 'during the 1970s,' 14 'during the 1980s,' four 'during the 1990s,' and two were established 'during the 2000s.' Eighty-three shop owners reported their shop's floor area: five answered 'less than 100 m^2,' six '100–200 m^2,' 23 '200–300 m^2,' 27 '300–400 m^2,' nine '500—600 m^2,' and 13 had floor-space of 'over 500 m^2' (Dwijendra and Yudantini 2007: 65). These data suggest the nature of the road primarily as a shopping strip with many privately-run shops of medium size that have taken root in the community over a fairly long period of time (see also Figure 6.2).

Ajeg Bali and Closed-off Town Planning 109

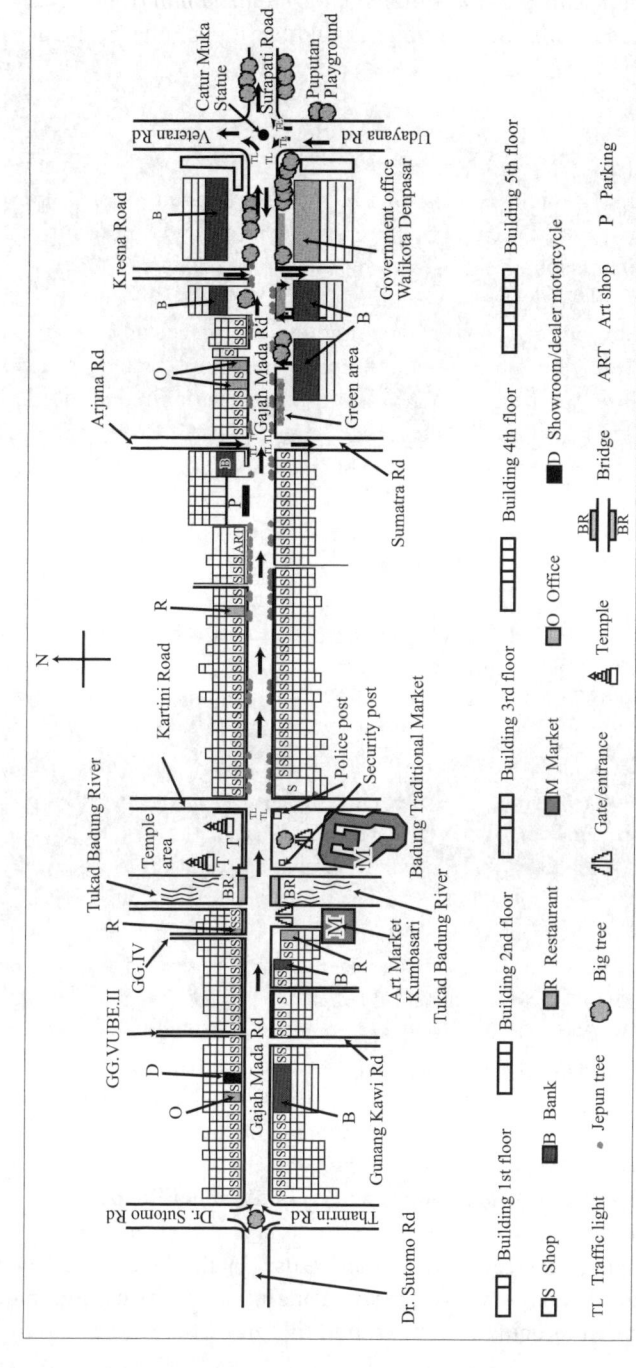

Figure 6.2: Built environment on Gajah Mada Road

Source: Mapped by author.

Photo 6.1: Gajah Mada Road in the Dutch colonial era

Source: National Archives of Indonesia.

Photo 6.2: Gajah Mada Road in the 1920s

Source: National Archives of Indonesia.

Development of global tourism and Gajah Mada Road

Following the beginning of the 1990s, Gajah Mada Road began to further develop as a street while maintaining its dynamism as a downtown precinct. From around this time, the whole of Bali was swallowed up by the wave of global tourism and rapidly emerged as a global brand. Coupled with the progress of resort development projects, commodities, people and activities became over-concentrated in the capital, Denpasar. Demographic data show that the population of Denpasar city increased by 22% between 1995 and 2004, a high growth rate similar to the 27% increase seen in Badung Regency that includes resort areas (Table 6.1).

The progress of urbanization in Denpasar in terms of population increase led to overpopulation, particularly in the central urban areas. At the same time, air pollution worsened due to traffic congestion and exhaust fumes. Crime became prolific. Under these circumstances, the biggest problem was that no official regulations were imposed on the urbanization process regarding population increase. As a result, Gajah Mada Road as a central urban area became extremely overcrowded, which even threatened to undermine the business infrastructure of retailers on the road. Residents and tourists who visited this road, most of who attended the prominent tourist spot, Badung Market, now had to contend with a degree of risk when accessing the area. Paradoxically, partly due to these circumstances, safe, zero-tolerance town planning became one of the main goals of urban restructuring/redevelopment.

Improving Gajah Mada Road: One 'form' of local initiative-based urban redevelopment

Toward road improvement

As described above, the development of global tourism brought an influx of people and commodities into central urban areas, including Gajah Mada Road, beyond social and structural limits. This resulted in chronic traffic congestion and frequent crimes, which very nearly paralyzed the town. However, the number of customers visiting the shopping strip did not necessarily increase, since many were attracted by other malls and shopping centers offering extensive parking facilities. Under these circumstances, redevelopment became an agenda. In June 2008, the Denpasar Urban Planning Bureau announced a tree-planting plan as part of the road redevelopment efforts. This represented an attempt to materialize an idea proposed by the last mayor (current vice-governor of Bali), based on the cultural city (Kota Budaya) project[3] to restore Denpasar as part of 'Bali in its former condition, richly endowed with nature.'

Table 6.1: Bali's urbanisation in terms of population (by regency)

Regency/second-class municipality	1985		1990		1995		2000		2002		2004	
	Population	Household	Population	Household	Population	Household	Population	Household	Population	Household	Population	Household
Jembrana	199,738 (95)	41,058 (82)	207,234 (98)	45,898 (91)	210,958 (100)	50,177 (100)	215,594 (102)	56,304 (112)	217,890 (103)	62,798 (125)	221,316 (105)	66,741 (133)
Tabanan	347,052 (93)	70,495 (81)	349,115 (93)	75,542 (86)	373,226 (100)	87,456 (100)	383,121 (102)	95,959 (110)	390,971 (105)	97,471 (111)	397,673 (107)	100,206 (115)
Badung	539,236 (191)	98,270 (167)	586,888 (208)	111,461 (189)	282,548 (100)	58,828 (100)	318,064 (113)	72,196 (123)	341,985 (121)	78,180 (133)	358,311 (127)	83,458 (142)
Denpasar	–	–	–	–	364,419 (100)	74,082 (100)	398,932 (109)	84,876 (115)	427,722 (117)	96,635 (130)	446,226 (122)	99,612 (134)
Gianyar	312,584 (91)	59,608 (85)	321,578 (93)	62,102 (89)	344,158 (100)	70,037 (100)	367,805 (107)	77,771 (111)	373,239 (108)	79,354 (113)	379,005 (110)	82,861 (118)
Klungkung	152,588 (95)	29,018 (93)	154,563 (96)	29,349 (94)	161,366 (100)	31,150 (100)	165,043 (102)	34,833 (112)	166,552 (103)	36,161 (116)	170,092 (105)	35,824 (115)
Bangli	166,840 (88)	34,094 (80)	173,065 (91)	38,066 (90)	189,879 (100)	42,527 (100)	198,579 (105)	47,527 (111)	199,268 (105)	48,037 (113)	210,103 (111)	50,306 (118)
Karangasem	326,920 (94)	67,030 (89)	339,545 (97)	71,922 (95)	349,415 (100)	75,733 (100)	369,320 (106)	86,767 (115)	384,208 (110)	89,208 (118)	389,576 (111)	93,319 (123)
Buleleng	513,521 (93)	109,226 (89)	524,661 (95)	120,239 (98)	552,057 (100)	123,200 (100)	582,312 (105)	136,819 (111)	588,662 (107)	143,575 (117)	607,616 (110)	148,963 (121)
Total	2,558,479 (90)	508,799 (83)	2,656,649 (94)	554,579 (90)	2,828,026 (100)	613,190 (100)	2,998,770 (106)	693,052 (113)	3,090,497 (109)	731,419 (119)	3,179,918 (112)	761,290 (124)

Note: Figures in parentheses are indices in percentage terms when the corresponding 1995 figure is taken as 100.

The announcement of the plan coincided with the aforementioned survey conducted by Gajah Mada University and the Denpasar Urban Planning Bureau seeking to ask residents how the road should be improved. Based on the survey results, it was recommended that the following measures be taken as local/community initiatives in order to retain the road's capacity as a business centre as well as maintaining the historic townscape: securing sufficient parking spaces; controlling traffic to ease congestion; developing pedestrian roads; preserving and regulating the townscape (signboards, buildings, etc.); and regulating roving vendors (*kaki lima*) and the homeless[4] (Dwijendra and Yudantini 2007: 70). These recommendations clearly comprise formal preparation for developing the tree-planting plan. However, most of the shop owners were not very interested in the proposal. The aforementioned survey contained an option that cited, 'increase flora,' as one of the measures that could be taken to improve the road. However, only 8.59% of all shop owners responded in the affirmative, indicating that the majority of local residents were passive supporters of the plan 'willing to accept the road improvement project if the authorities secured parking spaces' for them. To put it plainly, the tree-planting plan was, from the very beginning, established quite apart from the intentions of local residents or shop owners. As described below, it was, in a sense, expected that the implementation of the project would not lead to the revitalization or restoration of Gajah Mada Road.[5]

Progress of the road improvement project

The tree-planting plan was implemented during the period from December 2008 to March 2009 (Photo 6.3). At the same time, some buildings were demolished (Photo 6.4). These measures were implemented over quite a short time-span in New Gajah Mada (see Figure 6.2). In the end, however, no measures were taken to secure parking spaces, a development that was strongly requested by shop owners. Intriguingly, the road improvement project formally took 'form' through its promotion by the Denpasar Urban Planning Bureau with the approval of the two *banjar* (neighborhood units, or communities) with jurisdiction over Gajah Mada Road, namely, Banjar Wangaya Kelod and Banjar Titih which lie north and south, respectively, of the road. The road improvement project was thus conducted as such: by obtaining 'approval' from the communities, it would proceed as a locally-based urban redevelopment initiative. Incidentally, the city government obtained 'approval' from the two

Photo 6.3: Tree planting

Source: Denpasar Urban Planning Bureau.

Photo 6.4: Removal of buildings

Source: Denpasar Urban Planning Bureau.

banjar in very different ways (both are *banjar adat*, or neighboring customary units).[6]

Banjar Wangaya Kelod (450 households as of March, 2010) objected to the tree-planting plan when it was announced by Denpasar city authorities. The mayor of Denpasar did not approach the *banjar* directly; he asked a private company to negotiate with it, in response to which the company talked to the *kelian banjar* (head of the *banjar*) and the *kelian desa* (head of the *desa*). Both opposed the plan. However, this company did not convey their opposition to the mayor; instead, it forced the city's intention on the *banjar* and *desa*, saying that there would be no change. The Denpasar city authorities also made a direct request to shop owners, without going through the *banjar*, to attend an explanatory meeting. However, shop owners chose not to attend the meeting, thinking that their participation would be interpreted as acceptance of the plan. This rejection or silence consequently made it possible for the city government to assume that the local residents had 'approved' the project. Conversely, Banjar Titih (340 household as of March, 2010) totally accepted the tree-planting plan, through the positive response of the head of the *banjar* to the intention of the last mayor, with whom he had been in regular close contact. The main reason for the acceptance of the plan was that progress of the cultural city project promoted by the previous mayor would lead to the restoration/revitalization of Gajah Mada Road. In this case, the political connection[7] that had long been nurtured between the last mayor and the head of the *banjar* seems to have worked very effectively in obtaining acceptance of the project.

In any event, the local communities' response was divergent, with one opposing (ignoring) the project and the other approving it. However, the city government eventually succeeded in obtaining approval from both *banjar*/communities by cleverly avoiding the heads' intentions while cozying up to the community power structure. The communities' 'approval' was essential to allow the city government to advertise that the tree-planting plan was led by local communities, claiming that it was a local initiative-based urban redevelopment project.

Local reputation of the road improvement project

However, the road improvement project, which consists mainly of the tree-planting plan (Photo 6.5), does not so far necessarily seem to have resulted in the revitalization/restoration of Gajah Mada Road. In fact, it actually even seems to be accelerating the deterioration of the road. According to Mr. T, a shop owner whom I interviewed in March 2010, the number of shoppers decreased by 50% compared to before the implementation of the tree-planting plan. 'Balinese people use cars and motorcycles to shop. The number of customers decreased considerably because parking spaces have not been secured and because the planted

Photo 6.5: Gajah Mada Road after tree planting

Source: Taken by author.

trees prevent people on the road from looking into the shops.' Similar complaints were also often voiced by other shop owners.

In fact, more than a few shops now keep their shutters down. In addition, the cultural city project, which is superior to the road improvement project, has hardly progressed (it has actually been derailed). These circumstances again support the impression that the road improvement project has been abandoned, unfinished. The Denpasar Urban Planning Bureau, which forced the tree-planting plan on the communities, admits itself that local Denpasar residents and people coming from surrounding areas in their own cars tend to head to malls or shopping centers with large parking facilities rather than to Gajah Mada Road. In any case, these circumstances have exposed a bottleneck in the road improvement project and the tree-planting plan that failed to adopt local residents' perspectives, despite the city government's stance that it was a community-led, local initiative-based project.

Road improvement sympathizing with Ajeg Bali

'Form' of collaboration/governance

The road improvement project for Gajah Mada Road described above is characterized by the fact that, in terms of form, attempts were made or, at least seem to have been made, to implement the road improvement project based on collaboration between various stakeholders or, more precisely, based on governance entailing conflict and collaboration. Specifically, the project was promoted: (1) based on collaboration between the local shopping street, on the one hand, and the city government and university, on the other; and (2) by taking the 'form' of town planning 'from the inside,' conducted at the initiative of the *banjar* communities.

However, the road improvement project featuring 'horizontal egalitarianism,' and the view that it arose 'from the inside' were almost entirely fictional. In reality, the road improvement project was part of the town-planning project led by a city government that cleverly mobilized local communities. It is also undeniable that, because the road improvement project virtually specialized in the issue of 'green,' it was not easy to coordinate stakeholders who thus failed to reach even rough consensus. In other words, governance effectively failed to work. In any case, it would be fair to say that the improvement project for Gajah Mada Road was steeped in government over governance.

Ajeg Bali and road improvement

The above-described road improvement project, which substantially worked as government despite its facade of governance, sympathized with the Ajeg Bali movement, which advocates the protection of 'good old' traditional Bali. This further highlighted the project's governmental nature. The *Bali Post* newspaper, the largest local mass medium, consistently praised the Gajah Mada Road improvement project described above as an 'indigenous urban redevelopment project.' However, it was also the *Bali Post* group that had taken the initiative in promoting the Ajeg Bali movement (Yoshihara 2010a).

Ajeg Bali is an initiative that seeks the preservation of Balinese tradition. It became widespread during the 1990s, particularly in the latter half, promulgated by the *Bali Post* group. The factors behind this movement seem to include: (1) the compulsory introduction of Muslim short-term laborers called KIPEM (Kartu Identitas Penduduk Musiman), who emerged with the development of global tourism; and (2) the resulting appearance of new ethnoscapes (for example, a forest of mosques, too many *kaki lima*, the growing number of hijab-wearing women, bookstores flooded with Koran-related books, etc.). Most KIPEM were short-term laborers from Java who came to work on farms or at construction sites in place of local Balinese who had been drawn to jobs created with the development of global tourism (such as hotel or restaurant employees).

However, the terrorist bombing incident that occurred on October 12, 2002 triggered a new wave of Ajeg Bali. Specifically, the movement began to champion clearly social and political slogans. In the latter half of the 2000s, the movement came to focus on the dark side of global tourism, regarding it as 'evil' and attempting its eradication. Of note here is the emergence amongst some Ajeg Bali advocates of a movement to place KIPEM, short-term visitors from Java, in the same category of 'evil' as environmental destruction, widening disparity, etc. As a matter of fact, the Ajeg Bali movement is mediating the formation of a consensus that supports such measures as the exclusion of *kaki lima* and on-the-spot checks for KIPEM, called *sidak*, conducted at the initiative of local communities. These Ajeg Bali trends are undoubtedly rooted in the existing society's series of reactions—from zero tolerance to excessive security[8]—to the 'increasing Islamic impact on Balinese society.'

When we think about it, it is the multilayered social composition based on syncretism that is deeply rooted in the base of Balinese Hindu society. For this reason, Balinese society has an open nature even though it has been called the 'Hindu island.' However, in light of the current sympathy with Ajeg Bali, Balinese society has a stronger desire for an homogenous local culture that is incompatible with the aforementioned multilayered composition. This is neither an imitation of post-'Pancasila democracy' (officially, 'guided democracy' that aims at 'fair and cultural humanitarianism') nor 'distorted' or 'inverted' multiculturalism. It is exactly (a movement aiming at) the pure self-presentation of Balinese Hindus.[9] What is intriguing is the fact that the Gajah Mada Road improvement project sympathized with Ajeg Bali and proceeded as a town planning project which, on the one hand, sought 'Bali in its former condition richly endowed with nature' or the 'good old Bali,' while, on the other, protected local residents from 'invasion' by KIPEM, with consistent zero tolerance for 'foreign things.' While I refrain from going into detail here, the Gajah Mada Road improvement project has a strong global aspect.[10]

Closed-off town planning

For the very reasons described above, the 'local initiative-based urban redevelopment project,' a favorite catchphrase used by Denpasar city authorities, was in the end a pie in the sky, and the Gajah Mada Road improvement project had no choice but to actually become highly integrated and amenable to government from above. In other words, the project was based on community mobilization from above rather than being driven by the communities themselves, just like the Ajeg Bali movement. It is true that the road improvement project was itself based on struggles between various stakeholders and potentially was, for this reason, an experimental field of governance.

However, what was actually evident was a scheme in which the city government 'coordinated' the struggles of various claimants in advance through a private agent and community leaders (heads of *banjar*), and the development of a situation where 'foreign persons' came to be excluded by association with Ajeg Bali. At any rate, in the Gajah Mada Road improvement project, open governance that ensures competition between various stakeholders failed to work. Needless to say, the project did not provide a potential momentum for 'articulation,' as mentioned in the beginning of this chapter— articulation as an operating principle that works when different entities form a 'collective will' from disparate positions by changing their respective identities, without the privileging of any single entity (Laclau and Mouff 1985). The development existed exactly as a closed-off town-planning project.

In place of conclusion: Focusing on post-'development'

Assuming that the Gajah Mada Road improvement project constitutes a 'model case' of local initiative-based urban redevelopment, this example seems to indicate that governance, regarded as paralleling local initiative-based urban redevelopment in this chapter, is actually the other side of government, and that, in the first place, this model case can, in its nature, still be discussed within the framework of a development regime. In other words, the Gajah Mada Road improvement project, which was made to look like a local initiative-based urban redevelopment project by mobilizing local communities, was not, after all, completely independent from the system of government under the development regime,[11] no matter what new conceptual framework may have been used to describe it. The aforementioned scheme in which the road improvement project was arranged through the community power structure, in which community leaders were subordinate to their political superiors, was, upon reflection, actually widespread under the development regime.

At the same time, the fact that the project was made to look like a form of governance also indicates a 'form' unique to post-'development' that can no longer be controlled by centralized government. To put it plainly, after the development state exited the scene, government was only able to continue to exist by using governance as a bypass and working as if it were governance. Therefore, the phrase 'from government to governance' should refer to functional changes in light of the fact that government and governance structurally form a continuum.

In the present case, government was substantially the crucial player in the project, despite the facade of governance in procedure. Of particular note is that this case seems to more or less indicate a phase of locality that emerged with the development of globalization, in addition to the fact that it is unique to post-'development.' I will not reiterate the ways in which the present case sympathizes with Ajeg Bali. Upon consideration, however, it is Ajeg Bali that symbolically represents the present state of locality under globalization. Assuming that one of the outstanding achievements of globalization is multiculturalism as a form of universalism, Ajeg Bali represents an attempt to achieve multiculturalism at a peculiar level. This is exactly why this movement led to the communities' initiative that focused on the risks posed by the disappearance of 'boundaries' and differences and attempted to protect cultural tradition, which was becoming 'impure' as a result of the 'invasion' by immigrants, and to denounce foreign cultures. In any case, this was where the closed-off town planning was generated from a harmonious mixture of the 'good old town,' keenly advocated by communitarians, and the 'beautiful town' arising from zero tolerance ideology. This precisely represents local reactions to globalization.[12]

However, further analysis of the present case reveals that, in situations other than closed-off town planning initiatives based on government, a faint movement is emerging that intends to extricate intentional policy aspects of governance in order to achieve collective viability of individuals. This movement is seen mainly among those who are going under with the decline of the shopping strip and those who are being excluded under the 'beautiful town' slogan. In fact, despite the overcrowded condition of the road, there has been a move to create a diverse, lively street by inviting the participation of local community residents and visitors to the area. This movement is evident among shop owners who are on the verge of crisis due to the malls and shopping centers with large parking facilities that have drawn many customers from Gajah Mada Road. These shop owners have chosen not to easily rely on something like a cleanup plan for Tukad Badung River included in the superior cultural city project, based on their awareness that this plan will end up as a pie in the sky without improving the largest slum in Denpasar, located upstream. As if stimulated by this movement, the Denpasar city authorities began to construct parking facilities in 2010.

Stakeholders of or parties to the issue are no longer seeking government-led stereotypical, classic town planning or a 'beautiful town' formed by excluding 'foreign others.' Instead, they have begun to seek town planning based on governance that will enable 'local people to provide various solutions that can be changed and to form a new consensus, in response to which policy will change, which, in turn, will change people's relationships and their structure' (Hosaka 2005). This represents an activity at the ideological level, as mentioned at the beginning of this chapter, that attempts to establish the 'identity as party' to the issue through governance, and is also a predictor of what emergent town planning will be like in the post-'development' era.[13]

7 Economics of the Formation and Development of the Okinawan Urban Ethnic Community: From the Perspective of the Accumulation of Self-Employed Business Strategies

Kōichi Mori

Introduction

The purpose of this chapter is to describe and analyze the economics of the formation and development of 'Okinawan Village' in Vila Carrão or 'Carrão Village,' an Okinawan urban ethnic community established after the Second World War in the eastern part of the City of São Paulo, Brazil. According to the life strategy transition model of Japanese migrants (*nikkeijin*) developed by Takashi Maeyama (1983), Japanese migrants who changed their plans from *dekassegui* (temporary economic migration) to *eijū* (permanent residency) after the war began to aim toward socioeconomic ascension in São Paulo and other cities. They adopted a self-employed business strategy[1] in urban areas and attempted to climb the social ladder by investing family labor into their independent enterprises. According to the said model, the above accompanied another strategy, a white-collar technocrat-type socioeconomic ascension approach involving the operation of family businesses in order to send the younger generation to higher education institutions to achieve economic success as well as social prestige. This was due to the fact that offering better educational opportunities to the second generation in order to succeed in Brazilian society was a central goal underpinning the migrants' shift into urban areas.

Maeyama (1990: 217) points out the following characteristics regarding the initial choice of occupation by Japanese migrants (*nikkeijin*) in São Paulo after moving to urban areas:

A majority of the *nikkeijin* chose to become self-employed business owners in the early stages of urbanization. Their cultural and linguistic handicap was a major factor but it was also because European migrants dominated the more favorable industrial labor sector. Japanese migrants who did not have specialized skills in that field chose to operate small-scale family-run businesses by mobilizing wage-free family workers. In this respect, characteristic occupations among the *nikkeijin* are the laundry business (called the "laundry and dyeing business") and the sale of farm produce (wholesale at the central market, retail sale, street stalls, greengrocers etc.).

According to Maeyama, Japanese migrants who had relocated to the cities managed to establish economic niches in the laundry and farm produce businesses by way of small-scale family-run enterprises, and concentrated on them in view of their own situation (cultural and linguistic handicaps, lack of specialized skills, availability of family labor etc.) and market opportunities (domination of the industrial labor market by European migrants) in their economic adaptation. Maeyama's view is echoed by Aldrich and Waldinger (1990) who have studied the issue of immigrants in general and their entrepreneurialism in particular and concluded that immigrants' entrepreneurialism is a form of economic adaptation precipitated by an interaction between opportunity structure and group characteristics. Both Maeyama and Aldrich and Waldinger (1990), aim to construct a general model of one aspect, be it the life strategy of Japanese migrants in Brazil or migrants' entrepreneurialism, from a macroscopic viewpoint. I intend to consider the issue of urban economic adaptation among Japanese migrants from a microscopic perspective by focusing more intensely on local conditions (local market characteristics). As I mention below, the initial family businesses they established in Okinawan Village in Vila Carrão were not laundries and farm produce vendors as reported by Maeyama, but subcontract sewing businesses and *pastel* sellers at the *feira livre* (open market). I argue that their choices of business cannot be explained unless we consider the unique characteristics of the area into which early migrants moved and settled that shape some of the components of the opportunity structure.[2] I examine the actual state of urban economic adaptation on the micro level by reference to studies by Maeyama, Aldrich and Waldinger and others, particularly through critically utilizing Maeyama's macro model.

Incidentally, in recent years studies on migrants and entrepreneurialism from a 'microeconomic theory' approach have placed importance on actors and the collective outcome of their actions in migrants' entrepreneurial activities at the micro level (Higuchi and Takahashi 1998). These studies emphasize the importance of the presence of 'leaders' and 'preceding achievers,' and the existence of 'informal training systems' or skills and information acquisition systems developed under these predecessors. Through these predecessors and systems, the opportunity structure of a certain economic niche becomes recognizable to successors and entry barriers are lowered, facilitating concentration on a certain type of business. After entering into a particular niche, the group characteristics of the migrants and the formation of enclaves (economic generalization) consisting of horizontal and vertical labor division structures in that niche become more important.

The existence of predecessors and informal training systems appears important in explaining migrants' entry and concentration into a certain economic niche. Yet, neither Maeyama nor microeconomic studies on migrants' entrepreneurialism appear to adequately explain the formation and development process of self-employment-based local ethnic communities in certain localities. In this paper, I elaborate a more intensive urban adaptation process from the aforementioned viewpoint by relating the self-employment business strategies of Japanese migrants from Okinawa and their development in a certain locality to the question of the formation and development process of a local ethnic community.

Okinawan migrants in Vila Carrão, east São Paulo

A summary of Vila Carrão

From around 1946 Japanese migrants from Okinawa and their children began moving to and settling in Vila Carrão and neighboring administrative districts (Vila Matilde, Tatuape, Aricanduva, Vila Formosa, São Lucas, etc.) in the eastern part of the City of São Paulo. This area has become the region housing the largest number of Okinawan migrants in the city, currently inhabited by about 1,000 households of Okinawan descent. Okinawan migrants in this area form organizations, groups and networks based on various organizational principles such as multilayered homeland fellowships (from Okinawa Prefecture to *shima* (hamlet community)), clan and kinship relations, shared immigration experiences, trade associations and shared religious beliefs as an extension of Okinawa as the common

Figure 7.1: Map of São Paulo City, Vila Carrão and surrounding districts

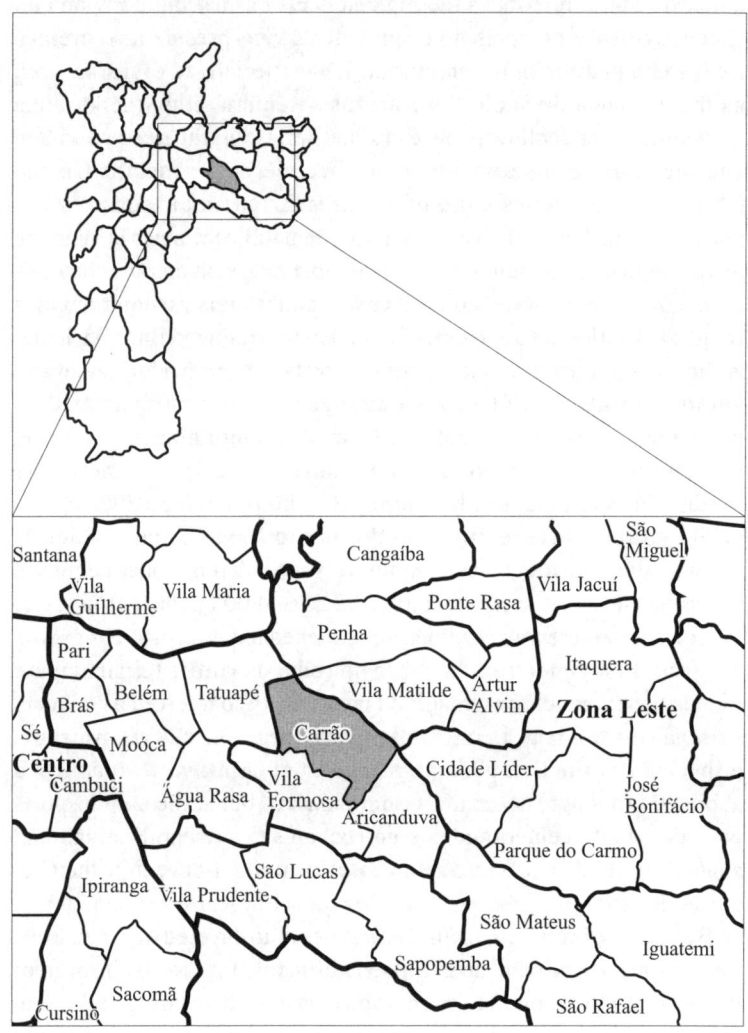

Source: Original Map published on the homepage of São Paulo Prefecture, 2010.

origem (origin). Among these Okinawan migrants' organizations, the Vila Carrão branch of the Okinawa Association of Brazil, organized on the basis of the shared Okinawan origin and a loose sense of neighborhood born from living in Vila Carrão and its neighboring districts, is recognized as the largest and most central ethnic organization, with about 450 member-families.[3] This branch is organized around a board of 50 directors as the highest decision-making body and an executive office comprising of president, vice-president, secretary, treasurer and director of secretariat. It has specialized divisions such as the women's division, the Kariyushi seniors' club, the karaoke division, the gateball (Japanese croquet) division, the dance division and the table tennis division, and effectively operates the Carrão Okinawa School consisting of a kindergarten and a Japanese language school. The branch area is divided into 21 sections based on the local community (neighborhood) principle and each member belongs to one of these sections.[4] It has its own 'hall' that is used not only for branch activities but also for individual members' weddings, Oriental zodiac-based birthday celebrations, entertainment, performance and karaoke events as well as a wide range of activities conducted by other local ethnic organizations formed through hometown, trade and immigration (shared experiences) relationships and networks (Shibu Sōritsu 50-shūnen Kinen Shi Henshū Iinkai (ed.) 2008).

The branch's recreational field day in Vila Carrão, which is reportedly the biggest event exclusively attended by local people of Okinawan descent, currently attracts 3,000–4,000 people as many of the families and relatives who have branched out, separated or moved out from first generation member households gather to participate. This is the extent of the 'imagined community' perceived as 'Carrão Village,' or 'Carrão is one *shima*,' by local Okinawan migrants (especially of the first generation). Festival Okinawa was launched about 10 years ago, not at the association hall but at the public sports park in the city center modeled on Hawaii's Okinawan Festival, and since 2010 it has been an official local community event of the City of São Paulo.

Besides the branch, Carrão District has multilayered organizations involving Okinawan migrants, including private schools for Ryūkyū performing arts (dancing, singing, drumming, classical music, snakeskin *samisen* playing and harp playing) and traditional Ryūkyū marshall arts (karate), a society of Bolivian re-settlers (who share the experience of migration from Bolivia to Brazil), the Zona Leste Association (Okinawa Seinentai migrants), hometown-based organizations from the hamlet level (Oroku and Tabaru communities) to the city/town/village levels (Yomitan village, etc.) and trade associations based on Okinawan trade relations. In the area of faith, the Spirit of Jesus Church and Inochi No Michi Kyōkai, both of which are Protestant churches from Okinawa, have set up in Carrão, and a number of *yuta* and *ugansā* (shamans) who have completed *michiake* (training) in Brazil are operating mainly in the areas of ancestor worship and problem solving.

Relocation and settlement of Okinawan migrants

Okinawan migrants began to move and settle in this area in 1946 immediately after the end of the Second World War, initiated by a family of migrants who had come to Brazil from former Oroku Village before the war, moved into this area and opened a laundry in the main street of Av. Conselheiro Carrão. Carrão District in those days was a *chacara* (small farming) zone on the periphery of São Paulo City, and although *loteamento* (residential subdivision) began in the early 20th century, it was very much a rural district with a small population concentrating in the only residential area along the main street of Av. Conselheiro Carrão. Still, there was a bus route connecting the district and the city that offered access via Bras District, established as the 'sewing base' in the 1930s, and Mercado District with its city-operated market.[5]

The move to and settlement in Carrão by Okinawan migrants began in 1946. Those originally from Oroku Village in Okinawa moved in through hometown relations (see Table 7.1) in the very early stages of this process. The opening of the *feira livre* in Vila Carrão in 1949 promoted the relocation and settlement process, mainly led by those from former Oroku Village. The number of Okinawan migrant households in Carrão reached 27 by 1956, and these families formed the Vila Carrão branch of the Okinawa Association of Brazil in the same year.

Table 7.2 shows changes in the number of branch members from 1957 to 2006. The membership expanded from less than 100 families in the 1950s to over 200 by the mid-1960s, over 300 by the early 1970s and to 430 by the mid-1970s. As the membership size has remained at around 420–450 to this day, it is possible to surmise that the relocation of first generation Okinawan migrant families to Carrão slowed or ceased altogether in the 1970s. Up to the early 1950s, the Okinawan migrants who relocated to Carrão District were mostly prewar migrant families from the inland districts of the State of São Paulo. Postwar migrants arrived from the 1952 resumption of immigration (1953 in effect), and many Okinawan migrants relocated from Bolivia from the 1960s to the early 1970s. The

Table 7.1: *The relocation and settlement of Okinawan migrants in Vila Carrão (early period)*

	Events and re-settlers
1946	The first relocation and settlement of Okinawan migrants in Vila Carrão. Saburō and Moushi Teruya (Oroku) (1946).
1947	Chain migration of the *urukūnchu* (Oroku people) began. The Kamieda family (Oroku), the Takara family (Oroku).
1949	The *feira livre* was established in Vila Carrão. It promoted a further relocation and settlement of the *urukūnchu*.
1956	The Vila Carrão branch of the Okinawa Association of Brazil was founded by 27 families in Vila Carrão. The number of postwar migrants from Okinawa increased rapidly from around this period using travel funds borrowed from the Ryūkyū Immigration Bank and the Japanese Government. The relocation and re-settlement of postwar migrants in Vila Carrão also began.

Table 7.2: *Changes in the membership size of the Vila Carrão branch of the Okinawa Association of Brazil*

Year	Members
1957	27
1958	27
1959	72
1960	84
1961	121
1962	132
1963	150
1964	204
1965	218
1966	234
1967	229
1968	236
1969	274
1970	310
1971	312
1972	347
1975	428
1984	429
1988	379
1995	450
2005	437
2006	450

membership exceeded 400 households from the mid-1970s, but this number temporarily decreased in the late 1980s when first generation migrants embarked on *dekassegui* (temporary work sojourn) in Japan, then hovered around 450 households from the 1990s to date (2,164 persons in 450 households in 2006).

As we will clearly see from the cases reported below, the relocation to and settlement in Carrão District by Okinawan migrants took place in the form of chain migration, mainly effected through the networks of kinship relations (including matrimonial relations) and hometown ties, and consequently exhibited a tendency towards the concentration of households originating from several communities. As at 2006, of the 421 member households where the head of the household's place of origin is known, the predominant group consisted of 142 households (33.7%) from Naha City and 140 from former Oroku Village (Oroku and Tabaru communities). They are followed by 27 households from Nishihara Town, 27 from Nakagusu Village, 26 from Nago City, 25 from Okinawa City, 24 from Yomitan Village and 19 from Yaese Town.

Occupational composition of Okinawan migrants in Carrão District

No statistical data exist on the occupational composition of all Okinawan households in Vila Carrão. The only resource that gives us glimpses in this regard are the occupational composition data of the Okinawa Association branch member households in 1984 and 2006, shown in Tables 7.3 and 7.4. Data have been collected based on actual surveys conducted at ten year intervals since 1977 regarding the occupational composition of households from former Oroku Village (Oroku and Tabaru hamlets in Naha City), accounting for one third of the total membership of the Vila Carrão branch. The data are not limited to the Okinawan migrants from Oroku in Vila Carrão, but they can be used as a secondary resource considering that about 40% of the Okinawan migrants from Oroku are concentrated in Vila Carrão (Table 7.5). Let us look at the characteristics of the occupational composition of Okinawan migrant households in Vila Carrão.

Table 7.3 shows the occupational composition of the branch members in 1984. The most notable features of this table are the predominance of self-employed businesses and the very low number of members in professional or white-collar occupations such as company workers (6), dentists (2), lawyers (2) and accountants (1). This demonstrates that the economic adaptation strategy adopted

Table 7.3: Okinawa Association members in Vila Carrão by occupation (1984)

Rank	Occupation	Actual number (persons)	Ratio	Rank	Occupation	Actual number (persons)	Ratio
1	*Custura* (sewing subcontractor)	155	36.1	21	Travel agent	2	0.5
2	*Feirante* (market seller)	76	17.7	28	Second-hand furniture shop	1	0.2
3	Supermarket	19	4.4	28	Grocery wholesaler	1	0.2
4	Bar	8	1.9	28	Electrical goods shop	1	0.2
4	Clothes shop	8	1.9	28	Priest	1	0.2
4	*Confeccion* (ready-made clothes shop)	8	1.9	28	Imported sewing machine seller	1	0.2
7	Cosmetics shop	7	1.6	28	Second-hand car dealer	1	0.2
8	Company worker	6	1.4	28	Camera shop	1	0.2
8	*Pasteleiro*	6	1.4	28	General store	1	0.2
10	Confectioner	5	1.2	28	Fish shop	1	0.2
11	Broker	4	1	28	Tofu producer	1	0.2
11	Real estate agent	4	1	28	Accountant	1	0.2
11	Hardware shop	4	1	28	Ironworks operator	1	0.2
11	Gasoline station	4	1	28	Woodworking plant operator	1	0.2
11	Café operator	4	1	28	Transport company	1	0.2
16	Eatery	3	–	28	Foundry operator	1	0.2
16	Itinerant trade	3	0.7	28	Sports shop	1	0.2

16	Acupuncture therapist	3	0.7	28	Radio/TV repairer	1	0.2
16	Trinket shop	3	0.7	28	Hairdressing salon operator	1	0.2
16	Grocery shop	3	0.7	28	Samisen shop	1	0.2
21	Dentist	2	0.7	28	Laundry	1	0.2
21	Auto repairer	2	0.5	28	Farming (vegetable grower)	1	0.2
21	Passador (iron operator)	2	0.5	28	—	—	0.2
21	Confectionery wholesaler	2	0.5	28	—	—	0.2
21	Building materials shop	2	0.5	28	—	—	0.2
21	Lawyer	2	0.5	—	—	—	—
21	—	2	0.5	—	Retired	38	8.9
21	—	2	0.5	—	Unknown	23	5.4
—	—	—	0.5	—	—	—	—

by the Okinawan migrants who settled in this district centered on self-employed occupations. The second notable characteristic is the high concentration in two occupations among the self-employed sector—*custura* (dressmaker) and *feirante* (market stall keeper) that account for 36.1% and 17.7% respectively, and comprise more than one half of the occupations of the entire membership. These two forms of employment can be considered to have characteristics that differ from those of the other self-employed occupations, in that they involve the production and sale of so-called non-ethnic goods (products not linked to the *origem* of Japan or Okinawa) and that they do not target the local market of Vila Carrão.

Table 7.4 shows occupations that account for relatively high proportions of the total occupations of the branch members and member households in 2006. According to the table, 98 households contain professionals and white-collar workers which formed the largest occupational category in 2006, followed by 41 households involved in the self-employed hardware and building materials wholesaler/retailer category, 31 households in sewing-related businesses (production, wholesale and retail) and 21 households in the cosmetics retail business. Although the households with self-employed occupations still predominate, the proportion of members who have professional and white-collar jobs has increased considerably since 1984. As mentioned in the Introduction, this probably relates to the fact that while their economic adaptation strategy in the postwar urban districts was based on self-employment, they also adopted what can be called a white collar technocrat-type strategy at the same time by organizing family labor in a flexible manner to allow their children to undertake higher education and obtain economic success and social prestige. The development of this white-collar strategy as part of the self-employed business approach is demonstrated in the occupational characteristic that shows a rapid increase in the number of professionals and white-collar workers among those from Oroku Village (in Table 7.5) from around 8% in the latter half of the 1970s to 29% by 1987 and 38% by 1997.

When we compare the self-employed occupations of 1984 and 2006, we notice a considerable reduction in the numbers of dressmakers and *feirantes*. Especially in 2006, only five households were engaged in the *feirante* business. Conversely, the occupations related to hardware and building materials and cosmetics retailing emerged to replace these self-employed occupations in 2006. Looking at the occupational composition of the migrants from former Oroku Village and their

Table 7.4: Number of workers in each member family by occupation (2006)

		Persons	Families
1	Cosmetics retailer	111	22
2	Hardware & building materials (wholesaler & retailer)	102	41
3	Sewing (producer, wholesaler, retailer)	90	31
4	Japanese foods & general merchandise (including supermarket)	51	7
5	*Feirante*	40	5
6	*Dekassegui* worker in Japan	35	8
7	Restaurant	17	6
8	Auto parts & repair	14	9
9	Travel agent	3	3
10	Professional & white collar	182	98
11	Student	345	–
12	Unknown & other	95	–
	Total	1085	–

Source: Shibu Sōritsu 50-shūnen Kinen Shi Henshū Iinkai (ed.) (2008: 328), partially modified.

children, we can identify a rising trend in cosmetics retailing from the 1980s, and in the hardware and building materials sector from the latter half of the 1980s to the 1990s.

The economics of urban ethnic community formation and development

As noted above, this paper examines the formation and development processes of Okinawa Village in Carrão, covering Vila Carrão and its neighboring districts by focusing on the cumulative development of the self-employed business strategies adopted as methods for economic adaptation and ascension. This section presents the self-employed business strategy adopted by the Okinawan migrants in this area in terms of *feirante* (market stall keeper) as the first strategy, the sewing business as the second strategy and hardware and building materials (wholesale and retail) and cosmetics retailing as the third self-employed business strategy, and provides a diachronic outline of the formation and development of each occupation through reference to

Table 7.5: Changes in the occupational composition of Oroku Tabaru Village Association members

	1977	1987	1997
Farming	23 (7.4)	18 (2.7)	17 (2.1)
Grocer & supermarket	79 (25.9)	71 (10.6)	51 (6.4)
Restaurant & café	22 (7.2)	21 (3.1)	14 (1.8)
Feirante (incl. *pastel* seller)	20 (6.6)	46 (6.8)	40 (5.0)
Sewing (wholesale & retail)	68 (22.3)	138 (20.5)	144 (18.0)
Hardware & building materials (wholesale & retail)	8 (2.6)	25 (3.7)	89 (11.1)
Cosmetics retail	2 (–)	42 (6.2)	88 (11.0)
Bazaar (miscellaneous goods store)	13 (4.3)	45 (6.7)	54 (6.7)
Hair salon operator	10 (3.3)	22 (3.3)	15 (1.9)
Confectionery wholesale & retail	1	2	4
Foods wholesale	15 (4.9)	9	3
Miscellaneous goods wholesale	–	–	3
Gasoline station operator	1	6	8
Professional & white collar	24 (7.9)	194 (28.8)	308 (38.4)
Total	305	673	802

Note: Figures in brackets indicate percentages.

case studies involving forerunners and new entrants. It then discusses how the individuals presented in the case studies tried to survive the period of economic crisis in Brazil from the 1980s, and looks at how a new self-employed business strategy emerged at that time.

Feirante as the first self-employed business strategy

Conditions shortly after relocation (the 1940s)
As mentioned earlier, the relocation of Okinawan migrants (families) to Vila Carrão began when a family from former Oroku Village relocated from an inland district of the State of São Paulo in 1946. This continued for at least several more years as prewar migrants from former Oroku Village moved in through their hometown connections. These early re-settlers began the early urban adaptation process by taking into account the absence of predecessors, the prevailing conditions in Vila Carrão and their own social and financial capital (language ability, funds, skills, labor, etc.). The first family who moved into the area in 1946 chose to rent a house in the only

Table 7.6: Major self-employed businesses of Okinawan migrants in Vila Carrão (2006)

Self-employed business	Emergence	Local market at the time of emergence	Product and market characteristics	Derivative self-employed business	Branch members (families) 1984	Branch members (families) 2006
Feirante (non-producer) *Feirante* (*pastel* seller)	End of the 1940s	Foundation stage	Sale of non-ethnic goods in non-local market. Enclave formation	Food and general merchandise. Cafe/restaurant. Sewing etc.	76	5
Sewing	Early 1950s	Foundation to growth stage. Population growth period	Sale of non-ethnic goods in non-local market. Enclave formation. Industrialization. Vertical integration from manufacturing to retail	Hardware trader. *Passador & entregador*. Sewing thread retail. Sewing machine repair and sale. Apparel shop etc.	155	31
Hardware	Early 1970s	Development stage. Middle class growth period.	Sale of non-ethnic goods in local market. Involution/specialization. Expansion to other districts	Building materials-related. Paint shop. Builder	6	41
Cosmetics retail	Early 1970s	→	→	–	7	22
Dekassegui	Early 1980s	Stagnation stage	Work in Japan and invest in Brazil	General *dekassegui* business (travel agency etc.)	–	–
Professional and white collar	Part of the self-employed business strategy since shortly after the Second World War. The children of postwar migrants began to enter these occupations from the 1980s.				11	98

residential strip along Av. Conselheiro Carrão and opened a laundry for local residents. The laundry business was the preferred 'work' for all Japanese migrants in the urban adaptation process, not only those from Okinawa. Two families (both from Oroku) who followed the first family into the district accepted a suggestion from their predecessor and began buying ready-made clothes from the 'sewing base' in neighboring Bairro (Brás District) and selling them from bicycle trailers. When the *feira livre* (open market) was built in Vila Carrão in around 1949, these families stopped itinerant selling and entered the market as *feirantes* (stall keepers) selling ready-made clothes. The launch of the open market in the district was of critical significance for the subsequent relocation and settlement of Okinawan migrants alongside the core group of former Oroku villagers. Entry into the open market during this very early phase was in the form of *feirante* selling non-farm products, ready-made clothes, herbs and spices and daily goods and, moreover in the form of illegal entry as *marreteiro/ ambulante* (unauthorized *feirante*), as they had no funds to purchase licenses. Let us look at the details in the following case of a prewar migrant family who entered the market business in the early 1950s.

Case 1: Feirante *as an initial urban occupation*[6]
A big factor for our relocation to São Paulo City was the information we got from the *urukūnchu* (fellow countrymen from Oroku) that there were so many opportunities to make money in São Paulo. We came here in August 1953 and we relied on my uncle on my mother's side who had moved to Carrão earlier and worked as a *feirante*. Our first home was an outbuilding behind his house. He and his family worked as *marreteiro feirantes* (unauthorized *feirantes*) selling ready-made clothes, daily goods and herbs and spices such as *alho* (garlic). Since we didn't even have enough food for the day, my mother followed my uncle to a wholesaler in Santa Rosa to buy garlic, pepper, toothpicks, etc. on the day after our arrival in São Paulo and started selling them from a crude table. Except the youngest brother who was too young, we children also contributed to the family income by walking around the *feira* and selling from *cestas* (baskets) such things as balloons, garlic and *bonés* (hats) made on an old Singer sewing machine my *papai* (father) had bought when we were at the farm. After the whole family had worked for one year, we bought a *lote* (a parcel of residential land) in Cidade Patriarca District jointly with another uncle on my mother's side and had a house built there. To purchase this land, our family set

up a *tanomoshi* (a type of rotating credit association) as *oya* (promoter) together with my uncles and the *urukūnchu* (fellow countrymen from Oroku) as *kodomo* (members) to raise funds. The *tanomoshi* was a mutual aid group.

Entry to the feira livre *(open market): The* feira livre *system*

The *feira livre* is a regular open market held daily except Mondays in the streets and squares of São Paulo City selling foods, general merchandise and flowers. *Feirante* indicates the merchants engaged in such retail trade. The history of São Paulo City's *feira livre* goes back to the 17th century, but the modern *feira livre* system was established when the then mayor Washington L. P. de Souza enacted a law for the introduction of open markets in 1914. The *feirante* licensing system was established in 1934, and the present *feira livre* system was founded in 1964 by Ordinance No. 5871. The *feira livre* was held at 315 locations in the city in 1967, 538 locations in 1976 and about 90 locations in the latter half of the 1980s. Merchandise traded in the markets include basic foodstuff such as vegetables, fruits, meat, eggs and seafood as well as various herbs and spices, dairy products, noodles and a wide range of basic daily necessities such as clothes, sewing supplies and kitchen utensils.

Feira livre *and Japanese migrants*

The entry of Japanese migrants to the *feira livre* as *feirantes* began as early as the 1920s. Japanese farmers in São Paulo City and regional cities within the State of São Paulo took their produce to the markets for sale. By the latter half of the 1970s, there were about 12,000 *feirantes* in São Paulo City and about 4,000 of them were Japanese *feirantes* (including Japanese descendants), the second largest group after Portuguese *feirantes*. This formed one of the predominant occupations for Japanese migrants and their descendants. There were two basic types of entry into *feiras livre* in São Paulo City. One was as the producer-*feirante*—a farmer selling his own produce at the market. The other type was the non-producer-*feirante* who bought his merchandise (farm produce) at São Paulo's central city market and sold it at the open market. Diachronically, the former has a longer history and the latter was basically chosen as the first occupation when the migrants relocated to the city. In addition to these two traditional types, Okinawan migrants created a new form of entry following the war, as sellers of *pastels* at the *feira*.

Feiras livre *and Okinawan migrants*

According to Yabiku (1988), it was estimated that about 2,000 Okinawan migrant households were working as *feirantes* in São Paulo City in the early 1980s, accounting for half of the 4,000 Japanese *feirantes* as at the late 1970s. It is possible to say that entry into the *feira livre* business was prominent among Okinawan migrants.

The relocation of Okinawan migrants to São Paulo and other urban areas which started immediately after the war and their entry into the *feirante* business chosen as their occupation in the early asset accumulation process in the city were closely linked to the human capital possessed by first generation Okinawan migrants. This process had the following characteristics: shortage (or lack) of investment funds; language barriers; lack of education, qualification and skills; prewar migrants' experience in farming and *feira* work in Brazil (recognition of employment opportunities); and the presence of a large number of Okinawan brokers and retailers at *mercado municipal/mercado cantareira* (São Paulo City's central municipal market) where many *feirantes* bought their products.[7]

According to Shimabukuro and Yonemori (1989), the number of *feirantes* among prewar Okinawan migrants increased rapidly in the early 1950s when migration from rural to urban communities increased markedly, and began to show a gradual decline in the 1970s after peaking at the end of the previous decade. In the case of postwar Okinawan migrants, the number of *feirantes* increased rapidly from the mid-1950s to the 1960s. Based on this fact, Shimabukuro and Yonemori (1989) define the *feirante* as 'the occupation at the initial stage of asset accumulation in the city.'

While the early form of entry as *feirantes* among the Okinawan migrants who moved into Vila Carrão was as unauthorized market vendors of non-farming sector products (clothes, herbs and spices and daily goods), the subsequent form of entry was characterized by the following. Firstly, the form of entry to the *feira* changed from non-farm product seller to farm product seller[8] and *pastel* seller (the latter is to be discussed in a separate section). Secondly, the form of entry transitioned from unauthorized *feirante* to authorized *feirante* through the purchase (or acquisition) of a market operator's license.

The entry of Okinawan migrants into the *feira livre* niche took place because employment opportunities emerged indirectly through the presence of a large number of prewar Okinawan migrants in the brokerage and retail sectors of São Paulo City's central market and more directly through the presence of predecessors (achievers), promoting the entry of more Okinawans to this niche. Thus the *feirante* formed the main occupation for Okinawan migrants' first business strategy in the city. It is possible to note that the presence of an enclave within the niche of *feira livre* was a condition that facilitated their entry into it (see Case 2 below).

Case 2
(This is the case of a migrant who was born in Yomitan Village, Okinawa Prefecture, and migrated to Brazil alone as a member of Okinawa Sangyō Seinentai (Okinawan Youth Association for Industrial Development) in 1961. He initially worked as a contract worker at a farm run by an Okinawan migrant in São Paulo's inland district, then as a tenant farmer before relocating to São Paulo City to work as a *feirante* selling vegetables.)

In 1964, I realized the difficulty of running a farm by myself and moved to São Paulo City where I had many friends from my home village. I initially stayed with a migrant family from my home village who were growing vegetables in Penha District in São Paulo and helped them. Then I stayed with an Okinawan supermarket operator from Yomitan Village and worked for him for a year or so. I thought I wouldn't be a successful migrant as long as I was a wage laborer, so I saved up funds by penny pinching while working at the supermarket to go on my own as a *feirante*. Through a fellow Okinawan, I was able to buy a *feirante licença* (license) from a Japanese person for "about twenty times the minimum salary." Anyone could become a *feirante* with this *licença* and some purchasing funds for the day. There was this convenient system called *carreto* in those days by which a *feirante* like myself who did not own a truck could pay a small fee to a private truck operator to have my purchased vegetables transported from the central market.

The entry to the feira livre *as* pastel *seller*
Selling *pastels* at the *feiras* was a new business within the *feira livre* system initiated by Okinawan migrants after the war. *Pastel* was traditionally made and sold by Chinese migrants at their shops in São Paulo City. While there was a strong ethnic image associating *pastel* and Chinese *pasteleiros* in the minds of São Paulo's citizens, they were familiar with *pastel* as a food product. *Pastel* is a *massa* (pastry)

made of flour and eggs filled with seasoned minced beef, *palmito* (heart of palm) and *queijo* (cheese) and fried in oil, and is also known as *kūki tempura* (airy tempura) among Okinawan *pasteleiros*.

In the City of São Paulo, *pastels* were traditionally sold in shops, and selling them at the *feiras* was a new concept introduced by Okinawan migrants shortly after the war and subsequently accepted within the city's *feira livre* system. Now it has become one of the 'attractions of São Paulo,' eaten by citizens while shopping at the *feiras*.

Let us consider why Okinawan migrants, who reportedly accounted for 99% of the 200 *pastel* sellers at the *feiras* at the end of the 1960s, entered this niche. As we know, Japanese migrants were regarded as enemy aliens during the war and the Japanese (as well as Germans and Italians) living in coastal regions such as Santos were forcibly removed, including many Okinawan migrants. They tended to live in clusters in Santos City and its surrounds or along the coastal railway line between Santos and Jequié. Some learned *pastel* making from Chinese *pasteleiros* in Santos City, and the selling of *pastels* at *feiras* is said to have started when they 'made *pastels* at home, walked around the market carrying baskets full of *pastels* to sell.' The entry to this niche increased subsequently under the following conditions: hardly any initial capital or special skills were required; employment opportunities were recognizable through skill acquisition by informal training under predecessors; and the *feira livre* system was expanded as the population of São Paulo City grew. The form of selling changed from the initial 'walking around the *feira* selling from a basket' to selling from fixed premises called *banca* (a type of tent), as in the case of other products sold by *feirantes* such as vegetables, fruits and daily necessities. However, *pastel* selling was an unauthorized business at the *feiras* at least until 1970, and the sellers were forced to operate under unstable conditions due to surveillance by city authorities and people soliciting bribes. In 1968, about 200 *pasteleiros* formed the State of São Paulo Pastel Union and lobbied the city administration through Okinawan city councilors for the granting of business licenses. As a result, the 200 *pastel* sellers were granted their business licenses in 1970, resolving the early-stage problem. Although *pastel* selling was subsequently banned in the same year due to hygiene issues, the sellers formed a union and had their operations allowed again in 1978. The business licenses were given to the group of *pasteleiros* that had by that stage grown to 400.[9]

The transition from illegal to legal operations was a factor promoting entry together with the formation of enclaves within the niche, to be discussed below.

Concentration and enclave formation in the pastel *selling niche*
The selling of *pastels* at the *feiras* was favored by many Okinawan migrants due to the aforementioned background factors. This was further promoted by the formation of an enclave within the *pastel*-selling niche. The enclave formation took place at the local market of Vila Carrão in which about 200 *pastel* sellers gathered in the beginning of the 1970s. The enclave formation involved the emergence of *pastel* production-related equipment manufacturers and purveyors, *pastel* frying tool manufacturers and sellers, *pastel* ingredient producers and vendors and large *pastel* refrigerator manufacturers and sellers within Vila Carrão, and this was linked closely to the formation and development of the hardware business, the main business category for the third self-employed business strategy to be discussed later.

Case 3: The selling of pastels *at the* feira
(This case involves the same person who appeared in Case 2 above. This postwar migrant changed his job from a *feirante* selling vegetables to a *pastel* seller at the feira. He began selling pastels at the *feira* in 1968.)

I wasn't able to make much money as a *feirante*. So I began to think about going into *pastel* selling at the *feira* which was popular among Okinawan migrants in those days, and in 1968 decided to help a *pastel* seller who was an Okinawan migrant from Bolivia. At the time, there were about 200 *pastel* sellers at the *feiras* in São Paulo City and 99% of them were Okinawan migrants. *Pastel* selling at the *feiras* was an unauthorized business and we were chased by the city authorities and the police and some people demanded bribes; it was an unstable job but anyone could go into it. In order to resolve this instability problem, *pastel* sellers formed the State of São Paulo Pastel Union and lobbied the city authority through Okinawan city councilors to issue formal licenses. The city issued the first lot of business licenses to 200 *pastel* sellers in 1968. The Bolivian migrant whom I was helping received the license also. In 1970 his family decided to leave Brazil to return to Okinawa and offered me his license for 5,000 dollars if I wanted to continue the *pastel* selling business. I was thinking about marrying an Okinawan woman at the time and I wanted a stable source of income, so I decided to buy the license. As our *banca* (a tent in which *pastels* are fried and sold) had regular customers and I had learned necessary skills while I was helping, I did not find *pastel* selling difficult.[10] Of course, *pastel* selling was hard work. In the year I bought my license (1970), the city issued an ordinance banning the sale of *pastels* at the *feiras* due to hygiene concerns, and we were faced with uncertainties. But *pastel* selling was permitted again in 1978 and business licenses were issued to about 400 *pastel* sellers at the time.

The *pastel* seller is a *feirante* and operates six days of the week at one of the *feiras* within the city just like other *feirantes*. In those days, the *pastel* seller got up at midnight, started making the *pastels* for sale on the day, went to the *feira* by five o'clock in the morning, sold *pastels* until some time after noon, then went to buy ingredients for the next day's *pastels* and prepared them; it was hard work. Still, we earned a daily cash income which was quite substantial.

About half of the 400 *pastel* selling families at the *feiras* were living in Vila Carrão. The number of *pastel* sellers grew from the 1950s to the 1960s, and half of them concentrated in Vila Carrão for particular reasons. One of these reasons was that specialist suppliers in ingredients, equipment and tools required for the *pastel* business appeared in Vila Carrão. Second generation Okinawan engineers developed *fechador* (*pastel* making machines), *cilindro* (rollers), pressers and *massa* (pastry) mixers. Vila Carrão was favorable for new ventures in terms of cheap land and housing.

I have been selling *pastels* at the *feira* since 1970, and I first bought a truck needed for *pastel* selling at the *feira* using my own profits and finance through the *tanomoshi* (rotating credit association), then I bought a house to get where I am now. My wife and I were the main sellers at the beginning and we soon employed some Nordestinos (migrants from northern Brazil) to help us. None of our children will take over our *pastel* selling business. They are all university graduates working for corporations.

The end of the feirante's *function as early stage of asset accumulation*
Whether it is the *feirante* selling vegetables and other farm produce or *pastels*, the background factors such as hard work, the decreasing importance of the *feira livre* system itself and the existence of the white collar technocrat economic ascension strategy through higher education within the self-employed business strategy have led to a steady expansion into other self-employed businesses out of the

feira livre niche and the younger generation's entry to professional and white collar occupations, and it is possible to say that its role as 'the occupation for the initial stage of asset accumulation' has now been played out. The *feirante* has become a small self-employment occupation among the Okinawan Association's branch members as their number has decreased from 76 families (17.7%) in 1984 to only five employed in that sector in 2006.

Sewing as the second self-employed business strategy:[11] The subcontract sewing niche and enclave formation, industrialization and vertical integration (from subcontractor to *patrão*)

A shift from the feira livre *to subcontract sewing*
As early as the beginning of the 1950s, the *feira livre* already contained opportunities for development into the second self-employed business strategy for Okinawan migrants in Vila Carrão. The self-employed occupations selected for the second strategy were *mão de obra* (sewing subcontractor), chosen on the basis of a recognizable employment opportunity brought on by the ready-made clothes *feirantes* at the *feiras* (through the provision of information etc.), and food and general merchandise retailers based on the experience of the *feirantes* selling *pastels* and other goods at the *feiras*. The former was started by a family with sewing skills acquired when they were prewar migrants in the South Pacific (Case 4). Conversely, the latter was prompted by population growth in Vila Carrão that started around that time.

The beginning of subcontract sewing and its subsequent development was closely linked to the geographical position of Vila Carrão. Jewish, Arabic and Syrian-Lebanese migrant groups established the 'sewing base of Brazil' in Brás District and Bom Retiro District on the route from Vila Carrão to the city center of São Paulo. Okinawan traders in ready-made clothes sales at the *feiras* procured their products in these districts, accumulated contacts with Jewish and Arabic ready-made clothes manufacturers, wholesalers and retailers and acquired industry information. This fact (including the proximity to Vila Carrão) made employment opportunities in this niche recognizable.

Case 4: From feirante *to sewing subcontractor*
Later on, some *urukūnchu* and uncles who were selling ready-made clothes at the *feira* advised us that it would be more profitable for us to go into sewing by utilizing my father's sewing skills and the children's

labor than continue working at the *feira*. This *feirante* introduced us to a Jewish shop from which he bought his merchandise. My father made a pair of children's trousers and took it to the shop as an *amostra* (sample). The shop owner looked at the sample and gave us work as a sewing subcontractor. In those days all orders were for *calça social* (slacks). We stuffed cut fabric into large jute bags and went home by bus, sewed them up, stuffed the finished products in jute bags, took them to the shop and were paid per piece. I walked to many places to take orders. It was my job because I was able to speak Portuguese. I liked order-taking better as I was at an age when I felt embarrassed to work at the *feira*. I carried samples made by my father and walked around Horizonte Precinct in Brás District and Jose Paulino Precinct in Bom Retiro District taking orders from Jewish and Syrian-Lebanese clothing shops.

In the beginning, my father sewed when he received orders, but we used profits from the *feira* and sewing to gradually buy second-hand sewing machines. My brothers learned sewing machine operation from my father and gradually quit the *feira* and moved into sewing. My father was in charge of the difficult stages of trouser making, and my brothers worked on their sewing machines by day and went to a night school by night. My parents hoped that they would get "clean" jobs when they grew up. Later on, my brothers became teachers after graduating from universities.

We established our credibility as a subcontractor after four to five years. *Patrãos* (bosses)[12] brought us jobs and we didn't need to go out to take orders. We children took turns to do *passa* (ironing) and thread-clipping at the beginning, but we began employing young *uchinā* (Okinawan) men and nearby *gaijin* (foreigners) as sub-contractors to do these simple tasks. When our work increased and became more profitable, some *uchinā*, especially *urukūnchu*, came to "learn" from us. They commuted to our workshop for several months to learn sewing skills and work processes, then went independent to work as *mão de obra* (subcontractor) from their own homes. *Uchinā* have the spirit of *yuimāru* (mutual aid), so they teach very diligently. My father was like that. All the children finished schooling and became public servants, factory workers and hairdressers, so he stopped subcontracting and started a high-end tailoring business. We bought a house in Carrão in early 1960 with the money we had saved by subcontract sewing.

The following characteristics are notable in this case: there was an established informal system of training, and this system was used by people from the same hometown through their networks based on homeland fellowship.[13] This fact must have been one of the main conditions which promoted concentration in a certain niche and furthermore one of the factors which facilitated settlement in the Vila Carrão area due to its peripheral nature.[14]

Concentration in the subcontract sewing niche
While food and general merchandise traders appeared as early as in the first half of the 1950s, using capital accumulated by working as sewing subcontractors or *feirantes*, the former were selling non-ethnic goods to the non-local market and therefore not restricted by the size of the local market. For this reason, the existence of predecessors (achievers) promoted the entry of subsequent re-settlers (migrants). Many migrants from former Oroku Village entered this self-employed business category of subcontract sewing in the very early stage because of the availability of information through hometown and kinship networks, support for urban relocation and settlement and the informal training system for the acquisition of skills, knowledge and information.

At that stage, the aforementioned self-employed occupation of *pastel* selling at the *feira livre* and subcontract sewing became the two major niches for Okinawan migrants in the Vila Carrão area. Concentration in these niches accelerated and enclaves (horizontal and vertical labor division structures) were formed in both niches during the 1960s to facilitate the entry of more people. Okinawan migrants in Vila Carrão considered entry into the two niches based on the availability of family labor; there was a tendency to enter into subcontract sewing if they had a relatively large family labor force and into *pastel* selling if they had a smaller labor force, for example in the case of a single person or a young couple.

Concentration in the subcontract sewing niche took place during the 1960s and the first half of the 1970s, and the number of families in the business reportedly reached 500 at its peak in Vila Carrão.[15]

Enclave formation (economic generalization)
Be it *pastel* selling at the *feira* or subcontract sewing, the existence of predecessors and achievers and the informal training system they offered promoted the entry of others to the niches and accelerated concentration. The existence of the high numbers of entrants gave rise to the formation of enclaves in both niches, further accelerating

the entry of subsequent parties. The enclave formation in the subcontract sewing niche led to the emergence of specialized labor in the subcontracting work stages of *passador* (ironing) and thread clipping, *entregador* (specialized deliverymen who cultivate customers, transport fabric and deliver finished products), sewing machine sellers, repairers, parts sellers, thread retailers and hardware traders (selling sewing tools such as scissors and blades). The enclave formation resulted in specialization in the areas of customer development, delivery and transportation and complicated sewing tasks and the improved availability of materials, tools and machinery that facilitated entry to this niche. In both *pastel* selling and subcontract sewing, these enclaves grew significantly during the 1960s and the 1970s.

Industrialization
When the number of subsequent entrants increased and surplus funds became available in the subcontracting sewing niche, people began to actively organize the *tanomoshi* (revolving credit association), a form of cultural capital. People raised funds through the *tanomoshi* to first purchase a house, firmly cementing their roots in Vila Carrão. In the case of subcontract sewing, they proceeded to expand their business from a cottage industry to a larger operation, employing non-family workers in what they call an 'industrialization' process. To Okinawan sewing subcontractors, 'industrialization' signifies the expansion of a subcontracting business by employing non-family labor. 'Industrialization' emerged as early as the beginning of the 1960s, and businesses employed several to 100 workers (mainly single migrants and non-Japanese-Brazilian migrants to this district from northern districts). With the advancement of the 'industrialization' process, sewing subcontractors clearly emerged as the middleman minority located between the Syrian, Arabic and Jewish Brazilians who held sway over the sewing industry as *patrão* (bosses) and the general Brazilian workers.

Case 5: From cottage sewing industry to "industrialization"
(This case involves a family of eight who migrated to Brazil in 1956 after the war from former Oroku Village in Okinawa Prefecture. The family was initially 'assigned' to the coffee plantation of a Japanese migrant in inland São Paulo, but as they witnessed frost-damaged coffee plantations from a train window on their way to the plantation,

they decided to begin their immigrant life relying on their cousin living in Vila Carrão. This interview was given by the first and second sons of the family.)

In Carrão District, we lived in the outbuilding of the house owned by my father's cousin. The cousin told us that an *urukūnchu* family, who were our relatives (the family in Case 1), was doing very well as sewing subcontractors in a place called Cidade Patriarca. We had a sewing machine and family workers and our mother had sewing skills as shown by the family business name of Mishinya (sewing machine operator), so we thought we could do that kind of work. My younger brother and I immediately went to Cidade Patriarca and applied for apprenticeships. We commuted there every day for a month and learned about sewing work as we helped with *passa* (ironing). Another brother (third son) went to our father's cousin, who was a ready-made clothes seller at the *feira* as well as a sewing subcontractor, to learn sewing and attended a *grupo* (elementary school) at night. This cousin helped us as our interpreter when we started our own business and tried to cultivate customers.

Once we learned the trade, we set up on our own. We had many family workers but only one semi-industrial sewing machine we had brought with us from Okinawa. We asked a relative, who was a former migrant (prewar) and successful hairdresser in São Paulo City, to lend us some money, bought several second-hand sewing machines and the whole family except our father and the youngest sister worked at sewing. The three older brothers also took orders and transported fabric for trousers and worked from seven in the morning to 12 at night without a break. Two and a half years later we bought a house in Vila Carrão. We continued to invest in machinery and equipment such as sewing machines and irons by organizing the *tanomoshi* with some *urukūnchu* and relatives to raise funds. Orders kept coming, as São Paulo City was growing larger.

When we were adequately equipped with industrial sewing machines, etc., we embarked on the 'industrialization' of our subcontracting sewing business beyond a cottage industry by employing non-Japanese women in the neighborhood as workers and single men from Okinawa as live-in *passadors* (sub-subcontractors who did ironing and were paid per garment). We were the first family who 'industrialized' subcontract sewing in Carrão, and employed 20 to 30 women at our peak.[16] We had been using *gaijin* (non-Japanese) as subcontractors for thread clipping, but we started doing it ourselves. As the population was growing in Carrão, we were never short of *gaijin* workers. In those days (around the early 1960s), many later migrants from Okinawa came to us to learn the trade and established on their own.

By then, some people had started a handy service called *entregador*, taking orders from *patrâos* (bosses/clients), delivering fabric to our workshop and delivering finished trousers to *patrâos* on behalf of new migrants who had language difficulties. There were sewing thread dealers. There were hardware shops handling sewing tools such as scissors and blades. They made the job of subcontract sewing easier. Since I was in the sewing business for many years, I learned how to repair sewing machines and made contacts in sewing machine companies. When my mother died and it was time for my brothers to become independent, I set up my own business in subcontract sewing, sewing machine repair and parts manufacturing and the youngest brother went into sewing machine sales. All my brothers and sisters run their own businesses in Vila Carrão.

From 'industrialization' to vertical integration

In the subcontract sewing sector, the number of families who invested in 'industrialization' as described in the above case increased and some also expanded into the retail and wholesale sector, as the product made in subcontract sewing changed from slacks to jeans (see Case 6).

Case 6: The establishment of the integrated sewing business from production to sales: From subcontractor to patrão
(This case involves a family who migrated to Bolivia from Okinawa in 1959 and relocated to Carrão District in São Paulo City 10 years later. They began working as sewing subcontractors, underwent 'industrialization' and expanded into an integrated manufacturing, processing and retailing business specializing in jeans.)

One year after we sent two of our brothers out on a "scouting" mission to the City of São Paulo in 1969, our family sold land and property in the Okinawan immigration district to raise funds for our travel and relocation, and came to Carrão relying on the family of our oldest brother's wife (1970). We rented a house through this family, bought second-hand sewing machines from a shop (Case 5) and turned our drawing room into a "factory" to start subcontract sewing (*mão de obra*). There were five or six Okinawan *entregadors* in those days who brought us jobs. We worked as subcontractors for a year and a half and saved enough money to buy a house. The population in Carrão had increased and the costs of land and housing were rising, so we bought a house in the newly developed Aricanduva District next to Carrão, established a sewing workshop behind the house and embarked on "industrialization" by employing 15 to 20 Brazilian workers. That was in the early 1970s when jeans became popular among young people and some Okinawan sewing contractors began to switch to jeans production. We also thought that jeans production was promising and went into it by investing in specialized machinery. The demand for jeans increased steadily as the economy of Brazil rapidly grew. We invited a younger brother who had moved from Bolivia to Argentina to come over and set up a joint business in 1976. From that time, we began to wonder whether we could expand from subcontract jeans production into apparel marketing (wholesale and retail), which was monopolized by the Arab, Jewish and Syrian Brazilians. After consultation with our colleagues and the Arab traders among our clients, we concluded that it was promising. We sold our investment properties (three houses) in 1980 to raise funds to go into the wholesale business and rented a wholesale shop in Emil Precinct in Brás District. From that time (1980) to 1985, many re-settlers from Bolivia raised 20,000–30,000 dollars through the *tanomoshi* and moved into Brás District. Thirty-four or five Okinawan jeans producers went into the wholesale and retail business in Brás District and 80% of them were re-settlers from Bolivia. The business was good and Okinawan jeans producers made one million pairs of jeans per month with sales reaching 15 million dollars at its peak.

Among the Okinawan migrants who undertook the integration of sewing operations from production/processing to wholesale/retail, a majority were former Okinawan migrants to Bolivia who had brought their families to Brazil to re-settle, as mentioned in the above case. This shift was based on the following factors: they were able to accumulate capital more rapidly than other sewing subcontractors because they had brought funds from the sale of their assets such as land and houses in Bolivia and used them to set up their businesses; there was a close-knit network of Bolivian re-settlers; and there were 'predecessors' among these former Bolivian migrants who succeeded with integration.

Even among the branch membership of the Okinawan Association alone, the number of entrants to the sewing niche reached 155 families (36.1%) at its peak in 1984, then it went into a recession phase and the number of entrants decreased to 31 families (90 persons) by 2006.

Hardware and cosmetics retailing as the third self-employed business strategy: Diversification of the self-employment niches, involution and geographical expansion

Diversification of self-employment and concentration in hardware and cosmetics retail

On the back of Brazil's rapid economic growth and the attendant growth of local markets (population growth and increased purchasing power) during the 1970s, Okinawan migrants entered into a wide range of self-employed businesses besides the *feirante* and subcontract sewing and expanded the scale and mode of operation through the active use of the *tanomoshi*, which was part of their ethnic cultural capital. The new businesses they entered into included hardware, with building materials retailing as its offshoot, cosmetics retailing, cafes and restaurants, *pastel* shops and bread-making, which are self-employed businesses targeting consumers in the local market. Their early mode of operation was selling non-ethnic goods in local markets. Among the self-employed businesses that emerged around this period, the entry to hardware (Case 7) and cosmetics retailing (Case 8) continued to increase after that (from the second half of the 1980s) through hometown networks and a further supply of entrepreneurs through 'informal training systems' based on traditional values such as '*yuimāru*' (mutual aid) and '*ichareba muru chōdē*' (all the people I meet are my brothers). They became the primary occupations of the third self-employed business strategy of the Okinawan families in Vila Carrão and continue to be the most common self-employed occupations today. The number of families in cosmetics retailing among the branch membership increased from only six (1.4%) in 1984 to 22 by 2006, and the number of families in the hardware business grew from just four (six if building materials shops are included) in 1984 to 41 by 2006, making this the most common self-employed occupation.

The following are case studies of the 'predecessors' in the main occupations of the third self-employed business strategy—hardware and cosmetics retailing.

Case 7: The entry to the hardware business (in the 1970s)
(The Okinawan hardware retail business reportedly emerged in Carrão District in the latter half of the 1950s when a prewar migrant opened his business in the main street of Conselheiro Carrão. The number of hardware businesses increased from the 1970s, and the industry later expanded through specialization (e.g., shops specializing in building

materials, paints etc.) and into wholesaling. This is one of the self-employed occupations favored by people of Okinawan descent today. The family in this case was among the first wave of Okinawan migrants who arrived in Bolivia in 1954, but they later relocated to Brazil due to the instability of agricultural production and recurring natural disasters (drought, flooding, etc.) in Bolivia.[17] Two members of the family relocated first in 1968 and the rest of the family followed two years later in 1970. They initially worked in subcontract sewing in Vila Carrão and later switched to hardware.)

I (the family's oldest son) came to São Paulo to "scout" in 1970 following my younger brother, who had moved to São Paulo on his own earlier, and his father-in-law. I bought a cheap house in Carrão through the father-in-law and looked around to determine what kind of work I should enter into. I had had a travel agency in Santa Cruz in Bolivia and I wanted to open a travel agency in São Paulo too but I had no information, so I decided to go into subcontract sewing, which my brother's family was engaged in. I returned to Bolivia, sold land and all my possessions from Okinawa and moved to Carrão District in São Paulo City with my family. I bought second-hand sewing machines from some *urukūnchu* (fellow Oroku people), and the whole family began to do subcontract sewing. We had to establish a stable financial base. However, subcontract sewing did not seem suitable for me. A nearby hardware shop came on the market and the younger sister of my brother's father-in-law told me, "the hardware business will grow because Carrão has a large sewing industry," so I decided to buy the business using proceeds from the sale of land in Bolivia as a down payment. I recall that the purchase price of the hardware shop was around 14,000–15,000 dollars. For the first three months, we sold hardware by day and sewed at night. We learned the know-how of the hardware retailing business from the previous owners during this period. We learned things every day, where to buy our merchandise, how to set prices and at what margin, etc. We organized the *tanomoshi* to raise working capital.

I ran the hardware business *socio* (in joint ownership) with my brother for three years in Av. Conselheiro Carrão. The business thrived as the population of Carrão grew and the area experienced a building boom. Looking at our success, people from Oroku and re-settlers from Bolivia came to us to 'learn' the trade. Some of them went on to run their own successful hardware and building material wholesale businesses. There were four or five hardware shops competing in

Carrão in those days, and since the local market was saturated some of them moved into wholesaling, switched to specialized paint or electrical shops, or shifted to other districts. We handed over our shop in Carrão to my brother's family and my family moved to the newly developed São Mateus District, bought a house with a shop and started a hardware business. We then handed on this shop to my eldest son's family and I returned to Carrão. I'm now running a travel agency for Okinawan customers. There are probably about 200 Okinawan hardware shops in the city now.

Case 8: The establishment and development of the cosmetics retailing business
(This case involves a single migrant who arrived in Brazil from Oroku Tabaru in Naha City, Okinawa Prefecture, in 1956 as a relative-sponsored migrant. After working in his relative's farm as a wage laborer for eight months, he moved to São Paulo City and found a *passador* job in a successful sewing business run by a family from his hometown through the Oroku hometown network. As a single migrant, he had no inclination to work as a sewing subcontractor or a *feirante*. He attended a hairdressing course at night to 'learn a trade' and once he became qualified, he opened up a hairdressing salon jointly with a senior hairdresser, who was a prewar migrant from his hometown. While working as a hairdresser, he went to a hairdressing teacher's course accredited by the São Paulo State Government to obtain a qualification to run a hairdressing school. He established a hairdressing school ('Hairdressing School A') and began to train hairdressers. He found it difficult to run the school on his own and sponsored his younger brother (single) to come from Okinawa to run the school jointly.)

At Hairdressing School A, we adopted the approach to purchase directly from wholesalers because our training program consumed a lot of cosmetic products and also for our students' convenience. As a result, we got to know a lot about the hairdressing and cosmetics retailing and wholesaling sector. I began to think that São Paulo's cosmetics industry had a bright future and handed over the hairdressing school to my brother in 1968 to concentrate on a cosmetics retailing business. It wasn't very profitable to start with and my hairdresser wife helped to make ends meet.

When I started the cosmetics retailing business, I didn't even think about opening it in the central São Paulo City. I was aiming to develop my business in the then *perifery* (periphery) areas in Carrão and its surrounds because I thought shops would cost less in these areas and the population growth would bring many customers. The business flourished on the back of the development of São Paulo City. I formed some *tanomoshi* with former Oroku people to raise funds for the opening of new shops and the purchasing of the merchandise. After my brother quit the hairdressing school he joined me, but we were still short of hands, so we invited another brother and his family from Okinawa. The three brothers were running a retail chain of nine cosmetics shops by 1970. By then, some former Oroku people (including some clansmen) had heard of our success and came to learn the know-how of the cosmetics trade. They went on to set up their own cosmetics shops.

Conversely, the expansion of the business size and the modernization of the management system occurred in the self-employed businesses that had achieved expansion into the food and general merchandise retail sector early on, using the capital they accumulated while working as *feirantes*. In short, Okinawan general store operators, especially those from former Oroku Village, entered the supermarket sector using the capital accumulated as general store operators and the funds raised through the *tanomoshi*. The entry into the supermarket sector was implemented through the introduction of the self-service system and cash registers and the provision of parking spaces. The businesses were later developed into chain stores with family workers assigned to individual stores employing non-Japanese-Brazilian workers.

Some self-employed businesses targeting the increasing numbers of Japanese and Okinawan settlers in Vila Carrão emerged during this period.[18] They included Japanese restaurants (karaoke), Japanese food and grocery shops, tofu (bean curd) shops and travel agencies. In other words, they were self-employed businesses offering ethnic goods[19] to the Japanese and Okinawan families in the local market. In particular, Okinawan travel agencies marketed tours to Okinawa before and after its reversion to Japan in 1972 and the Okinawa Oceanic Expo of 1975, creating a small Okinawa tourism boom in the latter half of the 1970s.

Involution (market development): Hardware and building materials and cosmetics retailing

In addition to the niches characterized by the sale of non-ethnic goods in non-local markets, the new niches emerging through enclave formation were characterized by, among other things, the production and sale of non-ethnic goods in local markets, the major examples including hardware (building materials) sales, snack food sales, cosmetics sales and supermarkets. A background factor to this was the growth of local markets through the increased number of mostly domestic migrants from northern Brazil settling in Vila Carrão. When certain levels of concentration were achieved in these niches, the process of involution began in local markets primarily in the hardware, cosmetics retailing and supermarket sectors. In the hardware sector for example, what was attempted initially was an involution for market development through specialization in building materials sales, paint sales and wholesales. As a result of the involution, local markets were saturated and there was no potential for the branching out of the existing family businesses within the district. The businesses therefore began to move into other local markets. The local markets targeted by the Okinawan self-employed in Vila Carrão were in the eastern area of the district, especially in suburbs such as São Mateus and Sapopemba that were experiencing a construction boom due to a marked increase in population. The shift into new markets was characterized by this eastward spread. The 1970s represented the fledgling stage in the family cycle for the 'migrant children' of postwar migrant families, and this spread to the periphery was mainly driven by the second and third sons who were going independent.

Chain stores and the growth into capitalist enterprises

The main businesses of the third self-employed business strategy such as cosmetics retailing, hardware and supermarkets achieved growth in the form of entry to the peripheral markets by taking advantage of the establishment and development of local markets in the eastern area of São Paulo City on the back of Brazil's rapid economic development in the 1970s.

Although the development (business growth) process through the sale of non-ethnic goods in the peripheral markets is common to the three sectors, cosmetics retailers and supermarkets were essentially family-based enterprises that assigned family workers to their chain stores while also employing non-Japanese workers. Some of the hardware dealers, however, albeit in small numbers, developed into more generalized companies through expansion into related sectors. For example, a postwar migrant started subcontract sewing in Vila Carrão, moved on to become an 'apprentice' at the hardware shop mentioned in Case 7, established his own hardware business, and later expanded into hardware wholesale. His successor (second generation) to the business entered into partnership with a non-Japanese-Brazilian capitalist to expand it into a hardware/building materials wholesale chain, retail home centers (10 stores), a spec-home and apartment construction business and a real estate business to market these spec-homes and apartments, and currently employs about 1,300 workers.

A crisis of the self-employed business strategy and the emergence of a new strategy

The defense of the self-employed business strategy: The founding of Okinawan trade organizations

After the rapid economic growth of the 1970s, Brazil experienced the 1980s referred to as the 'lost decade,' characterized by hyperinflation and economic instability. Brazil adopted a market liberalization policy in the 1990s that successfully held inflation in check, but the resultant economic recession and stagflation led to increased unemployment and decreased consumer purchasing power.

Hyperinflation in the 1980s had a significant impact on the self-employed business strategy of Okinawan migrants in Carrão. In order to deal with hyperinflation, the Okinawan self-employed in Carrão in the main sectors of supermarkets, sewing (wholesale and retail in particular), hardware and cosmetics retailing formed ethnic trade organizations (Table 7.7).

The common functions of these trade organizations included cooperative buying to reduce costs, exchanging industry knowledge and information and jointly hiring experts in commerce to improve management. While they tried to survive hyperinflation with these attempts, this phenomenon had both positive and negative effects on these businesses. The hardware (and associated) business, sewing wholesaling and retailing and cosmetics retailing were able to take advantage of inflation through stockpiling and investing and achieved further business expansion. Conversely, supermarkets faltered and many Okinawan businesses went bankrupt in the 1980s because they stocked many non-storable items such as perishable foods, and the government's anti-inflation policy prevented them from increasing the prices of daily necessities.[20]

As an aside, one of the great impacts of hyperinflation on the Okinawan self-employed was a marked decline in the efficacy of

Table 7.7: A summary of Okinawan trade organizations in Vila Carrão

	Year founded	Founders	Main functions
Gruppo Central	1982	28 supermarket operators from former Oroku Village, Naha City.	Joint purchasing to secure discounts comparable to large supermarket chains. Joint purchasing and stock management. Joint price-setting to avoid competition between members
Grūpu Hōsei (formerly Bras Hōsei Keizai Kyōkai)	Early 1990s	34–35 people among Okinawan jeans producers, wholesalers and retailers who had set up business in Bras District (80% were re-settlers from Bolivia).	Cost saving by bulk buying materials. Joint hiring of commercial lawyers and accountants to deal with unfamiliar legal and financial issues. Exchanging industry information, organizing workshops. Promoting joint product development and office automation. Fraternizing with industry.
Ferragem Okinawa (formerly Gruppo Okinawa)	1990	95 hardware retailers. Presently about 200 members.	Use collective influence over wholesalers. Cost saving by bulk buying products. Exchanging management information. Providing the management know-how to prospective operators, helping them with store site selection, and selling them a kit of the minimum required merchandise.
Gruppo T	1987	26 Okinawan cosmetics retailers (48 shops).	Bulk buying merchandise to compete with large capital-backed chains. Monthly meetings with suppliers. Information exchange and fraternizing.
The State of São Paulo Pastel Union	Mid-1960s	Pastel sellers at the *feira* in São Paulo City (about 120 people).	Lobbying for authorization of unauthorized *pastel* selling business.

the *tanomoshi*, which used to be an effective and important means of fundraising for new ventures, expansion and purchasing.[21] As monetary value dropped very rapidly under hyperinflation, the value of a *tanomoshi* fund could decrease substantially due to bidding time differences. Some *tanomoshi* operated in dollars in those days and produced successions of defaulters. Thus the *tanomoshi*, which had been providing a traction force to the Okinawan self-employed business strategy, lost its significance. The freezing of bank deposits in 1990 added to the predicament of the self-employed who found it difficult to raise working capital.

Besides these common factors, some changes in industry-specific conditions also had negative impacts on the self-employed business strategy. In the supermarket and cosmetics retail industries for example, large capital-backed supermarkets began to make inroads into the peripheral area to compete with Okinawan supermarkets and cosmetics shops. This proved to be a serious blow to the *feirantes*, which was the first ethnic self-employed occupation in Carrão. While the importance of the traditional *feira* system as an avenue for supplying daily necessities to citizens had been declining even before the entry of large supermarkets due to various reasons such as the social advancement of women (hence a decrease in the number of full-time housewives), an increased awareness of hygiene and changing lifestyles, the opening of these large supermarkets (many of them 24-hour operations) was a critical blow. In the sewing industry, new sewing bases similar to Brás and Bom Retiro emerged throughout the country, resulting in the reorganization of the domestic market and the declining importance of sewing bases in São Paulo. Moreover, the government's import liberalization policy let in cheap Chinese products to create competition.[22] These changes in the conditions had a significant impact on the continuation of the Okinawan self-employed business strategy in Carrão and acted as internal factors for the emergence and expansion of the *dekassegui* (those seeking temporary work in Japan) phenomenon that began in the 1980s. Many of the first generation Okinawan self-employed were forced to become *dekassegui* in order to rebuild their family businesses, repay debts and raise business funds.

Dekassegui *as a transnational self-employed business strategy*
Those who led the phenomenon of *dekassegui* to Japan from Vila Carrão were mostly first generation Okinawan self-employed. The phenomenon spread to second generation Okinawan-Brazilians in

the wake of the revision of the Japanese immigration control and refugee relief law in 1990.

Amid this trend, new ventures began to emerge based on the perception among the *dekassegui* workers and the self-employed business people in Vila Carrão that *dekassegui* represented an opportunity to develop a new phase of the self-employed business strategy, i.e., an opportunity to accumulate funds by working in Japan and to start new enterprises in Brazil. These ventures included the following: the Okinawan trade organizations that had been formed by the self-employed to defend themselves during the economic recession period of the 1980s established what can be called an 'entrepreneurialism support system' for returned *dekassegui* workers; and the Okinawan travel agencies which had been solely involved in the transportation of *dekassegui* workers and the Okinawan companies that had succeeded in the building materials wholesale sector began to develop new businesses targeting returned *dekassegui* workers.

In the case of the former, Gruppo Okinawa (presently Ferragem Okinawa), which was organized in 1990 by Okinawan hardware retailers as a counterforce to wholesalers, began to advise the returned *dekassegui* workers regarding the know-how of hardware retail management and shop site selection, sell a set of required minimum merchandise at a discount to start-ups and disseminate real-time information about the hardware industry through their website from the latter half of the 1990s. In the cosmetics retailing sector also, Gruppo T began to provide management guidance. These trade organization activities essentially form the traditional informal training system called '*narai*' (learning) that have been developed into more rational, modern and formal systems. The returned *dekassegui* workers are able to recognize employment opportunities in these industries through these systems. Many entrepreneurs have employed these systems to establish their own businesses.

While the former is a case of the modern development of Okinawa's traditional value system, *yuimāru* (mutual aid), the latter case involves entrepreneurial thinking to recognize *dekassegui* as a business opportunity. Okinawan travel agencies mainly selling tours to Okinawa appeared in Vila Carrão during the 1970s, and there were at least three companies operating there by the mid-1980s. All three companies were involved in outward trips of *dekassegui* workers, but one of them (tentatively called Company A)[23] took a more holistic approach to the *dekassegui* business and developed new types of businesses targeting returned *dekassegui* workers. The company initially set up a real estate division to broker the purchasing of homes and farmlands for them, and then expanded into business consulting for returned *dekassegui* workers who wanted to start up their own enterprises. Tanno (2007: 206) explains the consulting service as follows.

> Company A gives advice to those who are thinking about starting up new ventures and sends the clients to friends and acquaintances who are successful in the target industries to provide OJT (On the Job Training) for three to six months. The clients learn the actual business practices such as the purchasing of the merchandise and the customer service procedures, and the company asks them at the end of the OJT period whether they still intend to establish a business. [...] Company A provides management support to those who wish to continue with the business idea for about two years during the start-up phase.

Company A was not the only one to start this type of business. An Okinawan company with diversified interests ranging from 10 home centers, building materials wholesaling and spec-home and apartment construction to a real estate agency, which originally started from a hardware store, has also expanded into a wide range of services to help returned *dekassegui* workers readapt to Brazilian life. These include the sale of homes and apartments, consultation for would-be entrepreneurs in the building materials industry and the sale of the package of necessary merchandise.

Conclusion

I have examined the process of formation and development of a local ethnic community from the viewpoint of the cumulative development of self-employed business strategies (in relation to the opportunity structure mainly of the local market). Since I have already exceeded the allocated word limit, I shall include Table 7.8 below presenting a summary of the development of the self-employed business strategies and the growth of the community over time, from the latter half of the 1940s to today, in place of a 'conclusion.' In any case, I believe I was able to present one aspect of the decisive role played by the characteristics of the local area to which predecessors

Table 7.8: The formation and development of the Okinawan ethnic community in Vila Carrão (an economic perspective)

Indicator	Late 1940s–Late 1950s	1960s	1970s	1980s–Present
Type of settler	Prewar migrant. Early postwar migrant.	Postwar migrant. Re-settler from Bolivia.	Re-settler from Bolivia. Late postwar migrant.	Self-employed/second & third generation Japanese-Brazilians to Japan. *Dekassegui* worker returned from Japan.
Main self-employed businesses	(Very early) Laundry, itinerant clothes seller. Unauthorized *feirante* (clothes, herbs & spices, daily goods).	Sewing subcontractor. *Pastel* seller in the *feira*, authorized at the end of the 1960s.	Hardware and cosmetics retailers. *Pastel* sellers, finally authorized.	Hardware and cosmetics retailers.
Changes in the economic adaptation strategy centering on the self-employed business strategy	The search for self-employed businesses. The dawn of the subcontract sewing business through clothes sales at the *feira*. *Pastel* selling at the *feira*.	Two major economic niches (concentration on subcontract sewing and *pastel* selling). Early enclave formation within niches (hardware business etc.). Early self-employed businesses selling non-ethnic goods in local markets, e.g., food & general merchandise store, snack food shop.	Continuation of enclave formation in two major economic niches. Diversification of self-employed businesses (retail & wholesale of products for local markets). 'Industrialization' of subcontract sewing. Emergence of professional and white collar occupations out of the white collar technocrat strategy as part of the self-employed business strategy.	Concentration in new economic niches. Involution →market saturation → expansion to other districts and specialization. From sewing subcontractor to '*patrao*'. Dealing with economic crises. Formation of trade organizations. Emergence of *dekassegui*.	Increasing numbers of *dekassegui* workers among second-generation Okinawan-Brazilians. *Dekassegui* for a new phase of the self-employed business strategy. Emergence of businesses targeting returned *dekassegui* workers and capitalist enterprises.
Characteristics of the goods sold & market	Sale of non-ethnic goods in non-local markets.	Sale of non-ethnic goods in non-local markets. Sale of non-ethnic goods in local markets in an embryonic stage—emergence of general stores and cafés.	Sale of non-ethnic goods in non-local markets—sewing, *feirante*. Sale of non-ethnic goods in local markets—hardware, foods &	

Group characteristics	Hometown networks. The spirit of yuimāru (mutual help). (Mutual help) tanomoshi.	Hometown networks. The spirit of yuimāru. Informal training system. Utilization of tanomoshi for housing and investment.	general merchandise, cosmetics retailers. Sale of ethnic goods in local markets—Japanese foods and general merchandise, Japanese restaurant, travel agency. Hometown networks. Informal training system. Tanomoshi for investment (the height of tanomoshi activity).	A failure of tanomoshi (polarization).	Formal system for the supply of entrepreneurs.
Local market	Local markets in the foundation stage. Small population. Establishment of the feira livre in 1949.	Local markets in the growth stage—population increase, early stages of urban adaptation by settlers.	Local markets in their prime. Continual population increase. Middle class formation (increased purchasing power).	Stagnation stage (1980s–early 1990s).	Recovery stage (from the mid-1990s).
Changes in the ethnic community	Relocation and settlement by Okinawan migrants began in 1946. Postwar immigration began in 1952 (1953 in effect)—Settlement by early postwar migrants. The Vila Carrão branch of the Okinawa Association was formed by 27 families in 1956.	Relocation and settlement increased (274 family members in the branch at the end of the 1960s). Construction of the branch hall. Internal organization. Establishment of events and programs.	Relocation and settlement continued to increase. Postwar migrants' children went independent. People from the same hometown, shared immigration experience etc. began to organize themselves. Promotion of Ryūkyū culture—performance arts, karate etc. Okinawa tourism boom from 1972. Child migrants and postwar migrants' children went independent.	End of relocation and settlement. Move to create a new community-based culture—Festival Okinawa, Koshiyukkui etc. Establishment and development of ethnic trade organizations.	
Branch membership	72 families in 1959.	274 families in 1969.	428 families in 1975.	429 families in 1984 and 437 families in 2005.	

(achievers) relocated and settled. This was the subsequent selection of self-employed occupations by later migrants and the deep involvement of the migrants' group characteristics and the formation of enclaves (economic generalization) in the subsequent entry to and concentration in certain economic niches.

8 Migration, Economic Adaptation and Mutual Cooperation: Japanese Rotating Savings and Credit Associations in Argentina

By Masahiro Tsujimoto

Introduction[1]

Migrants who cross borders into foreign lands face numerous hardships, including language difficulties and insufficient finance, and for some, illness and natural disasters. What is needed to overcome these hardships is mutual cooperation among fellow immigrants. This chapter examines the rotating savings and credit associations (ROSCAs) of the Japanese in Argentina as an example of migrants' mutual cooperation. In the following section, the Japanese in Argentina and their ROSCAs will be explained and the purposes of this chapter will be fleshed out.

The Japanese in Argentina

The immigration of Japanese citizens to Argentina began in the early 20th century and continued after the Second World War. The majority of these immigrants came from the Okinawa Islands in the Southwest of Japan.

Japanese immigrants to Argentina can be grouped into those who directly immigrated to Argentina and those who initially went to other South American countries and then re-migrated to Argentina. Of those who re-migrated, many initially immigrated to Peru and Brazil prior to the Second World War, while others initially travelled to Bolivia and Paraguay in the wake of the war.

Currently, over 30,000 Japanese (i.e., Japanese immigrants and their offspring) live in various regions of Argentina. They differ in features from region to region. This paper focuses on those who live in Buenos Aires, the capital of Argentina, and its surrounding districts.

In the past, the majority of Japanese immigrants to Argentina ran their own businesses. Prior to the Second World War, many owned laundries and cafes in urban areas of Buenos Aires or engaged in flower cultivation and vegetable farming in surrounding regions. After the war, although fewer ran cafes, the majority have until recently remained in the abovementioned industries. However, the number of Japanese involved in these businesses has been declining amongst the second and third generations.

The ROSCA system

The Japanese in Argentina have actively formed ROSCAs, a customary form of monetary circulation that exists in various parts of the world (Ardener 1964; Ardener and Burman 1995; Geertz 1962). The following describes the system of a typical ROSCA. Meetings are held regularly in each ROSCA. At each meeting, members pay a contribution to raise funds to be received by a particular member. Every member receives funds in turn. Figure 8.1 shows how money is rotated within a ROSCA consisting of three members. (A), (B) and (C) represent each member and arrows indicate the flow of money. At the first meeting, (B) and (C) pay a contribution to raise funds to be received by (A). Likewise, (B) and (C) receive funds in turn, and the term comes to an end. The allocation of fund recipients is decided by a process of bidding or drawing lots. An actual ROSCA usually consists of more than three members, thus Figure 8.1 depicts a simplified version of the basic system.

Purposes of the current study

The first purpose of this chapter is to broadly examine the effectiveness of ROSCAs. The majority of Japanese immigrated to Argentina with almost no funds, qualifications or education valid in Argentina.

Figure 8.1: Rotation of money within a ROSCA

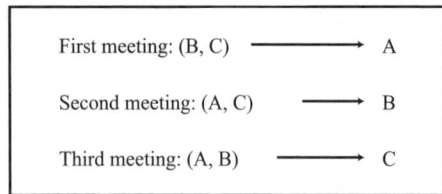

ROSCAs enabled them to establish the basis for life in such a difficult situation. This chapter explains how Japanese immigrants have used ROSCAs through their history in Argentina.

The second purpose underpinning this chapter is to investigate the adverse outcomes affecting ROSCAs. The main negative aspect inherent in this system is the occurrence of nonpayment of contributions by members who have already received funds. In this chapter, the nonpayment of contributions following the receipt of funds is referred to as 'default.' When a default occurs, members who have not yet received funds incur financial damage. This chapter describes how the Japanese have prevented defaults by looking at past instances of this phenomenon in their ROSCAs.

The above aims are closely linked. Frequent occurrences of default can lead to the collapse of a ROSCA. Defaulting must be prevented in order to increase the effectiveness of the system. Theoretically, an individual who defaults, namely a 'defaulter,' corresponds to the 'free-rider' discussed in studies of collective action. The findings presented in this paper are thus applicable to the free-rider problem as well as posing a solution to the issue of defaulting in the ROSCA system.

The data analyzed in this chapter are drawn from interviews and reference materials from Japanese newspapers and magazines published in Argentina. Though some of this material has already been examined and discussed (Tsujimoto 2000, 2006), this chapter attempts a comprehensive analysis of Japanese ROSCAs using this data as well as more recently collected information.

The terminology used in this paper is defined as follows. 'The Japanese in Argentina' are defined as Japanese immigrants to Argentina and their offspring. 'The Argentines' refer to those who are not 'Japanese' as defined above. Note that the offspring of Japanese immigrants born in Argentina hold Argentine nationality. 'Prewar' is defined as the period prior to the Second World War, and 'postwar' as that following that war. Although the Japanese in Argentina traditionally refer to ROSCAs as *tanomoshi*, *moai* or *muē*, this paper uses the term 'ROSCA.'

Effectiveness of ROSCAs

In this section, the effectiveness of ROSCAs will be examined by tracing the history of the Japanese in Argentina. As Figure 8.1 illustrates above, a ROSCA concentrates money owned by each member to a particular member. It is possible to raise a substantial sum of funds through this system, even if each member's money is scarce. This mutual aid system has enabled members to start their own businesses or deal with emergency situations.

Prewar ROSCAs

Firstly, an overview of occupations held by the Japanese in the prewar period will be outlined below. Figure 8.2 shows the occupational trends of Japanese in Argentina during this period (Tsujimoto 2006). The category 'Household work' includes those employed in domestic labor (e.g., cleaning and serving meals) at Argentines' houses. The category 'Farming' includes those engaged in flower cultivation and vegetable farming (both employers and employees). The category 'Accommodation/Restaurant/Entertainment' presumably includes those who owned or worked at cafes.

Prior to the 1920s, the majority of the Japanese were employed in manual labor. As Figure 8.2 illustrates, factory work was the most common occupation in 1914 and 1920, followed by household work. The majority of the Japanese lived in tenements in Boca and Barracas, downtown areas of Buenos Aires. In this period they probably lived in poverty and were not yet able to find a way to raise their status in Argentine society.

From the 1920s to 1930s, the Japanese began to establish businesses. As can be seen in Figure 8.2, the proportion of those engaged in factory or household work declined in 1928 and the laundry and cafe businesses, flower cultivation and vegetable farming had become the most common occupations by 1936. New migrants to Argentina initially worked for Japanese entrepreneurs while aiming to start their own businesses. During this period, although not yet wealthy, the Japanese were thought to have gradually paved their way for advancement in Argentine society.

A substantial collection of funds is required to start a business, yet the Japanese of the prewar period had almost no funds or support from the Japanese government (Japan International Cooperation Agency 1991). As a result, they had to obtain necessary funds from ROSCAs. According to a monthly magazine article published in the early 1970s (*Kigyō*, October 11, 1972), ROSCAs grew in number after the First World War and enabled the Japanese to expand their business ventures.[2] Articles on ROSCAs were published in Japanese newspapers from the late 1920s to 1930. The number and spread of these is

Figure 8.2: Occupations of the Japanese in the prewar period

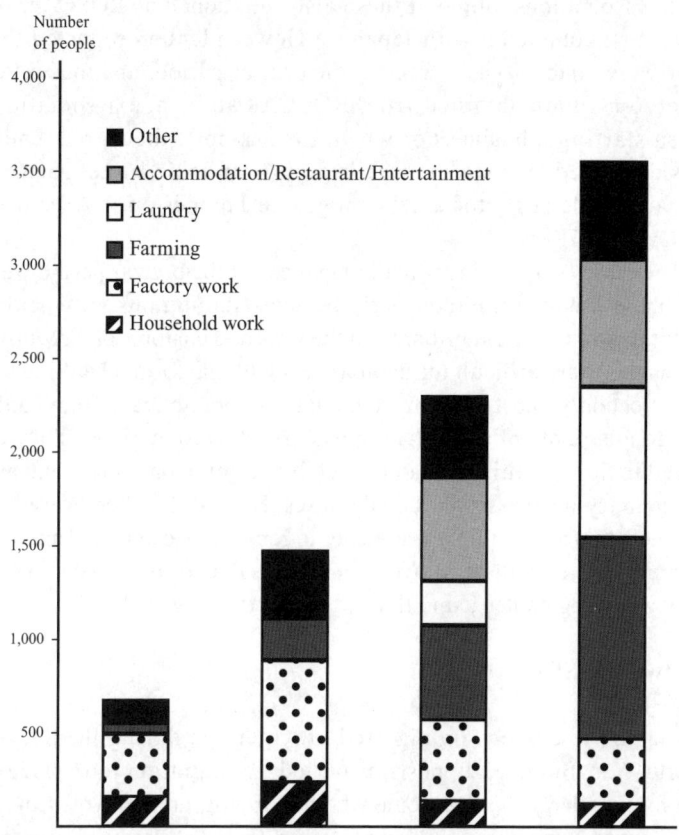

Source: Tsujimoto (2006). The data came from Ishikawa (1999). Various data in his book were reclassified and recalculated by excluding the family members of income earners.

as follows: one in 1926, seven in 1927 and two in 1930. The articles claim that the Japanese started their own businesses using the ROSCA system as their sole financial means, but that the adverse effects were numerous (see below for details). Many went into the lettuce farming business as a result of its sharp rise in price at the end of the 1920s. According to a newspaper article of that time, intense competition took place among ROSCA members to secure the funds necessary to enter this sector (*Aruzenchin Jiho*, September 27, 1930).

As Japanese entrepreneurs grew in number, they began to form trade associations. Some of these also functioned as ROSCAs. An interview conducted with Japanese flower planters reported that they were unable to use banks in the prewar period, and thus relied solely on funds obtained from ROSCAs and trade associations when starting a business or when, for example, their greenhouse was destroyed by a storm or hailstorm (Comité de Investigación y Redacción de la Historia del Inmigrante Japonés en la Argentina 2002: 277–278).

There are two reasons why the Japanese of the prewar period were unable to use banks. Firstly, early Japanese immigrants were neither fluent in Spanish nor familiar with the laws and customs of Argentina. It was therefore difficult for them to deal with the formal banking system. Secondly, most of them were unable to obtain loans from banks due to a lack of collateral (Gaimushō Tsūshōkyoku 1929). They engaged in flower cultivation and vegetable farming on rented land and ran laundry businesses in rented houses. Behind this there were also the facts that at the time it was easier to rent a house and land and that farmers had to regularly move to new fields due to soil exhaustion, as they grew vegetables using the 'extensive farming system.'[3]

Postwar ROSCAs

No Japanese citizens immigrated to Argentina during the Second World War. In the early postwar period, immigration took place in the form called *yobiyose*. Some who had immigrated to Argentina in the prewar period brought their families from the defeated war-torn homeland to be with them in Argentina. This form of migration came to be referred to as *yobiyose*. Prewar migrants sometimes covered the travel costs for *yobiyose* with funds obtained from ROSCAs. One Japanese interviewee described how he immigrated to Argentina: he was born in Okinawa in 1934 and arrived in Argentina in 1952 at the request of his father who had immigrated alone to Argentina during the prewar period. He also stated that his father obtained funds to cover his travel costs from a ROSCA.

Regarding the migrants' occupations in the postwar period, though fewer ran cafes, many remained in the laundry business or engaged in flower cultivation or vegetable farming. The results of a survey conducted in 1969 by the Japanese embassy were published in a Japanese newspaper the following year (*La Plata Hochi*, January 22, 1970). Though the survey did not include all the Japanese in

Argentina, it helps us to learn about the occupational trends at that time. According to this document, the most common occupation was the laundry business (11,700 persons), followed by flower cultivation (4,700) and farming (2,230).

Japanese who migrated to Argentina in the postwar period also used ROSCAs to start their own businesses in the laundry management and flower cultivation sectors. Figure 8.3 shows the records of 14 Japanese re-migrating from Bolivia to Argentina from the 1960s to 1970s (Tsujimoto 2000). The trajectory formed by horizontal and vertical lines corresponds to the record of each individual, and a vertical line indicates a change in his life. Each arrived in Buenos Aires with almost no funds, and yet most of these migrants, as represented in vertical lines from the 1960s to 1970s, managed to start their own business within a short period of time using funds obtained through the ROSCA system.

The Japanese of the postwar period also used ROSCAs to deal with emergency situations. For example, when a family member became ill or when operating funds for their business ran dry, a person's close acquaintances would suggest that they start a ROSCA and help them by allocating that they receive funds at the first meeting.

It is said that postwar ROSCAs reached the height of their prosperity from the 1960s to 1970s. During this period, some migrants reportedly belonged to multiple ROSCAs and rushed from venue to venue to attend meetings on Sundays (Aruzenchin no Uchinānchu 80-nenshi Henshū Iinkai 1994).

ROSCAs today

These days, fewer Japanese start a business using funds obtained through the ROSCA system. As Figure 8.3 shows, the number of Japanese in Argentina who go to Japan as guest workers has been on the rise since the end of the 1980s. The second and third generation Japanese have increasingly been employed by Argentine companies. Present-day Japanese do own real estate such as houses and land, and do deal with banks. However, Japanese ROSCAs continue to exist and not only first generation but also the second and third generation Japanese continue to use them on such occasions as emergencies or for the purchase of real estate and cars. The following discusses an example of a ROSCA in operation.

This ROSCA is run by Japanese who live in a town near Buenos Aires. In 2010, we conducted an interview with a male Japanese

Figure 8.3: Record of re-migrants from Bolivia to Argentina

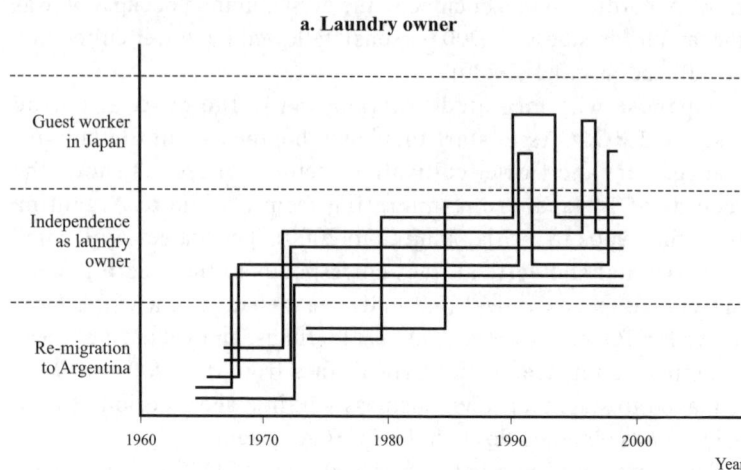

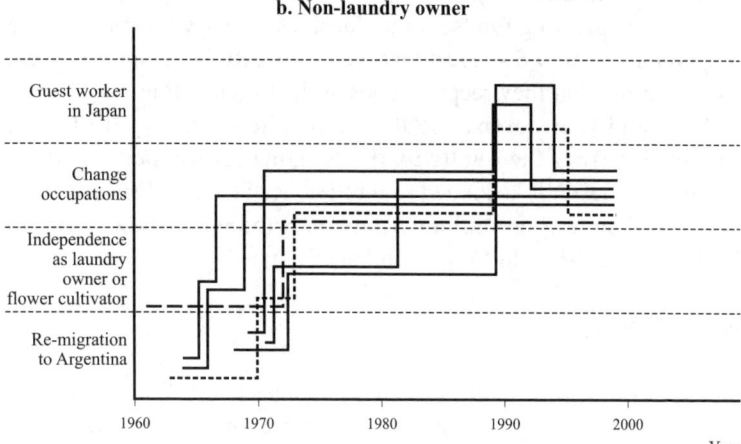

— — —   This person was fortunately able to start his own business from the outset

·······   This person underwent multiple career changes

Source: Tsujimoto (2000).

member of this ROSCA, consisting of 15 members. Of these, 13 are second and third generation Japanese in their 50s and 60s. Of the remaining two non-Japanese members, one is married to a Japanese and the other has many Japanese friends. The ROSCA meeting is held monthly during the day on Sundays. At the meeting, attendees enjoy an Argentine-style BBQ, called *asado*.

In this ROSCA, a fund recipient is chosen as described below. Those who wish to receive funds must make a request prior to a meeting. At that time, they must also give a reason as to why they require funds. Criterion for selecting a fund recipient is based on the reason given. The first reason prioritized is illness, the second is the purchase of a house and the third reason is the purchase of a car. Our interviewee had purchased a car and a condominium unit with funds obtained from the ROSCA. When he applied for funds to purchase his condo, another member also applied for funds to purchase a car. At that time, he was able to receive funds in accordance with the criterion.

Our interviewee cited the promotion of savings as the main reason why he belongs to the ROSCA. He claimed that if he had extra money he would waste it on luxuries such as clothes, but as he belongs to a ROSCA he could save it. According to him, banks are probably more favorable than ROSCAs in terms of interest; however, ROSCAs are advantageous as money can easily be obtained at his convenience.

Those who wish to join this ROSCA must be referred by an existing member. At first, the interviewee joined under his wife's name. He was not born in the town where the ROSCA was run, but his wife was. After he earned the trust of other members through attending meetings with his wife, he was able to join under his own name.

These days, the interviewee no longer attends the meeting. He asks his father-in-law, who is also a member, to pay contributions and receive funds on his behalf.

Adverse effects of ROSCAs

In the previous section, we discussed the ways in which the Japanese have used ROSCAs to start their own businesses and deal with emergency situations. There is, however, an adverse aspect of the ROSCA system. As evident in Figure 8.1 above, (A), the member who received funds at the first meeting, would be able to increase his profits by not paying contributions at the second and third meetings. In other words, those already in receipt of funds have a financial incentive to default. When a default occurs, those who have not yet received funds incur fiscal damage. In the following section, records of past defaults will be reviewed and ways in which the Japanese have prevented defaults will be examined.

Records of defaults

Records show that defaults occurred in Japanese ROSCAs throughout the prewar and postwar periods. Many Japanese started their own businesses using ROSCAs from the 1920s to 1930s. The previously cited references report the occurrence of defaults in this period. Some fled to Japan after receiving funds in the late 1920s (*Kigyō*, October 11, 1972). The Japanese newspaper articles discussed above cite the following as the adverse effects of ROSCAs: reckless business establishment relying on funds from ROSCAs; sharp rise in interest rates; occurrence of defaults; insolvent guarantors; shoestring operations run by financially-troubled members joining multiple ROSCAs in order to pay contributions; and intervention by extortionate money-creditors. Similarly, Gaimushō Tsūshōkyoku (1929) named the following as shortcomings of Japanese ROSCAs in Argentina: members fleeing after receiving funds; guarantors failing to fulfill their obligation; a sharp rise in interest rates; and an unsuitable monthly system of payment of contributions affecting farmers.

Those cited in the above references that fled after receiving funds can be considered defaulters. As these publications note, some ROSCAs require a fund recipient to secure a guarantor.[4] If the fund recipient defaults, their guarantor must pay outstanding contributions on their behalf. Records of guarantors failing to fulfill their obligations indicate the occurrence of defaults in ROSCAs. In an interview conducted by Tsujimoto and Kuda (2010), a second generation Japanese born in the 1920s, said that his father was involved in a great deal of trouble due to becoming a guarantor. When his father's acquaintance, for whom he had acted as guarantor, defaulted, his father had a hard time dealing with this problem.

Defaults also occasionally occurred in postwar ROSCAs. As discussed previously, ROSCAs were at their pinnacle from the 1960s to 1970s. The following cases during this period were referred to in Japanese newspapers and history books. A person who fled Argentina with money obtained from a ROSCA was featured with a photograph included (Nago Urawakai en la Argentina 1994); a defaulter reportedly lost his property through foreclosure (*La Plata Hochi*, April 30, 1970); and yet another incident occurred involving an individual absconding with ROSCA funds (*Akoku Nippo*, April 24, 1971).

Through ROSCAs, some were able to start their own business or cope with emergency situations, whereas others incurred damage from defaults or experienced hardship due to acting as guarantor.

Default prevention

Frequent occurrence of defaults discourages people from joining ROSCAs, and thus threatens their existence. In this section, the ways in which the Japanese have prevented defaults will be examined. A Japanese newspaper article provides a clue to this query (*La Plata Hochi*, April 30, 1970). It claims that: 1) members of a ROSCA must be carefully selected because a ROSCA exists based on each member's trust; and 2) in reality, the selection of members is neglected in order to increase the amount of funds.

As the first point suggests, the selection of members, namely 'peer selection,' would prevent defaults from occurring in ROSCAs. Peer selection is the process of excluding previous defaulters and those likely to run into difficulty paying contributions (e.g. low-income earners and potential absconders) from a ROSCA upon its formation. In other words, only those who are believed to be capable of paying regular contributions are allowed to join a ROSCA. The exclusion of previous defaulters from ROSCAs serves as a sanction against them. Preceding studies have pointed to peer selection as a means to prevent default (e.g., Hechter 1987; Koike, Nakamaru and Tsujimoto 2010).[5]

Peer selection has also been carried out in Japanese ROSCAs in Argentina. A particular ROSCA, reported in detail by Tsujimoto (2000), rejects previous defaulters, requires membership applicants to obtain a reference from an existing member and imposes an obligation to act as guarantor on referring members. Also, in another ROSCA cited in the previous section, membership applicants must obtain a reference from an existing member, and those without the trust of remaining members are rejected. It is said that the names of defaulters would be widely spread in the Japanese community. If such a reputation prevents them from joining other ROSCAs, peer selection serves as a stiff sanction against defaulters. Membership applicants who are low-income earners and likely to run into difficulty paying contributions may also be rejected. These examples indicate that the Japanese in this study have employed a peer selection process in the formation of their ROSCAs.

In order to carry out peer selection, those involved in the selection process must know each other well. If not, they cannot be sure as to whether potential members are previous or possible defaulters. Therefore, not all membership applicants, even if they are Japanese, are able to join Japanese ROSCAs. Members of ROSCAs often show reluctance to accept those they do not know very well.

As the second point suggests, the peer selection criterion was sometimes loosened in Japanese ROSCAs in order to increase the amount of funds. If the fund is too small, its recipient is unable to start a business or deal with an emergency situation. In order to increase the amount of funds, the number of members must also grow. Since the Japanese in Argentina previously had limited access to wealth, any one of them could have run into difficulty paying contributions, to varying degrees. To form a ROSCA with a sufficient number of members under such circumstances, they had no choice but to loosen the peer selection criterion. If the criteria for peer selection are loosened, the occurrence of defaults is to some extent unavoidable. This was the reason behind the occurrence of defaults in Japanese ROSCAs throughout the pre- and postwar periods.

What they probably needed was to keep the frequency of defaults below a certain level through loose peer selection criterion, rather than completely preventing it through strict peer selection rules.

Discussion

Effectiveness and adverse effects

Those who cross borders face difficult situations. The Japanese immigrated to Argentina with almost no funds, qualifications or education valid in that country. ROSCAs enabled them to establish the basis for life in such difficult circumstances. The Japanese established their own businesses or dealt with emergency situations with funds obtained from ROSCAs. Such effectiveness resulted from the concentration of members' money onto a particular member in a regulated fashion. It is possible to raise substantial capital through ROSCAs, even though each member's money may be scarce. ROSCAs make what is impossible for one person possible through the mutual cooperation of multiple people.

Conversely, some Japanese incurred damage from defaults—the adverse effect of ROSCAs. Peer selection has been carried out in order to prevent such defaults occurring. The peer selection criterion that applied in Japanese ROSCAs were considered to be loose. This was because the Japanese previously had limited access to wealth; if the peer selection process was too strict, none of them could join a ROSCA. On the contrary, if the peer selection criterion were loose, defaults were not completely prevented. Incurring the occasional loss from defaults can be regarded as a necessary cost in order to realize the effectiveness of ROSCAs.

Wealthy people may have been able to join ROSCAs, despite the strict peer selection criterion. However, they did not require ROSCAs in the first place. Those who sought to participate in the ROSCA system cannot be described as wealthy. The criteria of peer selection must have been loosened in order to enable such people to join ROSCAs. This way, those who earned a precarious living were able to further their financial position through utilizing the ROSCA system.

Future investigation

Another element of the effectiveness of ROSCAs not discussed in this paper is possibly the strengthened levels of solidarity among members. Members of ROSCAs often emphasize not only finance but also becoming acquainted with each other as the motivations behind joining ROSCAs. As Figure 8.1 exhibits, meetings are regularly held by ROSCAs. At the meetings, besides the rotation of contributions, attendees have a pleasant chat while enjoying food and drink for an extended period of time. The Japanese are considered to spread information widely through ROSCAs. Many belong to more than one group. For example, if one person obtains important information at the meeting of one ROSCA, they pass it on to others at the meeting of another group. These people then pass it on to some others at the meeting of yet another ROSCA. This way, information would be spread extensively throughout the Japanese expatriate community.

These ROSCA features are considered to have strengthened the solidarity among members and have had some influence on the development of the Japanese community in Argentina. This is, however, a subject for future investigation.

9 The Role of Ethnicity in International Migration: The Re-Migration of Latin Americans from Japan to the US

Ayumi Takenaka

Introduction

Ever since South Americans, mostly Japanese descendants from Peru and Brazil, began to 'return' migrate to Japan in the late 1980s, they have re-migrated in growing numbers from Japan to the US. Why do they re-migrate, despite their incorporation into Japan as ethnically privileged migrants (as descendants)? And why do they further migrate to the US, despite the two countries' relatively comparable economic status?

Much research has focused on economic factors as principal causes of re-migration.[1] Just as most voluntary migration is economically-driven, so, too, is re-migration induced by relative advantages, either real or expected. One important cause of re-migration oft documented is migrants' economic failure in the primary destination country (e.g. unemployment, unstable jobs), while another is the lure of greater economic opportunities in third countries (e.g. a higher income, larger labor market, more favorable tax system and reward structure) (Edin et al. 2000; Iqbal 2001; DeVoretz and Ma 2002). In her study of immigrants' re-migration from Sweden to third countries, Nekby (2004: 3) summarizes: 'Given the relatively high standard of living at the lower end of the earnings distribution, characteristic of Sweden, without an expectation of higher incomes or better employment opportunities in third country destinations, immigrants have little incentive to emigrate.'

The re-migration of South Americans from Japan to the US, however, cannot quite be explained by relative economic advantages, let alone by the economic and political instability that pushed migrants from South America to Japan in the first place. Most re-migrants leave Japan for the US to take up similar lower-rung occupations, such as factory work and in restaurant businesses, even earning lower wages. According to a report by the IDB (2005), on average Latin American migrants in Japan earn and save more than in the US, taking into account Japan's higher costs of living. Even though migrants themselves are often aware of the higher wages and greater monetary rewards in Japan (which lured them there in the first place), many still opt to re-migrate to the US.

The literature has also emphasized 'failure of social integration' as a determinant of re-migration. According to this, the propensity to re-migrate increases when the migrant does not speak the host language, does not own property in the host society or has not acquired citizenship in the host country (Beenstock 1996; Ramos 1992; DaVanzo 1976, 1983). In other words, failure to establish social ties in, and attachments to, the host society, engender re-migration (Beenstock 1996); for instance, well-integrated immigrants, such as those who speak German, have familial ties and citizenship in Germany and feel German are less likely to emigrate from Germany than those who lack these skills and connections (Constant and Massey 2002). This model, however, does not quite explain the re-migration of Latin Americans who entered Japan as 'privileged migrants.' As Japanese descendants, they were guaranteed automatic legal status, were provided with employment services and some language education by the government and, some claim, had greater familiarity with Japanese culture than other foreign migrants. As second or third-generation descendants of Japanese immigrants, moreover, they were more likely than other foreigners to have familial ties in Japan. Despite these privileges, Japanese descendants re-migrated from Japan more often than non-Japanese immigrants from Latin America.

In this paper, I explore the role of ethnicity to account for this re-migration. While studies of international migration have treated ethnicity as a consequence of movements (e.g. the post-migratory development of ethnic communities), they have largely neglected the role of ethnicity in inducing and regulating international migration (Bauer and Zimmerman 1997). In their studies on re-migration out of Germany, Constant and Massey (2002) and Steiner and Velling (cited in Constant and Massey 2002) cite 'feeling German' or 'feeling good in Germany' as a predictor of who stays and who re-migrates, though they do not explain these notions. According to Edin et al. (2000), African and Asian immigrants in Sweden are much more likely to re-migrate to third countries than Nordic migrants, even accounting for differences in levels of human capital and economic integration.

Ethnicity matters in shaping human mobility, but of course, there are many things ethnic. Brubaker (1998) discusses ethnic conflict and ethnic affinity in inducing 'migrations of ethnic unmixing.' Ethnic difference, expressed in the form of conflict or ethnic cleansing, pushes migrants out of countries of origin, such as in the case of refugee and forced migration; and ethnic similarity, perceived by migrants or the state, lures migrations of 'ethnic kin.' The state often uses a notion of ethnic affinity in implementing and justifying selective immigration policies, providing 'co-ethnics' with privileges, ranging from automatic citizenship to special language training (Bauer and Zimmerman 1997; Joppke 2005; Thränhardt 1999; Groenendijk 1997). Germany, Italy, Greece and South Korea do so in some ways, as does Japan, although Japan, unlike other states, does not automatically grant citizenship to its 'ethnic brethren.'

If ethnicity is important in inducing migration, what role does it play in migrants' adaptation, or what are the consequences of ethnicity-based immigration? According to numerous studies documenting the adaptation of ethnic migrants, even though (alleged) ethnic ties may induce migration, they do not always facilitate migrants' adaptation (Tsuda (ed.) 2009). In the case of ethnic Germans in Germany, for instance, Klekowski and Ohlinger (cited in Brubaker 1998) attribute their marginalized status to the social and employment privileges accorded to them, precisely because these privileges have deprived them of incentives. In many other instances, 'co-ethnic' migrants are often treated as foreigners and marginalized in their putative ethnic homelands; consequently, new ethnic identities are forged by migrants, and a new type of ethnic differentiation emerges in the host society (Fox 2004; Tsuda 2002; Zmegac 2005; Brubaker 1998). Thus, official understandings of ethnic affinity do not often translate into everyday practice. South American migrants of Japanese descent have experienced a similar fate. While their migration to Japan was directly induced in the name of ethnic affinity, the gap between the official and unofficial understanding of this notion rendered their ethnic adaptation rather problematic.

In the following section, I discuss the re-migration of Latin Americans from Japan to the US as a consequence of their *ethnic* integration in Japan. Their re-migration, I argue, was an ironic consequence of ethnically-induced migration. Following a brief discussion on how ethnicity played a role in inducing this migration, I first illustrate how ethnic privilege granted to 'co-ethnic' migrants provided them with the means to re-migrate to third countries. I then discuss the ways in which prior ethnic expectations and senses of affinity made the actual adaptation in ethnic homelands problematic.[2]

Ethnicity as a tool of immigration policies: Initial migration from Latin America to Japan

The so-called return-migration from South America began en masse as a direct response to Japan's ethnicity-based immigration policy of 1990. This policy allowed anyone with claim to Japanese ancestry (called Nikkeijin) within three generations (i.e. having one Japanese grandparent) to enter and work in Japan without any restrictions. One- or three-year visas (depending on the generation) granted to Nikkeijin and their spouses were renewable in perpetuity. As a result, migratory flows from South America peaked in the early 1990s; as of 2008, there were about 400,000 South Americans, mostly Brazilians (312,000) and Peruvians (60,000), officially registered in Japan.

The policy was officially justified on the grounds of ethnic ties. This meant two things. First, due to ethnic connections, descendants of Japanese immigrants shared 'blood' and culture with native Japanese, and this would supposedly facilitate their adaptation in Japan compared to other foreigners such as Chinese, Koreans and Filipinos (Ministry of Justice 1990, 1994). Second, because of their ethnic ties, it was proposed that Japanese descendants should have social and familial ties in Japan.

Although South Americans of Japanese descent were officially incorporated as 'family visitors,' economic factors nonetheless played a critical role behind their migration. First of all, the ethnicity-based immigration policy was introduced at a time of severe labor shortages fueled by Japan's expanding economy in the 1980s. Companies in need of laborers, especially in manufacturing and construction, pressured the government and actively recruited Nikkeijin workers from South America. Being admitted as blood-related relatives, most Japanese-South Americans, in reality, engaged in unskilled labor, often contracted through brokers. After all, they, too, had migrated to Japan to make money rather than to visit their distant relatives. Japan was an ideal place for them to make quick money—legally—where jobs offered an average of $3,000 per month in the early 1990s (see Takenaka 2003).

Faced with severe economic crises at home, Japanese community leaders in South America also pressured the Japanese government to allow later-generation Japanese descendants to work in Japan. In 1988, shortly before Japan's immigration policy was revised, leaders delivered their official request on the grounds of common descent and culture to help 'ethnic brethren' cope with economic difficulties. They also argued that migrating to Japan would help later-generation Japanese immigrants learn about Japan, appreciate their roots, and widely diffuse Japanese culture. This, they continued, would contribute to the prosperity of the overseas Japanese communities as well as to Japan's 'internationalization' process (Kaigai Nikkeijin Kyokai 1988: 27; Takenaka 2003).

Whether leaders and government officials truly believed in ethnic affinity, Japanese descendants were brought in as privileged migrants over other foreigners. Preferential treatment included the provision of employment services, some language training, skills-training programs and easier access to permanent residency and citizenship. Regardless of the motives of interested parties, then, this migration was ethnically induced, and it brought about a number of unintended consequences.

In response to the ethnicity-based immigration policy, many non-Japanese descendants, along with descendants, migrated to Japan. The number of non-descendants was particularly large among Peruvians who entered either on forged documents or as tourists, taking advantage of the visa exemption agreement before Japan practically abolished it in 1994 (Takenaka 2003). The inflow of this ethnic migration also included those who had little sense of prior ethnic affinity, or were not even aware of their Japanese background. A 'return'-migrant, Jorge Garcia, had never heard of the term 'Nikkeijin' growing up in Peru's rural area, but in trying to migrate to Japan, he discovered that he was Nikkeijin due to his deceased maternal Japanese grandfather. Ethnic migration, therefore, is not only generated by prior sense of ethnic affinity; it also generates, and reinforces, the requisite ethnic identity (Brubaker 1998).

Moreover, contrary to policymakers' prior expectations, more people came and many have stayed longer than anticipated. According to some officials interviewed, Nikkeijin were preferred to other migrants, not necessarily because of their descent, but rather due to their limited number and relatively high levels of educational attainment. Unlike the large populations of neighboring Asian countries, Nikkeijin were fewer, estimated at 2.5 million, and only up to the third generation, or grandchildren of Japanese emigrants, were allowed to migrate. Their high credentials may have meant that they were more likely to return than low-skilled laborers with a lower level of human capital. Despite these expectations, the number of Nikkeijin migrants has steadily increased, rather than decreased, over the years. Out of an estimated 1,300,000 Japanese descendants in Brazil and 80,000 in Peru, 10% and 35%, respectively, had already migrated to Japan by 1992 (and 21% and 65% by 2002, if we are to assume they were all of Japanese descent); although the number of migrants included non-Japanese descendants, especially in the case of Peruvians.

As a further unanticipated consequence, some re-migrated to other countries instead of returning home. Ironically, as described below, many of those re-migrants were racially 'unmixed' Japanese descendants who were expected to adapt well in Japanese society.

Ethnic ties as a means to re-migrate: Who re-migrated from Japan to the US and how?

The ethnically-triggered return-migration induced further movement away from Japan. This re-migration, destined primarily for the US, has been on the increase ever since the beginning of the wave of return-migration to Japan. The precise volume of this re-migration is difficult to estimate. Yet, among the 55 Japanese-Peruvian and -Brazilians I studied in the US, one third had migrated from Japan (the rest came from South America), and at least seven out of 44 Peruvians I interviewed in Japan in 1996–1998 have since migrated to the US. Meanwhile, the number of US non-immigrant visas issued to Peruvian and Brazilian nationals in Japan has steadily increased: from 169 (1990) to 394 (1995), 1,906 (2001) and 3,143 (2004) for Peruvians, and from 695 (1992) to 2,472 (2001) and 4,035 (2004) for Brazilians (US State Department).

While the total number of Peruvians and Brazilians residing in Japan has steadily increased, so has the number of departures relative to entries. As migrants increasingly move back and forth (Mori 1999; Ishi 2003), out-migration has become a salient feature and consequence of return-migration. During the period of 1990–2000, the out-migration rate was roughly 14.6% for Peruvians and 17.5% for Brazilians.[3] It is impossible to know what percentage of these out-migratory flows were return-migration or re-migration to third countries, or what percentage involved just temporary visits. Yet, in the case of Peruvian migrants in Japan in 2003, for instance, we can estimate that about 80% of those who left Japan returned to Peru (mostly for short visits), while 10% re-migrated to the US.[4]

Many of the re-migrants from Japan to the US were racially 'unmixed' Japanese descendants. This group were more likely than non-descendants to re-migrate to that country, because they more often had the means to do so. First, they tended to have extensive ethnic ties as a result of their prior migration. Second, compared to non-descendants, migrants of Japanese descent were better able to use Japan as a stepping stone to enter the US. Let me elaborate.

Utilizing ethnic ties

As personal networks play a pivotal role in inducing population movements, virtually all those who had concrete plans to migrate to the US had family members already residing there. By the same token, having families in Japan was a probable deterrent. Japanese descendants were more likely than other Latin Americans to further migrate to the US, in part because of extensive networks developed as a result of their prior migrations to that country. As a large number of Japanese emigrated to the US (and Hawaii) at the turn of the century, some Japanese South Americans, especially from Okinawa, had relatives residing in the US. Among the emigrants sent to Brazil and Peru, some headed north shortly after arriving in South America, often illegally crossing the US-Mexican border in search of better-paying jobs. Later, during the 1970s and 1980s, more Japanese descendants migrated to the US as part of the larger labor migratory flows from South America, pushed by that country's economic downturn and pulled by the growing labor demand in the US. As a result of these migrations, South Americans of Japanese descent had extensive ties to the US.

Personal networks were a key instrument in inducing the secondary migration from Japan to the US in two ways. First, migrant networks, or 'webs of social ties that link potential migrants in sending communities to people in receiving societies' (Massey and García España 1987: 733), facilitated relocation and settlement by providing financial and psychological support. By providing shelter, job information and contacts, networks lowered the costs associated with international relocation (Boyd 1989).

Second, within the current US legal framework for immigration emphasizing family reunification, family networks were a crucial means to gain lawful entry into the US. Over the years, it became increasingly difficult for many Latin Americans, in general, to obtain US entry visas. In this context, networks became an important tool to obtain family-sponsored visas. For instance, a Japanese-Peruvian migrant in Japan, Jorge Higa, had a mother and siblings living in the US. His mother, now a naturalized US citizen, left Peru for the US together with his elder brothers during the mid-1980s. He remained in Peru to finish his university training. Soon after the completion of his education, when he was ready to leave for the US, the return-migration boom began. His friends rushed for Japan, one after another, and he, too, decided to go there in 1989. It was his 'childhood dream' to see the country of his grandparents and he wanted to save money before joining his family in the US. A decade later in 1999, he finally left Japan for the US with the green card that his mother had applied for on his behalf.

Utilizing Japanese descent

At the same time, Japanese descendants were more likely to migrate, or aspire to migrate, to the US because of Japan's descent-based immigration and naturalization policies. That is, Japanese 'blood' facilitated entry into the US—the 'thicker,' the better, to borrow the words of Japanese officials—since it was generally easier to enter the US as a Japanese citizen than as Latin American. Those Japanese descendants who were racially 'unmixed' were better able to take advantage of Japan as a stepping stone to enter the US. Foreigners in Japan, in general, widely regarded having a Japanese visa, and particularly an official re-entry stamp, as increasing their chances of entry into the US. One Brazilian return-migrant who successfully visited Los Angeles as a tourist said, 'With a Japanese visa in your passport, American officials think that we will return to Japan.' A more secure way of gaining entry into the US was to obtain a Japanese passport or even permanent residency. Due to Japan's bilateral visa exemption agreement with the US, Japanese passport holders were able to enter the US freely as tourists.

Foreigners of Japanese descent were able to obtain Japanese citizenship and permanent residency more easily than other foreigners due to Japan's descent-based naturalization and immigration policies. For example, the minimum length of residence required for naturalization was reduced, on average, to three years instead of five, for the children or spouses of Japanese nationals (i.e. the second generation). This facilitated the naturalization process for Japanese descendants who could trace their Japanese heritage through both parents. Racially-mixed Japanese descendants, especially those with only one Japanese grandparent, were much less likely to be able to gain second-generation status because of their remote familial ties with Japan. Recently, the number of Latin American applicants for permanent residency increased, as did the number granted permanent residency each year (Ministry of Justice 2010).

Japanese descendants applied for permanent residency (and citizenship) partly to avoid the trouble of renewing visas, but mostly to facilitate their travel abroad, particularly to the US. Having had difficulty traveling with a Peruvian or Brazilian passport, many South Americans assessed that having a Japanese passport, or even permanent residency, would facilitate international travel. The savings they accumulated after years of work in Japan also whetted their appetite to 'explore the world'—as one aspiring migrant in Japan put it: 'We just want to travel around, as many (rich) people do.'

The return-migration provided South American return-migrants with an incentive to travel abroad, an opportunity previously denied to many of them either legally or economically or both. The Japanese ethnicity-based immigration policy offered Japanese descendants the special privilege to enter and work in their ancestral homeland. Japanese descendants, in turn, took advantage of this in order to further migrate to the US. While personal networks served as an important incentive for the re-migration, the return-migration itself provided them with the means to utilize their existing networks.

Problematic ethnic identity as a motive to migrate: Why did they migrate from Japan to the US?

Extensive ethnic networks provided the economic, legal and sociocultural means to migrate to, and settle in, the US. Yet, in themselves they do not sufficiently explain the motives of re-migrants. Why did Japanese descendants *opt* to utilize these means to further migrate to the US? Why did they *want* to migrate? The 'American dream' was frequently mentioned by migrants in their answers, and this was largely about socio-economic opportunities they associated with ethnicity in Japan and the US. As elaborated below, it referred to first their 'ethnic rejection' in Japan, and second to their perception of ethnic pluralism in the US. The 'American dream' was fundamentally a relative concept formed in contrast to what may be called 'Japanese disillusionment.' In other words, Japanese Latin Americans' re-migration to the US was related to the very manner in which they were incorporated into Japan as return-migrants; it was a specific outcome of return-migration.

Ethnic rejection as a push factor

Japanese descendants aspired to migrate to the US principally because they were disillusioned with Japan. Contrary to their prior expectations, upon arrival they were not treated as Japanese, but rather as foreigners. Despite their descent, they remained an 'ethnic minority' in their ancestral homeland. Worse still, being as such was closely associated with low-status occupations in Japan. Even though they were mostly of middle-class backgrounds in their home countries with higher educational attainment, they engaged in dead-end manual factory work in Japan. A Peruvian re-migrant in New Jersey said, 'Nikkei (descendants) in Japan feel deceived because they are not treated as descendants, but only as foreigners. You see, we all went to Japan as if going home, but the Japanese discriminate against us as foreigners and as the children of emigrants.' Japanese descendants in the US often experienced similar discrimination as members of a racial minority. Yet, the shock they experience in Japan was not due to the act of discrimination itself, but the fact that they were denied the very identity they formerly cherished in return-migrating to their ancestral homeland. This sense of 'deception' drove many to migrate out of Japan.

Their assessments of Japan and the US varied according to ethnic and class background. 'Racially unmixed' descendants with middle-class backgrounds were particularly appalled at being deprived of their ethnic *and* middle-class identities in Japan, and tended to view the US with greater illusion. Poorer Latin Americans, who were often racially mixed and had lower expectations of Japan, were less likely to aspire to migrate to the US. Generally from modest economic backgrounds, these migrants experienced little, if any, downward economic mobility in Japan. Juan Ruiz Shiroma, a migrant of mixed racial background in Japan, said that he was happy enough with the money he was making in Japan not to dream about the US. He learned through his brother, living in one of Los Angeles' 'poor Black neighborhoods,' that 'Latinos earn only $1 per hour washing dishes, anyway.' Thus, views of the US depended much on class and ethnic background as well as prior expectations.

Ethnic pluralism as a pull factor

The notion of the 'American dream' was further reinforced by Japanese descendants' negative experiences in Japan. The US was portrayed as utopian in contrast to 'too much work' and 'too rigid and monotonous a life' in Japan. Unlike Japan, it was perceived that the US simply 'must be better' with 'less cold people.' 'There must be more life' in the US, and ultimately, 'the US must be more like home.' When Japanese Latin Americans talked about the 'American dream' like this, they were primarily referring to socio-economic opportunities associated with ethnic pluralism in the US.

This was commonly expressed as freedom and opportunities in association with how they were treated by others. By freedom, Japanese Latin Americans primarily referred to the way they were treated with regard to their social status. Some meant the right to 'argue with your boss' or to have a 'carefree work environment,' characterized by a lack of punctuality and a lax code of hygiene in factories in the US in contrast to 'too many norms' and the 'rigid work style' in Japanese factories. Others referred to the contrast with various constraints they experienced in Japan as 'foreigners.' As one aspiring re-migrant expressed, 'People in the US treat you as one more person, not as *gaijin* (foreigner). But in Japan, people constantly make you aware that you are *gaijin*; they treat you as *gaijin*; they look at you as *gaijin*.' As a result, he sighed, 'I just can't express myself freely because I am a *gaijin*.' He wanted to migrate to the US to gain freedom from that label.

Closely associated with freedom were the perceived opportunities. Even though most Japanese Latin Americans in the US engaged in low-skilled labor such as factory work as in Japan, they nonetheless perceived greater economic prospects in the US than in Japan where they, as *gaijin*, expected little chance of upward social mobility. One Japanese-Peruvian in New Jersey, who worked in factories in both countries, well illustrated this point:

> The system of work in Japan is more rigid than in the US. I used to be a welder in Peru, but the Japanese didn't even ask me about my skills and experience. They just treated me as one of many laborers. But in the US, they ask you what skills you have and what kind of job you

want to do. Yes, even if you don't speak English [like himself], they find ways of communicating.'

In Japan, conversely, 'if you are a foreigner and don't speak Japanese, they automatically put you in a position where they make you work like a robot.' Likewise, another re-migrant in Los Angeles said he decided to leave Japan for the US for the future of his children: 'I think there are more opportunities for my kids here. In Japan, I will always be a laborer and my kids will be the sons of a laborer. But here in the US, if you go to school and get educated, I think you will have opportunities beyond a laborer.' Carlos Tateishi, a university graduate from Peru who worked as a factory laborer in Japan, also hoped to re-migrate to the US because of the relative advantage there for professionals: 'If you are educated, you have more opportunities in the US than in Japan. In the US, it's up to you, but in Japan, the labor force is rigidly structured so that if you are out of the [promotional] ladder, you are out for good.' Latin American re-migrants, therefore, perceived that it was class, rather than race or ethnicity, that mattered in the US. In Japan, on the other hand, their ethnic (foreign) background would forever prevent them from upward social mobility.

Their perceived 'American dream' was also about cultural opportunities. By this, some Japanese-Peruvians meant relative linguistic ease. The large Spanish-speaking population in the US made it easier for them to adapt to that country. Ricardo Nakasone, who arrived in Los Angeles from Japan in 2000, had not learned English, and it was even unnecessary, he said, 'because there are so many Latinos.' After a five-year-long language struggle in Japan, he felt at greater ease in Los Angeles. Japanese Latin Americans, in general, also referred to the diversity of American society. Reinforced by Japan's narrower notion of ethnic and national identity, American ethnic pluralism was idealized and praised as a symbol of freedom, individualism and equality. It particularly mattered to those Japanese Latin American return-migrants who fell into a state of limbo after experiencing an identity crisis in Japan. Ricardo Nakasone expressed a sense of satisfaction: 'There are so many different kinds of people here, and no one cares who you are and where you are from, so you can be the way you are. I am neither completely Japanese nor completely Peruvian, but it doesn't really matter here.' A Japanese-Brazilian in New York shared a similar view. Working in a Japanese restaurant while studying at college, she praised New Yorkers' 'openness' toward foreigners in comparison to the Japanese.

> Here in New York, people also ask me where I am from because of my background. Even though I look Japanese, I don't have a Japanese accent [when speaking English]. But here, they find my background interesting. It's positive, unlike in Japan where people consider anything different as negative.

Another re-migrant in Los Angeles talked about the difference in treatment in terms of speech.

> Americans are used to different accents and they are tolerant of foreigners" accented English. What matters is how you make an argument. People listen to you and respect what you say. But the Japanese are perfectionists; if you have a slight accent, they look at you and begin to wonder where you come from. And the moment they find out that you are not Japanese, they change their attitudes.

In sum, the US offered diverse systems to adapt to, in their view, unlike in Japan where there was only one system—Japanese. American pluralism, as re-migrants perceived, allowed them to exercise more ethnic options; they could be Asian *or* Latino, or simultaneously Japanese *and* Peruvian or Brazilian, retaining Japanese traditional cuisine while speaking Spanish or Portuguese. In other words, their ethnic/racial identity in the US entailed more symbolic elements in association with freedom of choice (Waters 1990), coupled with pragmatic advantages. One Peruvian re-migrant stated: 'Usually, Nikkei in Los Angeles first find housing in urban Latino areas, because it's cheaper and later they move to more affluent Japanese communities.' Depending on their needs and resources, they were able to exploit opportunities and resources in both communities. Indeed, such options were the biggest incentive luring Japanese Latin Americans to re-migrate to the US.

Japanese Latin Americans could enjoy diverse patterns of ethnic adaptation in part because of the diverse ways in which they were incorporated into the US. Unlike in Japan, where return-migrants were incorporated en masse by the state's policy of ethnic migration, Japanese Latin Americans migrated to the US relatively free of state intervention. Also, Japanese Latin American migrations to the US occurred over a relatively long period, from the 1970s on to the late 1990s and from different countries. More established immigrants who arrived during the 1970s and 1980s mostly came directly from South America, while newcomers increasingly arrived via Japan.

Among the Japanese-Peruvians I interviewed in the US, 32 out of 43 were from Peru, and 10 from Japan. Some entered the US as tourists, family-sponsored immigrants, or students, while others crossed the US-Mexican border without documentation. Legally, some were naturalized US or Japanese citizens, while many remained Peruvian citizens or combinations of the above. Residentially, they were also more dispersed geographically than in Japan, although they tended to settle in two primary locations: New York/New Jersey and Los Angeles (and to a lesser extent, Miami). Socio-economically, too, they engaged in diverse occupations; whilst most were employed in low-skilled labor as in Japan, a greater proportion of Japanese Latin Americans in the US were in highly-skilled occupations, such as medicine and law, particularly in New York.

Diverse modes of entry resulted in diverse patterns of ethnic adaptation. In Japan, where Japanese Latin Americans were incorporated in a specific manner as factory laborers, they were collectively labeled 'Dekasegui workers' (temporary contract workers). In the US, in contrast, they largely avoided being branded, partly because of their small numbers and also due to their ambiguous and flexible racial and ethnic categories, both in terms of self-identification and classification by others. They were typically treated as 'Asians,' but as a new breed of 'Asians' who spoke Spanish or Portuguese like 'Latinos.' They were 'Japanese' so long as they kept their mouths shut; but as soon as they opened their mouths, they became Latinos. At other times, they were treated as 'Asians who spoke Spanish' or 'Latinos with a Japanese face' (from interviews) or, to reflect their mixed backgrounds, as 'Asian-Latinos' (*Los Angeles Times* 2/5/95) or 'Japanese Latin Americans' (US Department of Justice).

Japanese Latin Americans' own racial/ethnic identities were also ambiguous and flexible. Sometimes 'Asian' and other times 'Latino,' they chose and manipulated their identities according to their needs. They opted to be 'Japanese' whenever they 'wanted respect,' as a Peruvian re-migrant explained, 'since Latinos have a bad reputation anyway. So whenever I want respect, I say I am Japanese.' In addition to Asians' higher socio-economic status relative to that of Latinos, association with Japan granted them membership in the 'First World.' Establishing contact with the Japanese (Japanese companies), moreover, would enhance their prospects for job hunting, especially in Los Angeles where there was significant presence of Japanese capital.

Japanese Latin Americans could enjoy racial and ethnic options in the US also because of the nature of existing ethnic communities.

Although Japanese Latin Americans were generally treated as a racial/ethnic minority both in Japan and in their respective South American countries, they were more readily accepted in Japanese or Latino communities in the US. Sharing status as a racial or ethnic minority vis-à-vis the white majority, Japanese as well as Peruvian or Brazilian group membership was more inclusive. Consequently, being in the US, Japanese descendants' social distance from the Japanese (from Japan) diminished. Although they were treated as foreigners in Japan, in the US, they found they shared more commonalties. One re-migrant who worked for a Japanese company in Los Angeles said that while in Japan, speaking with a slight accent automatically put him in the position of a foreigner; in the US, however, even a limited command of Japanese made him 'Japanese' relative to others, since the majority in the US do not speak any Japanese. Another Japanese-Peruvian, too, found it easier to enter Japanese circles in the US: 'In Japan, the Japanese treated me as a foreigner. In Peru, the Japanese (e.g. businessmen from Japan) treated us as inferior children of emigrants. Here in the US, I'm still not 100% Japanese, but I feel more welcome [among the Japanese], I guess because they don't speak English and feel vulnerable, and I speak some Japanese, so they appreciate it.' Likewise, those Japanese-Peruvians who moved around Peruvian social circles in New Jersey frequently commented on their narrowed distance from other Peruvians. Although their social distance remained wide both in Peru and Japan, it decreased in the US through their shared status as immigrant workers and racial/ethnic minorities. In fact, the kind of ethnic factor that divided these groups in Japan made little sense in the US. While South Americans were incorporated into Japan as 'ethnic Japanese' (regardless of their actual descent), they migrated to the US as general laborers from Latin America. Thus, in the US, Japanese descendants had little 'ethnic affinity' or expectations to feel 'just at home' as they often did prior to return-migrating to Japan.

Many Latin Americans re-migrated, and aspired to re-migrate, from Japan to the US with positive perceptions of the latter reinforced by their experiences in Japan or by their desire to escape their unexpected realities in that country. Their perceptions of the US remained relatively positive, even though, in reality, most of them engaged in similar types of low-rung occupations in the US. Carlos Tateishi, who spoke earlier about greater opportunities in the US for university-educated professionals, wound up working night shifts for a Japanese manufacturing factory in Los Angeles doing 'exactly the same job' he did in Japan and even earning a lower (minimum) wage.

Antonio Yamamoto, another university graduate, found a job as a security guard in New Jersey, also making less than he had earned in Japan. But it did not seem to matter much. After all, they did not re-migrate to make more money. They still perceived that there were possibilities to do better in the US, at least more so than in Japan. It was this hope that mattered more to them.

Conclusion

Re-migration is likely to continue growing in the foreseeable future. For one reason, once people migrate, subsequent moves become easier to adjust to. As many industrial countries implement restrictive immigration policies, migrants increasingly use another country as a stepping-stone to enter their final destinations. Technological advancement in travel, as well as greater access to information, also facilitate multiple movements.

Through the ethnically-induced return-migration and subsequent re-migration, Japanese Latin Americans have also begun to migrate repeatedly between multiple countries. Now with extensive networks across the Pacific, they migrate back and forth to meet their different needs. They went to Japan when they 'needed money,' and to South America to 'have a good time with family.' And when they wanted something in-between or a combination of both, they opted to migrate to the US. So, no matter how unhappy they said they were in Japan, many tried to obtain Japanese permanent residency 'just in case, to leave more doors open' (a Japanese-Peruvian migrant in Japan). Also, they frequently aspired to engage in international businesses involving Japan and Latin America. While desperately hoping to leave Japan for the US, one Japanese-Peruvian dreamed about running an export-import business dealing in tropical fruits between Japan and Peru. Another planned to start a Japanese-style inn in Peru for Japanese tourists.

As they increasingly opted for transnational lives, the US became an even more attractive site. First, the US was a geographically convenient site to lead a transnational life across the Pacific; it was situated between Japan and South America, and flights connecting the two regions typically required a stop-over in the US. Second, the US was economically advantageous; areas such as southern California, where Japanese economic influence was strong, provided greater access to both Japanese and Latin American markets, thus affording better opportunities for people who wished to engage in jobs linking the two areas. Furthermore, the US was an ethnically convenient site for transnational migrants. Because of its ethnic pluralism, Japanese Latin Americans, particularly in Los Angeles, were better able to utilize their mixed cultural backgrounds. One Japanese-Peruvian re-migrant worked for years in a Japanese sushi restaurant in Los Angeles. Since most employees were Spanish-speaking Mexicans, he served as an interpreter and a 'cultural mediator' between the Japanese employers and Mexican employees, despite his limited command over the Japanese language. The US also provided a good cultural middle-ground. Japan and Latin America were 'culturally polar opposites,' as many re-migrants claimed, but the US fell between the two. Thus, to many multi-migrants with mixed backgrounds such as Japanese Latin Americans, the US was an ideal destination; coupled with the economic opportunities it offered, the US was where they perceived they would be able to exercise more economic *and* ethnic options than other countries.

As re-migration continues to increase, the US may further attract such multiple-migrants with multicultural backgrounds. That is because re-migration, compared to primary (one-off) migration, is shaped more by familial, cultural or ethnic reasons, rather than simply by economic factors.

Part III:
Migrant Education and Generations

10 The Development and Use of Resources in Educating Immigrant Children

In ja Lee

Introduction

Most immigrants relinquish nearly all of their resources when they leave their home country. They lose their mother tongue. People who are normally capable of expressing even the subtleties of the heart in their native language are often at a loss as to how to communicate things in the way that they would like once they migrate to a foreign culture. They lose the relationships that they have cultivated from childhood. Immigrants must leave their relatives and close friends behind along with the networks of support they represent. Those who had been practicing a profession may need to re-acquire their hard-earned, nationally recognized qualifications and certificates in the new country. Only those people who have, to some extent, been able to temporarily relinquish the various resources that are essential to survive can undertake immigration.

The above is a typical image of immigrants, used by people who are not immigrants themselves, to depict this group. It was, however, probably more accurate in a slightly earlier era; a period when cross-border migration was still physically, politically and economically difficult. Today's immigrants cannot, however, be rigidly placed within the confines of this image. Indeed, there are a considerable number of immigrants who have made even better use of the resources that appeared to have temporarily given up or who, through their own efforts, have managed to replace the resources they lost. Riding the wave of globalization, they expand their sphere of activity, augment their store of the resources that they need to live and create a second home base for themselves.

The aim of this chapter is to depict the various tensions experienced by immigrants by focusing on how they create and use resources. The case of the education of the children of newcomer Korean immigrants living in Japan will serve as the vehicle for achieving this aim. This example has been chosen because children's education is an extremely troubling issue for immigrants and at the same time a critical one in terms of the resources available to future generations.

While we lump them together as 'newcomer Koreans,' this group includes many types of immigrants. For this reason, researchers generally adopt wide-ranging subjects for their surveys; however, this chapter limits itself to looking at the intellectual class who have found employment in Japanese universities and research institutions following their time as foreign students in Japan. This group has been selected because its members have been the most strategic in their approach to education. Thus far, 18 families and 12 individuals have been interviewed as part of this survey. While this is not at all a large number, the sample is sufficient to paint a picture of the trends in children's education and also of the creation and use of resources for this purpose.[1]

Between Japan and Korea: The case of Family A

Let us begin by examining the case of one particular family.

Mr A currently teaches at a national university. He came to Japan to study in 1987, accompanied by his wife. Their eldest son was born the following year and their youngest two years later. After completing his doctoral studies, he worked as a tutor before securing his current post, in the same year that his first son started primary school. Because both Mr and Mrs A had always intended to return to Korea after Mr A finished his studies abroad, they continued to pay careful attention to their children's Korean education even after Mr A secured a permanent position in Japan. They taught Korean to their children using picture books and other educational materials that they had ordered from their homeland.

This did not, however, result in them paying scant attention to what their children were doing at school. Culturally, Koreans take education very seriously and as a consequence of the rapid pace of economic growth, Koreans have displayed a zeal for education that outstrips even the levels seen in Japan, tending at times to be viewed as excessive. As members of the intellectual class, Mr and Mrs A were also very earnest about education. In order to help with their children's schooling and out of consideration for the fact that they were in a foreign country, they engaged someone to act as the children's guardian at kindergarten, actively participated at their primary school and did their best to interact with their children's teachers and the parents of their classmates.[2]

Also, in an attempt to encourage their children to mix with the local school children, they created an environment in which there was an incessant stream of neighborhood children visiting their home. An interesting result of this has been that the associations forged with these children became the starting point for those created between this Korean mother and Japanese mothers in the neighborhood. Serving a few Korean sweets or some Korean cuisine had quite an impact, and the circle of friends grew steadily. Mrs A reports that she did not set out with the intention of creating this situation, but rather it was the natural outcome of simply acting as she would have in Korea. Possibly thanks to the special environment created by government housing, the number of close family acquaintances grew; the family were able to acquire an understanding of Japanese customs and mores, manners and ways of thinking in the course of unreserved conversations, and Mr and Mrs A were able to glean a significant amount of information regarding Japanese education. Family A's immigrant status most likely accounts for the expansion of their close circle of neighborhood acquaintances to this extent, in a country where interpersonal relations have been generally weakening.

Family A, blessed as it was with a wealth of local human connections, did not waver from its original plan of returning home at some stage in the future. As the school years went by for their eldest son, the couple began to worry. Their anxieties were the result of assorted data and reports that they were viewing in the various media about Korean education. The gist of what they had gleaned was that if Korean children living abroad did not return home while they were still of primary school age at the very latest, this would lead to a number of problems in areas such as their ability to adapt to Korea and their ongoing education in their home country. The father's ability to return to Korea was constrained by work considerations, but they felt a sense of urgency about the children returning ahead of them; that is, going either on their own or with their mother. So it was that in the summer of the eldest son's fifth year of primary school that the mother and children went back to Korea.

In line with their earlier plans, they returned to Korea at the beginning of July. This was so that the children could experience a short taste of their new school life before the summer holidays. The family lived with their mother's parents, and the school that the children attended had been their mother's school. Having explained their situation to the school, the family asked for the children to be given home teachers with some knowledge of Japanese. During the summer holidays, the children were sent to undertake supplementary studies. At the beginning of the summer holidays, they purchased their own home near the mother's family home. The ability of this family to construct a conducive educational environment for the children while rapidly implementing all their plans was entirely facilitated by the existence of the mother's family network.

The Mrs A's parents, siblings and other close relatives pitched in by sharing the various tasks amongst themselves, thus managing to provide a range of support to Mrs A and her two children. Although they had not made regular trips home during their time as migrants in Japan, the rich network of relatives functioned just as well as it had before, or actually even better, once they returned to their own country. These are the kinds of resources that migrants are grateful to have. Associations between Korean relatives are even richer today than they have been in the past, and while there may be times when these associations seem cumbersome, they continue to flow like an underground stream, providing a lifeline to which one can turn for help whenever the need may arise. For the majority of Korean immigrants, the networks of relatives that they appeared to have lost upon migration to Japan still exist; the ties have simply been left dormant.

Mrs A's siblings frequently visited their new home in Korea, and it also became the meeting place for the family's female cousins. It seems that it was thanks to this situation that Mrs A and her children did not experience loneliness or isolation while they were living on their own. Mr A also visited Korea once every two months to spend time with his family. According to the children, he acted even more 'like a father' than when they had all lived together in Japan.

The children's adaptation to their new environment had gone well. This was in part due to the appropriate action taken by their parents and family network, but it would also seem that some of their success was down to the skills that the children had acquired while living in Japan. Although the eldest son did not particularly experience any language difficulties, changing schools during his fifth year of primary school did leave him at something of a disadvantage. However, his skills in using the Japanese abacus, which he had learnt along with his neighborhood friends in Japan and which practically no one had learned in Korea, led to him being in the spotlight in class for his mastery of mental mathematics. With this recognition behind him, he was able to mix confidently with his classmates in no time at all. Once the children had settled in at school, Mrs A made them undertake a series of extra lessons. As long as they did not dislike going, she sent them to a rapid succession of after-school activities including taekwondo, computer, mathematics and English classes at 'cram' schools. At the time of their return to Korea, the country had just experienced the peak of an education fever resulting in a large number of training centers and cram schools being established in their neighborhood. They said that buses to these various centers and schools regularly passed by their house, and that while they were at first surprised by this situation, they too soon became a part of it. In this way, the brothers accumulated the same set of experiences as other ordinary Korean primary school students. This was considerably more difficult than their experience in Japan had been, but both of the boys were able to steadily acquire a range of knowledge and skills. Amongst these achievements, the younger brother distinguished himself in the study of mathematics, going on to be overall champion in a national mathematics competition.

After the boys and their mother had been living in Korea for about three and a half years, Mr A made a momentous decision regarding plans for their lives; he decided to continue his current work in Japan. That it had not been as easy to change jobs in Korea as he had thought was an important factor, but so too were Mrs A's objections to the family continuing to reside apart. Consequently, Mrs A and the children returned once again to Japan. The eldest boy was in the second year of middle school and the youngest in the sixth year of primary school. It might be assumed that these sudden changes in the plans for the children's education would have some degree of negative impact on them, but in the case of Family A they were, fortunately, able to readjust to their old lives. This meant that despite some minor difficulties in adapting, the children were able to fit right into life and school in Japan without experiencing any major problems. Quite the reverse, they ultimately felt delighted at the relatively lenient Japanese curriculum. For these brothers who had experienced the difficult Korean education system, study in Japan was something that they could easily handle, and as evidence of this both were accepted into the area's top university preparatory school, and are now studying at Tokyo University.

News from home and mixing with the neighbors

As we have seen, the education of the younger generation in Family A was a resounding success, despite the changes of strategy along the way. One can imagine that there would certainly have been difficulties in aspects of their lives that we have not discussed here. These were not, however, problems particular to migrants. What is rather more vital is the fact that Family A, aware that as migrants they were at a disadvantage in a number of areas, responded to these issues as they arose; they acquired the resources that they were lacking and made effective use of those that they did possess.

Having always assumed that they would return to Korea, Mr and Mrs A needed to prepare for their children's education following their return. Fortunately, there were abundant picture books and various other educational resources aimed at early childhood education on the market at that time in Korea, as it was in the grip of an 'education fever.' Korea was also producing increasing amounts of information and materials concerning the education of children who have lived abroad. Even though these sorts of educational resources may have been plentiful, it would probably have been difficult for anyone other than Koreans in Korea to obtain accurate information. This was not difficult for Mr and Mrs A, who had not yet been away from Korea for an extended period of time. As a consequence of Mr and Mrs A having been able to make effective use of resources in the form of abundant information about education available from the home country, their two children were able to acquire a certain level of Korean language competence and they also managed to time their return to Korea appropriately.

The children's neighborhood bonds created and fostered by their parents using the characteristic ethnic resources of Korean food and Korean-style hospitality are also precious resources for migrants. As a result of the constant stream of parents that they knew visiting their home, the parents in Family A became well informed about matters concerning education and were able to share concerns and solutions regarding parenting issues. Mr and Mrs A understood the value of making their children study the abacus as a result of these interactions, and thus sent them to lessons. It could be said that the 'special talent' that the eldest son displayed on the family's return to Korea was a product of these neighborhood bonds. The presence of large numbers of Japanese people in their neighborhood who were able to speak openly not just about education and parenting but a range of other issues was reassuring for the children, but even more so for the parents. These local human resources would prove of tremendous assistance at the time of their return to Japan from Korea. They enabled Mr and Mrs A to acquire advanced notice of detailed information regarding the local middle school that their children would be attending and also other information on the curriculum and high school entrance examinations. It was also these local human resources that cushioned the children's process of readapting to a new environment upon their return to Japan.

Japan, Korea and then abroad: The case of Family B

Family B moved to Japan at the end of the 1980s with two young children, and the parents took up positions as foreign students at different graduate schools. Mr and Mrs B placed their children in a nursery and spent their days conscientiously pursuing their studies. Since, as with Family A, they intended to return to Korea one day, Family B set about educating their children in the Korean language by taking the time to read them picture books and making them study the writing system. The parents recount that although the children were very young, they understood that their parents were tired from studying and accordingly would say to each other, 'let's play quietly as mum and dad are still asleep,' and take care not to make a sound. Realizing this, their mother could not help saying to them, 'I am pleased to be your mother.' Their mother said that although the relationship between them was one of parent and children, it also felt like they were friends.

During their time living in Japan, they felt like guests. Because they were both foreign students in universities that were representing Japan, the couple felt they were always treated with special consideration and kindness by those around them. They were not able to form many bonds with people in their neighborhood because they were so busy with their studies, but this did not cause them any particular inconvenience and their children managed to mingle with the Japanese children around them and had a very normal upbringing.

During their seventh year in Japan, when they judged that it was time for Mrs B to get on with writing up her thesis and when she seemed to be on the verge of getting her degree, they sent both children back to Korea ahead of themselves. The eldest son was in his fourth year of primary school and the youngest in his second year.

They sought help with childcare from the wife's family. Whilst they did not experience any difficulties with everyday conversation, it appears that the children were puzzled by the 'foreign culture' of the country to which they had returned. The younger boy, in particular, was preoccupied by the small differences between Japan and Korea, and complained about various aspects of Korean life.

Mrs B achieved her degree without any difficulties the following year and returned to Korea with the aim of finding work at a Korean university. She set up house near her parent's home, where she had left her children, but her attempts to find a job were unsuccessful. During this time she enlisted the help of her parents and employed a home tutor to care for her children. Partly due to her parent's affluence, her family's standard of living did not suffer despite the fact that she was unable to find work. Her husband, Mr B, already had a teaching position at a Japanese university and would be able to return and look for work once his wife had secured employment in Korea. Mrs B, who repeatedly made it to the final stages of job interviews only to be rejected, time after time, and who had begun to feel that if they kept on like this the family would always be apart, changed tack and set about trying to find employment at a Japanese university. However, the children, who were now in grades six and four of primary school, were opposed to this change of plans. It was thus only on the condition that she would concede to all of the children's demands (these included a big house in nice surroundings, getting a pet and the latest game consoles) that the three ended up moving to a Japanese regional city where Mrs B had secured employment.

During the summer of the eldest boy's second year of middle school, Mrs B's elder sister's son (who was in the second year of high school) went to New Zealand to study. The couple decided to ask Mrs B's sister to let their eldest son accompany his cousin to New Zealand to study for just six months. Their son telephoned home after having arrived at his destination and told them that New Zealand was paradise. It seemed that in New Zealand he had found the surroundings that he had been unable to find either upon his return to Korea or when he repatriated to Japan for the second time. The fact that he headed straight back to New Zealand on a holiday immediately after getting back to Japan following his six months of overseas study is evidence of how he felt.

Fortunately, this coincided with Mrs B's younger sister moving to New Zealand as an investment migrant to open a boarding house for foreign students, thus enabling them to place him there. A short while after their eldest son had departed on his extended period of overseas study, their younger son also began asking to be allowed to study abroad. Although his parents attempted to persuade him to wait a while, as he was still only in his sixth year of primary school, he pleaded tearfully that he wanted at all costs to be allowed to join his brother in New Zealand. Mrs B reflected that she had not been able to help feeling that the boy felt a stronger attachment to his older brother than to his parents. After discussing the matter with each other, in the summer of the boy's sixth year of primary school, the couple decided to send him off to study in New Zealand.

In addition to their mother's younger sister, a couple who were Mrs B's friends from graduate school also lived nearby, and took the boys on outings to a variety of places. They also formed close bonds with local classmates and other foreign students from Korea, and managed to complete their studies while also enjoying themselves immensely in their social milieu. The children were able to spend their middle and high school years in this privileged environment. The elder son then went on to university study in the United Kingdom, returning temporarily to Korea during this time to do his military service. After graduation, he began working for a major Korean trading company and he now lives a busy life in Seoul. Upon his return from studying in New Zealand, the younger son gained entry to a prestigious Japanese university. As a result of Mrs B getting a position at a Japanese university and Mr B changing jobs, once the boys had completed their study abroad, the parents and the younger son were able to live together in Tokyo during the latter's university study. Currently, the younger son has also suspended his studies to complete his military service in Korea.

Family networks and conscription

As we saw with Family A, the family network left 'lying dormant' in the home country serves as a valuable resource for immigrants. Family B also made ample use of this resource in educating their children. Family B differed from Family A in that the father was also looking for university work, and this resulted in Family B having an even greater need for assistance in raising and educating their children. However, a particular characteristic of Family B was that their family network was not limited to within the borders of Korea.

The late 1990s, when the children of Family B went to New Zealand as foreign students, is referred to in Korea as the 'early study abroad' period. It was a time in which increasing numbers of students began to be sent abroad to study before beginning university at home, a period of acquiring knowledge about the world. The explosion in the numbers of predominantly primary and middle school students being sent overseas is a phenomenon that began in the 2000s, after the Korean economy had survived the 'IMF Crisis.' It represented an attempt to raise a new generation able to respond to a world situation characterized by increasing globalization. Mrs B's sisters were at the forefront of this trend.[3]

There is no doubt that Mr and Mrs B, who lacked a support network in Japan as described above, were struggling to find the best approach to their children's education in that country. Opportunity presented itself in the form of an invitation from their family network, which was supposedly 'lying dormant,' to make use of their resources. This represented, moreover, an invitation to participate in that era's vanguard early study abroad education strategy. This was most certainly a godsend for Family B. Borrowing from the strength of their family members to send their children to study abroad, a move that seemed full of good future prospects, was considerably more attractive to Mr and Mrs B than struggling on their own with the children's education in Japan.

Cases like that of Family B increased steadily following the year 2000. Today, Korean families in which multiple siblings are abroad either as overseas students or immigrants are certainly not rare. If we extend the scope to include aunts, uncles and cousins, then we have a situation that depicts many Koreans living overseas. Moreover, despite it being claimed that there has been some loosening of ties, the connections between relatives appear firmly intact. It will be very interesting to see how Koreans living overseas, whose numbers have increased rapidly over the past 20 years, and their relatives in Korea go on to make effective use of their family networks in their children's education.

Another point of considerable interest is the fact that the children of Family B had joined the army. Conscription exists in Korea, and it is established practice for all males to serve two (previously three) years in the army. There are, however, numerous exceptions: for example, children such as those in families A and B with permanent residence rights in Japan are allowed to decline when drafted. Those born in countries such as the US where a principle of *jus soli* applies are also exempted.[4] Males granted this exemption, however, are only allowed to reside in Korea for less than six months at a time until they reach the age of 35; therefore, those who wish to use Korea as the base for their activities have no choice but to do their military service.

The children in Family B both have permanent residence rights in Japan and, given their histories, would seemingly have no difficulty living in a country other than Korea until they were 35. Despite this, they both undertook military service of their own free will. It would seem that each of the brothers had a variety of reasons for doing so, but we could sum up their motivations as seeking to equip themselves with the resources that they lacked as a consequence of having grown up as the children of immigrants. There is also the fact that military service is, in a sense, seen as a finishing school where all Korean males receive their social education. In Korea, at least, having been in the army is one of the criteria involved in being considered an adult man. Having served together in the army as members of the same intake of recruits are also experiences that lead to the forging of a powerful sense of camaraderie between the brothers of Family B. The vertical and horizontal relationships formed at this time often continue to operate as solid bonds throughout a person's lifetime, even after the end of military service. The brothers, who moved to New Zealand and then the UK after their period of coming and going between Korea and Japan, probably felt that they lacked these socially valued and stable human relationships that existed within Korea.

As Korean males, both considered that a military record, which served as proof of their having come of age, and solid human relationships that would last a lifetime were important resources. It would not be an exaggeration to say that the success of Family B's eldest son in adding these resources to his ability to speak three languages fluently underpinned his employment as a key player in one of Korea's leading trading firms.

Family C: Mainly Japan and a short stint in the US

Mr C came to Japan as a foreign student in the mid-1980s, and currently works for a national research institute in that country. His eldest daughter was born after his arrival in Japan and his eldest son a short time later. As Mr and Mrs C had not intended to live in Japan for an extended period of time, they conversed in both Japanese and Korean at home, bringing up their children to be bilingual. The children initially showed signs of confusion, but soon grew accustomed to using two languages. They were sent to a kindergarten in part because Mrs C went out to work, and she felt that this led to the children's feelings of loneliness.

Several years after taking up his current post, at a time when his work was going according to plan, Mr C was on the verge of accepting a position in Korea. However, he put off returning to Korea at that time because of his wife's strong opposition and as it would have been difficult to end his research project part way through. They subsequently had the opportunity to live in the US for about two years, when their eldest daughter was in middle school and eldest son in the second year of primary school, but Mr C says that he and his family felt that the US did not suit them. When it came time to return to Japan, they had serious concerns regarding how to best go about their children's education. They considered enrolling them in international schools and Korean schools but, ultimately, the children attended local public schools. Thereafter, the children followed the same, general path taken by ordinary Japanese children living in the suburbs of Tokyo.

The only strange thing was that when it came time for the eldest daughter to go to university, she selected Seoul University as her preference. Several Korean universities have set up a special quota of places for students who have received their 12 years of school education outside Korea. Whilst the number of available places is small, this fixed quota is also used at Seoul University. It tended to be the framework under which second and third generation Japanese Koreans gained admission but, more recently, these places have come to be filled by Koreans who have studied abroad. When the eldest daughter was fortunate enough to gain entrance to Seoul University, she was reportedly very happy at the thought of having been able to establish her own pathway for returning to Korea. It seems that in the beginning she enjoyed the fact that everything was new to her and she experienced various new stimuli. However, whether because she was unable to fit in with Korean culture and lifestyle or whether due to the fact that she could not overcome the gap in academic ability between herself and the students in the regular courses, she steadily lost her will to continue studying and after about two years she withdrew from her studies and returned to Japan. She has now re-enrolled at a Japanese private university and is conscientiously taking her studies in a different direction. The eldest son is currently in his second year of high school and plans to attend university in Japan; despite being able to speak Korean, he appears to have no interest whatsoever in returning to a country in which he has never lived. Mr C reports being equally divided between feelings of wanting to return to Korea and a desire to continue living his present life in Japan.

Special university quotas and family networks in the home country

In two of the preceding examples, the children had the opportunity to be educated in Korea before attending middle school. The children in Family C meanwhile had no experience at all of returning to Korea for their education. Of the families that I was able to survey for this study, the majority of cases (seven out of 12 families) were like Family C. Moreover, more than half of these families had lived in the US for about two years after the husband found employment there. They resided in Japan as immigrants and also spent some time living as temporary migrants in the US during this period.

This experience of layering one immigrant status on top of another might at first glance be viewed as broadening the educational opportunities for the younger generation, but in reality the resources available for the children's education are reduced. Place of residence in the US is determined according to employment concerns, and this can affect the amount of contact possible in cases where close relatives may already be living in the US (and there were actually cases like this amongst the families in this survey). In addition, as a result of a succession of changes within a short period of time to the base of family life, in some cases there is no scope for creating new resources.

If the conditions are right, then possibilities for the children's education are considerably expanded. Some families were able to gain acceptance into solid Korean communities already established at their destination point in the US. As a result, the younger generation's Korean became more polished and they were able to adapt easily to school life in that country. These types of ethnic communities can become powerful resources for immigrants.[5] However, they have not been established everywhere and, when the period of immigration is out of synch with these developments, there are also occasions when newcomers remain outsiders in their communities. It could be said that families that manage to make connections are quite fortunate. One cannot deny the possibility that in the future these sorts of communities of Koreans will spring up all over the US, and that the fortunate cases will become the norm, but this is something of a dream.

As mentioned earlier, Korean universities allow students who have completed all of their education outside of Korea to take examinations under a specially prepared framework. These students are able to gain entrance into Seoul and Yonsei Universities, which, as far as high school students taking the ordinary examinations within Korea are concerned, are the most difficult educational institutions to enter. Because of this it is possible to say that the entitlement to take an examination under a special framework is a special resource unique to immigrants. It was by making use of this resource that the eldest daughter of Family C was able to progress to attend a university in her 'native country,' where she was able to receive the best higher education available. Unfortunately, however, she voluntarily put an end to this university pathway that she had striven to achieve. There was actually a similar case in another family in which the eldest daughter also discontinued her studies at a top university in Korea before graduating and returned to Japan. Understandably, this special resource can only be used once. Equally, it stands to reason that what is vital is the extent to which one is subsequently able to utilize or generate other resources.

In contrast to Families A and B, Family C failed to make use of the powerful resource represented by the family network. There was certainly a lack of situations in which they could make use of this resource, and the couple may well have had their own issues with their respective families. In retrospect, however, it was very regrettable that they did not attempt to make whatever use possible of this resource when their daughter began her university studies (she entered a student dormitory). Even though they are able to speak the language, adapting to life in their 'native country' is in many regards an unexpectedly difficult process for immigrant children who have grown up in foreign countries.

On reflection, the approach taken by Families A and B increasingly appears extremely sensible in terms of the education of immigrant children. Both families exhibit a different set of circumstances and numerous disparities in their abilities to make use of and create resources. What is interesting, however, is that they both use the wife's family network as their major resource. Generally speaking, more emphasis is placed on the patrilineal family network in Korea, with children being regarded as structural members of this framework.

The assumption, therefore, is that the family network on the father's side would be expected to play a major role in the education of children. This notwithstanding, both Family A and Family B chose to rely on the mother's family network. One reason for this may be the fact that it would have be easier for the mother, who was returning to Korea on her own with the children, to live under the same roof as her own family. An additional reason might be that this choice made it easier to utilize the family network as a resource. The explanation for this lies in the fact that if they were to rely on the husband's family network, the wife as well as being the children's mother would simultaneously have to fulfill the role of 'daughter-in-law' to her husband's family. There are too many drawbacks inherent in the 'daughter-in-law' position for a mother in the position of attempting to facilitate the education of her immigrant children, a task that is more fraught with concerns about the children's ability to adapt than is generally the case in the education of children. If these disadvantages could be sufficiently overcome through the use of the family as an advantageous resource, then that would be another matter; but when this is not the case, choosing one's own family where the emotional ties are stronger and where character flaws might be overlooked, is indeed the sensible course of action. This aspect of the findings calls for a reanalysis from a gender perspective, and it is my hope to redraft along these lines at a later stage in this survey, after having collected more data.

Conclusion

We have used case studies about the education of the children of newcomer Korean immigrants living in Japan to look at how immigrants make use of the resources available to them, and also at how they create the resources that they lack. There is a certain bias in the subject matter of this survey, and I have, therefore, not dealt with matters such as the way in which economically successful immigrants make use of financial assets as resources. I hope, however, that I have managed to provide at least a partial sketch of immigrants engaged in difficult struggles in order to forge a better life.

From the outset, the main aim has not been to come to some sort of conclusion or generalization and therefore, in ending this discussion, I would like to record the personal impressions that I formed in the course of carrying out this study. Twelve immigrant families served as the subjects of this survey, and depending on the family, I interviewed the couples separately and where possible I asked if I could also interview the children. As is common during interviews, there are gaps in the accounts given by a husband and wife of the same family. These types of gaps occurred frequently in this survey material but, in most cases, it was the wife who gave the most detailed account and whose reminiscences were most accurate. Perhaps because the conversation centered on children, I have the impression that the wives (mothers) reliably picked up on aspects that the husbands (fathers) had failed to notice. I have a feeling that in writing this I will be criticized for dealing in role stereotypes based on gender differences, but it does seem that the role played by the mother is far more considerable in creating stability for an immigrant nuclear family than is normally the case.

Another related impression that has stayed with me concerns the differences in the characteristics and abilities of the wives/mothers. Is it not the character and ability inherent in women who are wives and mothers that are the important factors controlling not only children's education but also the overall quality of immigrant life? The more the survey progressed, the more convinced I became of this fact. Cheerfulness in dealing with everything, a brightness of spirit making everyone around them happy and the ability to act to ensure that a goal once set can be achieved promptly: these aspects of their characters and abilities heightened not only the quality of the family but also that of their own lives. This is not something that is confined to immigrants. However, in the case of immigrants the presence or absence of this cheerfulness, openness and activeness leads to major differences in outcomes.

We have the famous words of Hiratsuka Raichō, 'In the beginning woman was the sun.'[6] Do not today's immigrant women need to act as both moon and sun? I cannot help thinking that if the trend of the times sees an increasing number of immigrants, then the capacity of migrant women to use their inherent qualities can lead to a bright future for this society. They shine as they live their lives, using their natural gift of cheerfulness that brightens up their surroundings and their ability to act in a way that is so energetic that it fairly engulfs all around them.

11 Japanese Immigrants in Brazil and 'Colonia-go': Japanese as an Immigrant Language

Yasue Nakato

Introduction

The following dialogue is from a conversation between Japanese immigrants in Brazil (Ōta 1959: 65). I wonder how many people will be able to understand what they mean.

"*Kazamento* no *fesuta* de *serubēja* ga *basutante* demasuyo." (There will be a lot of beer at the wedding celebration)
"Sorya *muito bon* desuna." (That sounds very good)
"Aa, *shin, shin*." (Oh, yes, yes)

All of the words shown here in italics are loanwords from the Portuguese language; kazamento: *casamento* (wedding), fesuta: *festa* (celebration, festival), serubēja: *cerveja* (beer), basutante: *bastante* (ample), muito bon: *muito bom* (very good), and shin: *sim* (yes).

The language that is commonly heard in the Japanese-Brazilian community is often called 'Colonia-go,'[1] a mixture of Japanese and Portuguese. 'Colonia,' a loanword from the Portuguese *colônia*, has the following meanings according to Handa (1970: 790, glossary).

Colonia
The word is equivalent to "colony" in English, but it is used in this book to mean three things. Firstly, it is an area in which *colonos*, family workers of a coffee farm, live. Secondly, it is a collective settlement of owner-farmers, which is called "shokuminchi" (colony) in Japanese because the word *colono* also means "settler" and "agricultural immigrant." Thirdly, it is a short form of *colonia japonesa* ("Nikkeijin"/ Japanese-Brazilian community). Prewar terms such as "zairyū dōhō" (resident countrymen) and "hōjin shakai" (community of Japanese

nationals) are no longer appropriate to describe a community that now includes the second and third generation Japanese-Brazilians.

In Japan, very few people know of the existence of the 'Colonia-go,' not to mention its meaning. Indeed, 'Colonia-go' is in the process of vanishing from the Japanese-Brazilian community due to the declining population of first generation immigrants and the aging of second generation immigrants. In this chapter I discuss the linguistic characteristics of 'Colonia-go,' the background of the linguistic contact that led to its formation, and its position in the Japanese-Brazilian immigrant community in light of the history of Japanese immigration to Brazil and social conditions at the time. Source material is drawn from documents and records kept by Japanese immigrants in Brazil.

Generational change and language shift

The Federative Republic of Brazil (*República Federativa do Brasil*) forms the largest territory and population in Latin America, with a land area of 8.51 million km^2 and a population of about 190 million people. This vast country is divided into five regions—North (*Norte*), Northeast (*Nordeste*), Southeast (*Sudeste*), South (*Sul*) and Central West (*Centro-Oeste*), and about 40% of the population are concentrated in the Southeast where Brazil's largest city, São Paulo, is situated.

The mass immigration of Japanese to Brazil began when the first immigrant carrier *Kasato Maru*, carrying 790 or so people, docked at the Port of Santos on June 18, 1908. The number of 'Nikkeijin'—Japanese immigrants and their descendants—who continue to live overseas is estimated to be 2.6 million people worldwide, of which 1.4 million currently reside in Brazil.[2] According to two nationwide population surveys of the Japanese-Brazilian community conducted in 1958 and 1988, as shown in Table 11.1, the Nikkeijin population increased from about 430,000 in 1958 to around 1.23 million in 1998, but the place of residence did not significantly change with about 80% living in the Southeast Region (Burajiru Nikkeijin Jittai Chōsa Iinkai (ed.) 1964; Sanpauro Jinbun Kagaku Kenkyūjo (ed.) 1989), the majority in the State of São Paulo. Although Brazil has the largest Nikkeijin population in the world, this group currently accounts for just 0.7% of Brazil's total population, and represents less than 2% in the Nikkeijin-concentrated area of the Southeast. In this sense, the Nikkeijin in Brazil can be considered a minority ethnic group.

Let us examine generational change and shifts in language use in the Nikkeijin community in Brazil. The ratios of generations in the 1958 and 1988 surveys are shown in Table 11.2, and those of languages used at home are presented in Table 11.3. It is clear that the first and second generations constituted the majority in 1958, whereas the second and third generations form the largest group in 1988. The main language used at home also shifted considerably from Japanese to Portuguese.

According to our survey on language life[3] conducted at two rural locations in the State of São Paulo in 2003, there was a marked difference in intergenerational language use in that the first generation predominantly used Japanese, the second generation both Japanese and Portuguese and the third generation predominantly Portuguese. The language shift from Japanese to Portuguese was almost complete over the course of three generations. This generational shift in language use is also related to linguistic ability. As the younger generations use Japanese less frequently, their fluency gradually declines and it becomes more difficult to maintain the ability to read and write Japanese in particular.

The age of immigration to Brazil ended in the 1980s. As the first generation ages and diminishes in number and the second and third generations take center stage, the lifestyle of the Nikkeijin has changed greatly in terms of the diversity of occupations, population concentration in urban areas, higher educational backgrounds, the common occurrence of marriage to non-Japanese and so on. Now that the fourth, fifth and sixth generations are entering the scene, the Japanese language has almost become nonfunctional in terms of basic interpersonal communication. The growth of a younger generation with no sense of belonging to the Nikkeijin community has led to the loss of the centripetal force of the community as an ethnic group and the phenomenon of *dekassegui* (traveling to Japan for temporary work) that began in the second half of the 1980s and spurred the decline of the *colonia japonesa*. This situation is described in Imin Hachijūnen-shi Hensan Iinkai (ed.) (1991: 271) as follows.

> As the first generation decreases and the second and third generations increase further within the Nikkeijin community, there will be more interracial marriages. ...As a result, there will be more mixed-blood

Table 11.1: The Nikkeijin population in Brazil and population ratios by region (1958 and 1988)

	1958 survey	1988 survey
North (*Norte*)	5,227 (1.21)	33,000 (2.68)
Northeast (*Nordeste*)	1,765 (0.41)	28,000 (2.28)
Southeast (*Sudeste*)	334,201 (77.70)	974,000 (79.32)
South (*Sul*)	78,097 (18.16)	144,000 (11.72)
Central West (*Centro-Oeste*)	10,679 (2.48)	49,000 (3.99)
Unknown	166 (0.03)	–
Total	430,135 (100.0)	1,228,000 (100.0)

Note: Figures in brackets indicate percentages.

Table 11.2: Ratios of Nikkeijin generations (1958 and 1988)

	1958 survey (%)	1988 survey (%)
First	32.3	12.5
Second	52.1	30.9
Third	15.5	41.3
Fourth	–	13.0
Fifth	–	0.3
Unknown	–	2.0

Table 11.3: Ratios of languages used by the Nikkeijin at home (1958 and 1988)

	1958 survey (%)	1988 survey (%)
Japanese	53.2	6.3
Japanese & Portuguese	32.0	19.7
Portuguese	14.8	56.0
Unknown	–	18.1

Nikkeijins and the border defining the *colonia japonesa* will become unclear (borderless). ...When the border of the *colonia japonesa* is blurred, it means that the Nikkeijin community as an ethnic group can no longer be defined by the term *colonia*.

Linguistic characteristics of 'Colonia-go' and the background leading to its creation

Changes in the number of Japanese immigrants to Brazil

A total of about 240,000 Japanese immigrated to Brazil before and after the Second World War. Figure 11.1 is a graph showing the number of Japanese immigrants who arrived in Brazil each year over a period of about 70 years from the start of immigration in 1908 (based on Mita and Horisaka 1986: 264). Immigrant numbers are shown along the vertical axis and arrival years along the horizontal axis. The number of Japanese immigrants to Brazil varied according to the political, economic and social situations in both Japan and Brazil at the time, and the period can be divided broadly into four phases. The number of immigrants and the ratio for each phase are shown in Table 11.4.

Phase I covers the early period from the start of immigration to Brazil in 1908 to 1923, during which many Japanese immigrants entered the country as 'colonos,' or contracted farm workers. Phase II covers 1924 to 1941 when immigration was encouraged as part of national policy, the number of immigrant arrivals peaked and the 'colonies' of collective Japanese settlements flourished. Phase III is a 'void' period when immigration from Japan was stopped due to a diplomatic break between the two countries in 1942, through the end of the Second World War to 1951. Phase IV is a period of 'postwar immigration' that began from the restoration of diplomatic relations in 1952. The number of postwar immigrants began to decrease after peaking in 1959, and less than 100 immigrants arrived each year during the 1980s. At that point, the age of immigration spanning about 70 years virtually came to an end.

The linguistic characteristics of 'Colonia-go'

How did 'Colonia-go' take shape in the Japanese immigrant community in Brazil? Here is a typical example of 'Colonia-go' (Satō 1957: 82).

"Sā hayaku *merukādo* sa itte iki no yoi *pēshe* wo *konpura* senya." (Let's go to the market quickly to buy some fresh fish.)
"Tsuide ni ajinomoto ba *un ratta* kawanya naran, imanara nihyaku *miru* mo suru be ne." (I must also buy a can of Ajinomoto [a monosodium glutamate product]; I suppose it costs 200 mil or so now?)

Figure 11.1: Annual change in the number of Japanese arrivals in Brazil

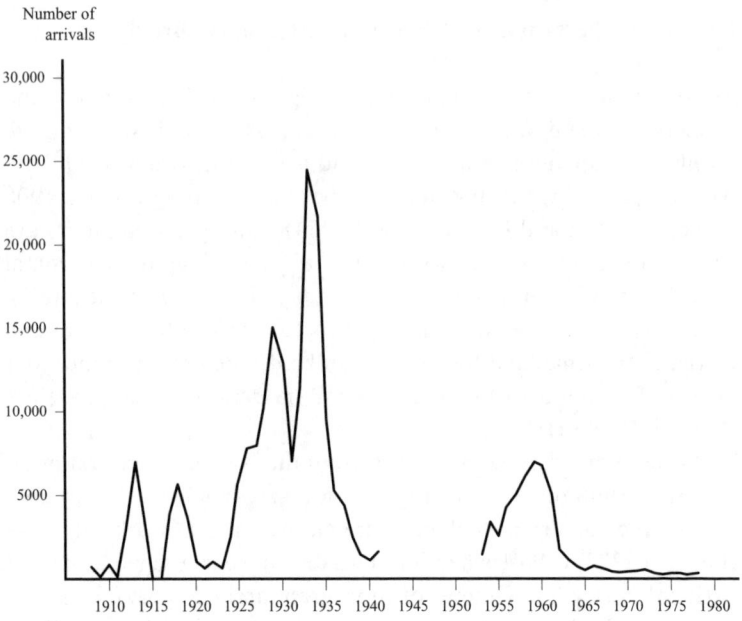

Table 11.4: Periods of the Japanese immigrant community in Brazil and number of arrivals

	Year of arrival	Number of arrivals
Phase I: Colono period	1908–1923	32,590 (13.7)
Phase II: Colony period	1924–1941	153,676 (64.4)
Phase III: Void period	1942–1951	0 (0.0)
Phase IV: Postwar immigration period	1952–1978	52,387 (22.0)
Total		238,653 (100)

In the above dialogue, all of the italicized words are loanwords from Portuguese; merukādo: *mercado* (market), pēshe: *peixe* (fish), konpura: *compra* (the verb 'comprar' (to buy) in the third person singular present tense indicative mood), un ratta: *um lata* (one can; '*um*' (one) is an adjective preceding a masculine noun and '*lata*' (can) is a feminine noun), and miru: *mil* (Brazil's currency at the time).

Incorporating numerous words borrowed from Portuguese into the Japanese grammatical structure is one of the major linguistic characteristics of 'Colonia-go.' As an aside, 'un ratta' (*um lata*) should be 'uma ratta' (*uma lata*) with a feminine form of the adjective, *uma*, according to the grammatical rules of Portuguese. This offers us glimpses into the way Japanese immigrants spontaneously acquired the Portuguese language in their daily lives.

Another major linguistic characteristic of 'Colonia-go' is the mixed use of various Japanese dialects in its grammatical construction. In the above example, 'hayaku' (a non-euphonic form commonly found in eastern Japanese dialects), 'merukādo sa' and 'nihyaku miru mo suru be' (postpositional particles '-sa' and '-be' in the Tōhoku dialect), 'ajinomoto ba' (a postpositional particle '-ba' in the Kyūshū dialect), and 'konpura senya' and 'kawanya naran' (grammatical features of western Japanese dialects spoken in the Chūgoku, Shikoku and Kyūshū regions), are used together.[4]

Background to the language contact (1): Contact with the Portuguese language of Brazilians and foreign immigrants

The large amount of lexical borrowing from Portuguese was inevitable to allow the Japanese to go about their daily lives in Brazil. Handa (1952: 8–12) explains as follows.

> We were bound to use the language of Brazil when we set our foot on its soil. …The Brazilian words that come with a new lifestyle gradually drive out and replace their Japanese equivalents. They are turned into Japanese-like words, or used as if they were Japanese and come to replace the original.

Loanwords from Portuguese not only supplemented words and concepts that did not exist in the Japanese vocabulary but also substituted the names, kin names, and words representing quantities and time which existed in the Japanese language (Higa 1982). Even though some words can be translated into Japanese, a Japanese word 'chawan' (bowl) and its equivalent loanword from Portuguese 'chijēra' (*tigela*) are separate things, and the Japanese 'okatte' (kitchen) sounds more Japanese than the loanword 'kojīnya' (*cozinha*), for example.

When the Japanese began to immigrate, many European and other foreign immigrants were already working on coffee plantations. The importation of foreign immigrant workers had begun to increase from around 1850, 50 years prior to the arrival of the Japanese immigrants, with many coming from Italy, Portugal, Spain and Germany. Japanese immigrants had contact with the languages of these foreign immigrants in addition to Portuguese. *Koronia manyōshū*[5] (Collection of Colonia poems) (1981) contains the following Colonia '*tankas*' (31-syllable poems) (author's name, year of publication and page number in brackets).

> Waga sumeru mori wo hedatete Itariya no korono no moyasu kemuri agareri (Across the woods in which we live, the smoke rises from the fire made by Italian colonos) (Ichirō Noguchi 1957: 238–239)
>
> Doitsugo namari ōki Hakugo[6] no Doitsujin to irikumeru kōshō shitsutsu iradatsu (Irritating is a complex negotiation with Germans who speak Brazilian with a heavy German accent) (Keishū Tokuo 1939: 33)

In those days, Japanese immigrants were an outright ethnic minority in Brazilian society as they accounted for less than 1%, and foreign immigrants accounted for only about 10% of the total population of Brazil. As might be expected, Japanese immigrants faced a language barrier and tried desperately to learn Portuguese as a means of survival.[7] The following is a quote from the chapter entitled 'Shoki tokōsha to Burajiru-go' (Early immigrants and the Brazilian language) by Aoyagi (1941: 398).

> None of the immigrants who arrived on the Kasato Maru could speak the Brazilian language. …They all made strenuous efforts to earn their living among the Brazilian people with whom they could not communicate. They managed to get things done using signs and gestures most of the time. Since they experienced hardship due to lack of language proficiency, they all felt the need first and foremost to learn the Brazilian language. Whenever immigrants gathered, they taught each other new words and tried to use the Brazilian words they knew in place of their Japanese equivalents. Their children who were born in that environment learned the Brazilian language rapidly and made their parents proud …they moved from place to place to earn a livelihood and could not undertake education at home. The second generation grew up under these circumstances and in the end became non-speakers of the Japanese language.

What was the Portuguese language spoken by the early Japanese immigrants like? The following essay entitled 'Dai 1-kai imin no arubaito "Nippaku kongō-go" de kekkō shōbai dekiru' (A side job of the first group of immigrants: Can do business using the 'mixed Japanese-Brazilian language') is found in *Kasato Maru* edited by Nihon Imin Gojūnensai Iinkai (1958: 64), which was compiled to commemorate the 50th anniversary of Japanese immigration to Brazil.

> Those who were young and active among the first group of immigrants who were assigned to the plantations in Guatapará came up with what we now call a side job. ...On Sundays and public holidays, they visited nearby Brazilian farmers and asked if they wanted them to "castrate pigs" by saying as follows. "*You, Guatapara*, noe, mejiko, *kappādo*, noe, shunōru, ten, *poruko* ka, *non ten* ka... ten nara *ten* to *fāra paramī*." It is quite an odd use of Portuguese with some Japanese words mixed in, but what they were trying to say was "We are pig castration experts at Guatapará plantations; do you breed pigs? If you do, please let us castrate them." Oddly enough, they managed to do business using this "mixed Japanese-Brazilian language" that seems hardly intelligible to listeners.

The above Portuguese passage spoken by the Japanese immigrants to Brazilians, in which the words written in italics are Portuguese words, is constructed as follows; '*Eu* (I), *Guatapará* ([place name]), *não é?* (right?), *médico* (doctor), *capado* (castrated pig), *não é?* (right?), *senhor* (master), *tem porco* (has pork) or *não tem* (not has), if *tem* (has), *tem* (has), *fala para mim* (speaks to me).' It is just a list of Portuguese words, or Portuguese words arranged in Japanese word order. It is said that the Portuguese language spoken by Japanese immigrants was acquired spontaneously through contact with Brazilians and European immigrants living at coffee *fazendas* (farms), and contained much crude language and slang, as they were mostly exposed to language spoken by low-class laborers called the *colono* (Handa 1970).

As mentioned by Aoyagi (1941) above, the immigrant parents in the early *colono* period were too busy to think about education for their children and were rather more eager to learn Portuguese themselves (Wako 1939: 51–52).

> In early 1918 when I was the editor of *Burajiru jihō* (one of the Japanese-language newspapers in Brazil), I went on a research trip for a period of 40-odd days to find out about the education of the children of Japanese immigrant families in and around Ribeirão Preto out of my personal interest. It was because the Japanese were still immigrant workers at coffee plantations and many of them were living in this region in those days. I visited nearly 1000 families at more than 40 farms,

and found that none of them taught Japanese to their children; and although parents wanted their children to learn the Brazilian language, very few Brazilian schools existed outside of large plantations.

Background to the language contact (2): Contact between the regional dialects of Japanese immigrants

The life of the *colono* as short-term immigrant laborers at *fazendas* was extremely harsh and difficult. Japanese immigrants gradually changed their aspirations towards medium- and long-term work and began to live as tenant and independent farmers. During the 1920s, Japanese 'colonies' or settlements were formed one after another along the railway line extending into the hinterland of the State of São Paulo. There were five to six hundred settlements at peak, gradually forming the 'Japanese community in Brazil.' This process was boosted by the influx of large numbers of Japanese immigrants based on the national policy from 1924, and encounters between Japanese immigrants inside and outside of colonies brought about the language contact between their regional dialects.

Table 11.5 shows the number and ratio of Japanese immigrants who arrived during the period from 1908 to 1962 by their place of origin, according to each phase (Burajiru Nikkeijin Jittai Chōsa Iinkai (ed.) 1964). Although geographical division does not always coincide with dialect division, these data can reveal an approximate pattern. The largest group through all the phases is immigrants from the Kyūshū region, especially Kumamoto Prefecture (10.2% of the total number of immigrants) and Fukuoka Prefecture (8.4%). The second largest group came from the Chūgoku region, especially the Sanyō area (Hiroshima Prefecture 6.0%, Yamaguchi Prefecture 3.2%, Okayama Prefecture 2.8%). This group is followed by those originating from the Tōhoku region, particularly Fukushima Prefecture (5.3%). Looking at each phase, those from Western Japan (mainly Kyūshū, Okinawa and Chūgoku) alone accounted for 80% of the total number of immigrants during Phase I. The ratio of those from Eastern Japan (mainly Tōhoku) began to increase during Phase II. The 'mixed use of dialects, mainly Western Japanese dialects' noted by many researchers as a characteristic of the Japanese language used by the Nikkeijin in Brazil is understandable, based on the immigrants' place of origin ratios.

While the mixed use of dialects is a common characteristic of the Japanese language used in Japanese immigrant communities throughout the world, there are some identifiable variations between

Table 11.5: Number and ratio of arrivals by phase and place of origin (1908–1962)

	Phase I	Phase II	Phase IV	Total
Hokkaidō	704 (2.2)	12,329 (8.0)	2,670 (6.3)	15,703 (6.9)
Tōhoku	1,840 (5.6)	20,435 (13.3)	4,269 (10.0)	26,544 (11.6)
Kantō	1,035 (3.2)	9,519 (6.2)	4,681 (11.0)	15,235 (6.7)
Chūbu	3,501 (10.7)	16,061 (10.5)	2,953 (6.9)	22,515 (9.8)
Kinki	1,610 (4.9)	14,690 (9.6)	3,199 (7.5)	19,499 (8.5)
Chūgoku	4,455 (13.7)	22,557 (14.7)	3,857 (9.0)	30,869 (13.5)
Shikoku	1,556 (4.8)	10,615 (6.9)	2,943 (6.9)	15,114 (6.6)
Kyūshū	12,209 (37.5)	38,879 (25.3)	13,230 (31.0)	64,318 (28.1)
Okinawa	5,680 (17.4)	8,591 (5.6)	4,829 (11.3)	19,100 (8.3)
Total	32,590 (100)	153,676 (100)	42,631 (100)	228,897 (100)

the communities. According to Higa (1983), the Chūgoku dialect became the common base for the standard Japanese spoken in Hawaii for the reasons that about 50% of Japanese immigrants in Hawaii came from the Chūgoku dialect zone, that they were the early arrivals, and that the Chūgoku dialect was relatively similar to the standard Japanese language. By contrast, Japanese immigrants in Brazil did not have a dominant dialect that could form the foundation for a common Brazilian Japanese language, because none of the dialect groups accounted for more than 10% of the total Japanese immigrant population. In both Hawaii and Brazil, the Okinawa dialect did not become a common language of the Japanese immigrant communities, despite the fact that Okinawans were the largest group among the early arrivals, as it is very dissimilar to standard Japanese. Handa (1952: 7–8) comments as follows.

> The Japanese language in Brazil is above all a language used by immigrant laborers. The dialects used by immigrants from all over Japan were mixed together and those words that were most widely understood have survived and formed our Japanese. However, our language has not achieved full standardization in the way that occurred in Hokkaidō, and we can see that the dialect of a numerically or culturally dominant prefecture in each district is represented more strongly in the mix of various dialects. In the Noroeste region for example, the language has achieved a certain level of standardization with a high representation of the Kyūshū dialect in Lins and Promissão

and there is a detectable level of the Tōhoku dialect in Araçatuba. The Japanese language spoken in the City of São Paulo appears to be somewhat standardized just as in Hokkaidō, but some Shikoku dialect is detectable in Pinheiros as many of the immigrants came from Cotia.

Many organizations were formed in Japanese immigrant communities, including Japanese associations, Japanese schools, youth associations, women's associations and trade unions. It is likely that through increased contact between colonies on various occasions, including at sports events such as *sumō* and baseball matches, the Emperor's Birthday, athletics meets and entertainment shows organized by Japanese associations and other bodies, active contact between dialects was promoted and the elements of these dialects that were incomprehensible to many were gradually eliminated. However, these regional differences in the dialect mixture and the language's failure to achieve 'full standardization' were greatly influenced by the geographical conditions under which Nikkeijin communities were formed and developed over the vast land centering on the State of São Paulo, in addition to the aforementioned absence of a dominant dialect. Moreover, a majority of the immigrants were dialect speakers from rural villages and small regional cities. Thus, in contradiction to the progressive national standardization of the Japanese language in Japan, Nikkeijin communities did not have a 'foundation language' (Handa 1952: 10), such as standard Japanese. The immigrants were rarely made aware of the difference between standard Japanese and their dialects, therefore their language failed to develop towards standardization.

Status of 'Colonia-go' in the Japanese immigrant community

From 'Japanese community in Brazil' to 'Colonia': Through the 'void' period

The Japanese colonies reached full bloom during the 1930s. Japanese arrivals began to increase from the second half of the 1920s and came to account for one half of the total foreign immigration to Brazil by the mid-1930s. The following Colonia *tankas* in *Koronia manyōshū* offer some glimpses into life in the Japanese community in those days.

Hōjin no ōki kono chi wa Hakujin[8] no shōhin kōkoku ni hōbun no miyu (In this district with many Japanese residents, even Brazilian shops include Japanese in their advertisements) (Chibaji Kawada 1952: 123)

Nihongo de "bora wa dōkane" to koe kakeru Hakujin ni waraitsutsu kawasareteiru ("How about some mullets?" a Brazilian says in Japanese and makes me smile and buy some) (Kikuo Fukazawa 1965: 256)

Amid the stabilization and growth of the Japanese community, increases in the numbers of immigrant children and those of the second generation heightened interest in children's education and led to the establishment of many Japanese schools in the colonies. There were 486 schools attended by as many as 30,000 pupils as of 1939 (Aoyagi 1942). While the then prevailing approach for children's education was 'nisshu hakujū shugi' (Japan first, Brazil second), prioritizing Japanese education in view of their eventual return to Japan, various arguments were put forward about the direction of children's education. These included 'hakushu nichijū shugi' (Brazil first, Japan second), emphasizing Brazilian education for permanent settlement and assimilation and 'wakon hakusai' (Japanese spirit, Brazilian learning), influenced by ultranationalism following the Manchurian Incident.

Conversely, the rise of nationalism in Brazil during this period led to the strengthening of immigration restrictions and assimilation policies. All Japanese schools were shut down by 1938, and the publication of Japanese-language newspapers and magazines and the use of the Japanese language were banned by 1941. Diplomatic relations between the two countries were severed in 1942. In the end, Japan was defeated in the Second World War. Although the Japanese community regrouped once the 'kachigumi-makegumi' conflict (the conflict between two factions, one of which accepted defeat, 'makegumi,' and the other not, 'kachigumi') that occurred immediately after the war had settled, the immigrants gradually began to feel that they should give up on the idea of returning to their homeland and live in Brazil permanently. The immigrant community, members of which used to call themselves 'zaihaku dōhō shakai' (A society of Japanese countrymen in Brazil), came to refer to members of the Nikkeijin community, including the immigrant children who grew up as Brazilians, as 'Colonia.' The term 'Colonia,' which is a Portuguese word for 'colony,' is not merely the name the Nikkeijin community adopted after the war, but also represents the determination of the immigrants to live as members of Brazilian society and slowly established their new identity as 'Japanese-Brazilians.' Paurisuta Shinbunsha (ed.) (1958: 3–4) describes as follows.

> Well-worn phrases such as "zaihaku nihonjin" (Japanese residents in Brazil), "zairyūmin" (resident Japanese) or "zaihaku dōhō" (Japanese countrymen in Brazil) have become far removed from the actual state of the Nikkeijin in Brazil. ...Although the period during and after the war is called the "void" period, it was in fact the most enriching era of growth and served as a character building period for the Colonia. When they emerged from the tunnel of war and saw the blue sky again, the Nikkeijin in Brazil were no longer "resident Japanese" nor "Japanese nationals in Brazil." We had grown into the Colonia.

From the 'nippaku kongō-go' to 'Colonia-go': 'Colonia-go' for the Japanese immigrant community

During the 1950s, the Nikkeijin community, which made a fresh start as the Colonia, called its own language 'Colonia-go' instead of 'nippaku kongō-go' (the mixed Japanese-Brazilian language), and began to keep records of it.

> While everyday speech is thus messy, I realize that "Colonia-go" that developed under various living conditions in the past has consolidated into one form and seeped into almost every household. Yet, this messy "Colonia-go" is somewhat endearing to us as we see in it reflections of the history and images of our Colonia itself. (Satō 1957: 81)

Positive sentiment towards 'Colonia-go' as 'messy' yet 'endearing' grew from the 1960s, and people actively looked for the significance of its existence, despite the criticisms leveled at it.

> The characteristic of the Japanese language of the second generation is its very democratic expression without the use of "desu" or "masu," whether the person you are speaking to is senior or junior to you. ... Many more new words and expressions will be created for the second generation's convenience from now on, and criticizing this on the grounds that they are not used in Japan is a type of nostalgic sentiment. It is impossible to control a language that is like a living creature that continues to change with time, location and environment. ...It is right

for Colonia Japanese to be different from Japanese spoken in Japan. It is the inevitable fate of a language. (Andō 1966: 46)

Words are not simply "corrupted" and mixed in. As a strategy for living, we deliberately and painstakingly mix and knead the two languages together. The language currently in use in the Colonia as the result is called "Colonia-go." Other than "Colonia-go" as the greatest cultural heritage of the Colonia's sixty-year history, there is no language for writing plays that can appeal simultaneously to both segments of the community ...a population who primarily use Japanese and a population who primarily use Portuguese. ...it is not a simple mixture of the two languages nor is it completely permeated with dialects. A breakdown of language is a laughable claim. There is no language that does not change. (Maeyama 1972: 116)

'Colonia-go' came to occupy an important position in Japanese language education. *Zenpaku jidō sakubun-shū* (Collected compositions of Japanese children in Brazil), published in the Colonia for the first time in 1954, contained essays written in 'Colonia-go' using 'rekishi-teki kanazukai' (the historical kana orthography) and was regarded to be 'most suitable as a composition reference book for school children in the Colonia.' The following is 'Boku no uchi' (My family), selected as the best composition in the first year primary school student division (Zenpaku Kyōiku Kenkyūkai (ed.) 1954: 13).

Boku no uchi wa mekaniko desu. Otōsan no hokani Jukia no nīchan to, Kanpo Rinpo no nīchan to, sorekara mada hokani 5 nin imasu. Mise dewa itsudemo isogashisōni hataraite imasu. Okāsan wa, Jukia no nēchan to, Tomichan to kujinnya wo yatteimasu. Ura no uchi wa kondo gakkō ni narimashita. Boku wa gakkō ga sukidesu.
(My family are *mecânico* (mechanics). Besides my father, there is an older brother from *Juquiá* ([place name]), an older brother from *Campo Limpo* ([place name]), and five others. They always work busily at the shop. My mother does *cozinha* (cooking) with an older sister from *Juquiá* ([place name]) and Tomi-chan ([person's name]). The house behind us has been turned into a school. I like my school.)

The Nikkeijin's attachment to 'Colonia-go' culminated in the compilation of a Colonia version Japanese language textbook for primary school *Nippon-go* (Japanese) (eight volumes for the introductory level and four volumes for the intermediate level), edited by Nippaku Bunka Fukyūkai from 1961 to 1964. The following is a partial quote from the 'Onibusu' section in Volume 1 for the introductory level, published in 1961 (1961: 62–63).

> Otōsan to, onibusu de San Pauro e ikimashita.
> Atokara kuru jidōsha ga zunzun oikoshite ikimashita.
> Pasuto no soba wo tōrimashita.
> (I went to São Paulo by *ônibus* (bus) with my father. We were overtaken by many cars that were coming behind us. We went past a *pasto* (pasture).)

The central idea behind the Colonia version textbook was to 'cultivate the unique spirit of the Colonia based on the character of the Brazilian nation and nurture men and women committed to the prosperity of Brazil.' The textbook was mainly characterized by the inclusion of 'the histories of immigration to Brazil and the Colonia for the purpose of instilling love for Brazil and an awareness and right sense of pride as the Nikkeijin,' and 'Brazilian words of everyday use in the Colonia such as *milho* (corn) and *ônibus* (bus) in the volumes for lower grades.' The Nikkeijin praised the textbook highly, claiming 'the establishment of the basic principle for correct Japanese language education by the use of this textbook offers a great hope for the future development of the Colonia,' and the Colonia version of *Nippon-go* quickly spread to all corners of Brazil once it was approved as a textbook by the State of São Paulo in 1963 (Hakkoku Nichigo Gakkō Rengōkai (ed.) 1966: 76–78). This textbook, made for children of Japanese descent for the first time after the war, was truly a book written for the Colonia children by the Colonia people in 'Colonia-go.'

Rejection of 'Colonia-go': A conflict with 'Japanese in Japan'

As academic exchange between Japan and Brazil increased from the 1970s, the introduction of the visiting Japanese expert system and the training of Nikkeijin teachers in Japan provided an upgrade in earnest to the conditions for Japanese language education. Although 'Colonia-go' became the subject of academic studies by Japanese researchers, it came to be rejected as a language for teaching in Japanese education as it conflicted with 'Japanese in Japan.' In particular, various comments about 'Colonia-go' made in 1969 by Kikuo Nomoto, a visiting professor at the University of São Paulo, sent shock waves through the Nikkeijin community at the time and sparked lively debate on the pages of Japanese language papers and magazines. The following is one of Nomoto's comments (1969: 69–70).

> "Colonia-go," Japanese in Colonia, in particular has so many Portuguese words. ...I do not believe that this fact itself warrants criticism since the ability of the Japanese language to incorporate many loanwords is a sign of its vitality in my view, but I believe we must always keep Japanese in Japan in mind and teach how the language is used in Japan. For example, "*onibusu*" is not understood in Japanese. We must say "*basu*" (bus). ... If people are not taught a standard form of Japanese, they may write Japanese, but they may not be understood by Japanese people in Japan, who constitute the majority of Japanese speakers.

Nomoto justifies the abundance of loanwords from English in the Japanese language spoken in Japan as 'a sign of its vitality,' but he criticizes the abundance of loanwords from Portuguese in 'Colonia-go' on the grounds that it 'may not be understood by the Japanese people in Japan, who constitute the majority of Japanese speakers.' On the subject of lack of linguistic politeness in 'Colonia-go,' he commented that 'I cannot ignore the impression that Brazilian Japanese is very rough,' against the view that it constitutes 'very democratic expression.' Nomoto concluded that 'Frankly speaking, the Japanese language spoken in this place seems destined for extinction,' in opposition to the aforementioned expectation in Andō (1966) that 'Many more new words and expressions will be created for the second generation's convenience from now on.'

The criticism of 'Colonia-go' by Japanese language experts from Japan diminished its status as 'the greatest cultural heritage of the Colonia's 60-year history' described in Maeyama (1972), led to the rejection of Japanese language education in the development of 'Colonia-go' by the Nikkeijin and destroyed their ideal for Japanese language education. The Japanese language that it was thought should be taught was 'proper Japanese' or 'Japanese in Japan,' and 'Japanese-Brazilian's Japanese' or 'Colonia-go' was eliminated as a language for teaching and subsequently vanished altogether from Japanese language education in Brazil. The change in the status of 'Colonia-go' in Japanese language education is represented by the following passage from the teacher's handbook of a Japanese conversation textbook published by Nihongo Fukyū Sentā (1990: II).

"Never use *chanpongo* (mixed language)"
You should never use mixed language such as the use of intermediate language in place of nouns (e.g., "Sensei wa, ano *sāra* de *uma ōra, aura* suru." (The teacher has a class for an hour in that classroom.)). It will have a negative impact on your students. ...Every time you use mixed language, it is as if you are wiping out the proper Japanese language you have just taught. Japanese language teachers must not do things that may accelerate the extinction of the Japanese language.

Negative appraisals of 'Colonia-go' were also made in the context of Japanese language education in Japan. Yamashita (1993: 131), looking at the Japanese language spoken by Japanese-Brazilian language students in interviews, said that 'commonly used Japanese in Brazil,' or Colonia Japanese, was an 'unnatural Japanese' that 'should be corrected,' and that Japanese-Brazilians needed to think about 'starting Japanese language education all over again.'

In this paper, [...] while already widely used as standard Japanese in Brazil, I would like to take some examples of expressions which may prove problematic when one comes to Japan and uses them in everyday life, because of their anachronism in extreme cases or strong influences from regional dialects, and consider what practice is needed to correct them.

Japanese in Brazil: From an immigrant language to a foreign language

Japanese language education in Brazil changed dramatically from the second half of the 1990s. According to surveys conducted by the Japan Foundation on overseas organizations involved in Japanese language education, a majority of Japanese language students in Brazil traditionally learned Japanese at 'non-academic' institutions, i.e., at private Japanese language schools operated by Nikkeijin organizations or individuals. The ratio was 98.4% in the 1990 survey and 96.5% in the 1993 survey, and most of the students were the children of Japanese-Brazilian families. This was the peculiarity of Japanese language education in Brazil, a country with a large population of Japanese descendants.

However, the commencement of foreign language education programs at primary and secondary education institutions and Japanese language courses at higher education institutions from the second half of the 1980s saw a rapid increase in the number of students learning Japanese as a second foreign language. As a result, the ratio of Japanese language students at non-academic institutions was down to 76.2%, and the ratio of those at 'public education institutions' accounted for 25% of the total in the 2003 survey. The growth of the Japanese language student population at primary and secondary education institutions was particularly remarkable, with their number jumping from only 130 in the 1993 survey to 2,299 in 1998 and steadily increasing thereafter to 3,154 in 2003, 3,538 in 2006 and 3,852 in 2009. This represents an almost 30-fold increase over a period of 15 years. Many of the Japanese language students at public educational institutions are not of Japanese descent, including adult students. The increase in the number of non-Japanese and adult learners is a tendency also found at non-academic Japanese language schools. Whether of Japanese descent or not, a strong interest in Japanese pop culture such as *anime* and *manga* has been identified as a major motive for Japanese language acquisition which, together with the ongoing availability of *dekassegui* opportunities in Japan,[9] continues to support the steady growth of Japanese language student numbers.

In the old days, the Japanese language in Brazil was Japanese immigrants' Japanese, i.e., 'Colonia-go,' and Japanese language education in that context was education given to children of Japanese descent. Much time has passed, and Japanese has become a foreign language not only to learners but also to Japanese language teachers of Japanese descent. 'Japanese as an immigrant language' has faded and given way to 'Japanese as a foreign language.' Yet, over 70% of Japanese language learners in Brazil are still learning at non-academic Japanese language schools supported by the Nikkeijin community and forged by Japanese immigrants in Brazil.

Conclusion

In days past, the study of Japanese language centered on the prescriptive study of standard Japanese and the historical study of Japanese within Japan. Due to the increased interpersonal contact through population mobility after the period of Japan's rapid economic growth and the dissemination of nationally-standardized Japanese, it became apparent as to just how diversified the Japanese language had become in the language life of the Japanese. Together with the rise of sociolinguistics, this realization led to the active study of the regional variation and transformation of the Japanese language from the 1970s. The national standardization of Japanese was mostly completed by the 1990s, and the rapidly declining regional dialects ceased to function as language systems. An inferiority complex about dialects suffered by many provincial people has faded away, and a renewed sense of importance has become attached to regional dialects.

In Japanese language education, standard Japanese was the only language that it was deemed should be taught, and variants such as regional dialects and youth language used to be excluded from Japanese language education. However, the number of foreign residents in Japan rose rapidly from the 1980s through the government's plan to increase the number of foreign students to 100,000, coupled with the influx of foreign laborers during the bubble economy. The arrival and settlement of technical/skills trainees and South American people of Japanese descent during the 1990s saw the previously concentrated population of foreigners in large cities spread to all regions of Japan. This prompted an expansion of Japanese language education from mainstream language education for foreign students at universities to teaching Japanese to foreigners seeking to learn the language spontaneously in local communities. As the status of regional variants has improved, television and radio, which used to disseminate standard Japanese to all corners of Japan, are now overflowing with regional dialects and youth language. The recent boom in Japanese subcultural materials such as *anime*, *manga* and computer games and the popularization of the Internet provide those overseas with many opportunities to learn living Japanese without going to Japan. These major changes in the Japanese language acquisition environment have created a new need for the teaching of variants other than standard Japanese in the classroom.[10]

In parallel with the circumstances surrounding the study of Japanese and Japanese language education, a growing interest in the study of disappearing languages and language contact on the back of globalization has further broadened the field of Japanese language studies. In addition to the languages of Japanese immigrants in countries such as Hawaii, Canada and Brazil, remnants of the Japanese language spoken in former Japanese territories such as Micronesia, Taiwan, the Korean Peninsula, Northeast China (former Manchuria) and Sakhalin are now actively studied. These languages were previously treated as subordinate variants of Japanese that had undergone contact with other languages and transformed, and were considered unimportant as the subject of linguistic studies. Their complex historical backgrounds would also have made the implementation of such studies difficult. It is no exaggeration to say that the time limit for the surveying of these languages has already expired. As I think of the state of 'Colonia-go' of the Japanese-Brazilian community, I see the need to keep records of its use, together with memories of the Japanese immigrants who were repeatedly dislocated by history, before it vanishes completely.

Note: This paper is part of the outcome of research supported by a MEXT Grants-in-Aid for Scientific Research for Young Scientists (B) [KAKENHI 20720140].

Notes

Chapter 1

1 This data was obtained from the staff member of a large Indian firm in charge of visa and immigration, and is calculated based upon the arrival and departure dates of all 183 engineers.
2 In this regard, the person responsible for visas at one Indian branch firm reported that a number of their engineers had come seeking advice regarding their card. It seems that the engineers can retain their registration card without issue; however, when they return to Japan and request an extension to their visa, they may run into trouble when queried as to why their income was so low and as to whether they had properly paid their taxes.
3 To protect the informant's privacy, a pseudonym is used.

Chapter 3

1 The original phrase is 'rain of gold in another country, rain of stone at home, yet I choose my home country.' This is an old saying that describes the spirit of nationality.
2 Quote from UNDP's Human Development Report (2009: 9).
3 The official name for such private agencies is Pelaksana Penempatan Tenaga Kerja Indonesia Swasta (private agency for the placement of Indonesian migrant workers), abbreviated as PPTKIS.
4 From the 2009 data, compiled by the Research and Development Unit of *Kompas*, reported in the edition of November 26 (2010: 46).
5 As reported by the National Survey of Remittance Patterns of Indonesian Migrant Workers, conducted in 2008 by the Central Bank, quoted in *Kompas*, November 26 (2010: 46).
6 Based on a true story, told by the PhD student in December, 2010.
7 Based on a true story, as reported in *Kompas*, November 26 (2010: 45).
8 Based on a true story, as reported in *Kompas*, November 26 (2010: 47).
9 This section is largely summarized from the 2009 Human Development Report of the UNDP.
10 Following the argument of Morokvasic (1983, 1984), who had conducted research on international migration focusing on women. She concluded that reasons for migration revealed the consequences of capitalist expansion, which dislocate and disrupt rural social relations.
11 Based on her research, Lan (2006) points to a racial stereotyping that occurs in Taiwan concerning domestic migrant workers from the Philippines and Indonesia. Filipinas are considered smart and unruly, while Indonesians are thought to be stupid but obedient. This stereotyping indicates the perceived low skill level of Indonesian migrant domestic workers.
12 Findings from Chin's research (1997: 372) shows that for Malaysians, Chinese and Indians to gain membership into the middle-class community,

they must possess three things: 1) a certain annual household income level; 2) a white-collar occupation and/or university-level education; and 3) a 'lifestyle' that is defined as having overseas travel experience or knowledge and appreciation of different cultures and peoples and ownership of a house/condominium and imported cars and the latest consumer items, in addition to a live-in domestic servant.

13 According to Rudnyckyj (2003) and Lyons (2007), the third entity, which is the NGOs, should also be considered. However in this chapter, the argument will focus only on the two entities cited.

14 From T.H. Marshall as quoted by Wibowo (2003). On the other hand, Stasiulis and Bakan (1997) point out that current debates on citizenship are commonly based on the work of T.H. Marshall published in 1950. According to Stasiulis and Bakan, Marshall's framework presumes an evolutionary expansion of citizenship rights (p. 114), which start with the experience of post-Second World War Britain and the development of the modern welfare state. Stasiulis and Bakan also point to the critics of the concept of citizenship identified by Marshall, quoting Turner (1990) who argued that the premise of Marshall's work (its presumption of the emergence of the equality of citizenship rights within post-war Britain) does account for the importance of class, ethnicity and gender as differentiating elements.

15 This section follows the argument of Stasiulis and Bakan (1997: 115).

Chapter 4

1 The name of this temporary resident ID card has been changed from 'ID card for seasonal resident' (Kartu Identitas Penduduk Musiman) to 'ID card for incomer' (Kartu Identitas Penduduk Pendatang). The acronym of the card has thus been changed from KIPEM to KIPP. However, the term KIPEM as a reference to migrant workers has taken hold, without being replaced by the new short name, and is used regardless of whether or not the worker actually possesses such an ID card.

2 A number of people from East Java and Lombok migrate to Malaysia to work as laborers on estates (plantations) or as housemaids, as there are not enough farmland or employment opportunities in their hometowns to support their livelihoods. In this regard, see Hugo (1993, 2006) and Sudibia (2005).

3 The term 'kampung' originates from a Malay word meaning 'village' or 'rural area.' In Indonesia, kampung refers to a residential quarter whose residents have come to the city from the same rural hometown and live there in a cluster. Kampung is not an administrative district but a natural residential quarter formed by the clustering of people with the same ethnicity, in such terms as language, lifestyle and religion. In Bali, the term 'kampung' is used to refer exclusively to a residential quarter inhabited by Muslims, as opposed to 'banjar,' inhabited by Hindus.

4 For residents of the Kampung in Pemogan village, see Nagano (2009: 158–161) and Yoshihara (2008: 143–165).

5 For the harmonious coexistence by segregation of Hindu and Muslim original inhabitants in Bali, see Kurasawa (2009).

6 All cases discussed here are based on a series of interviews conducted in Pemogan village during the period from December 2005 to December 2008. All names have been changed to protect the privacy of participants.

7 Farmers in Bali belong to irrigation associations, called *subak*, that are unique to the Balinese. There are two *subak* in Pemogan village: Subak Cuculan and Subak Kepaon. For more information on *subak*, see Lansing (2006), Sutawan (2006) and Nagano (2008).
8 For details of solid waste collected in Pemogan village, see Mangrove Information Center Report (JICA 2002–2003: 19–22).
9 The fact that this association was named 'full moon,' a holy day for Hindu Balinese, reveals that it was not formed voluntarily by Muslim Javanese batik workshop owners.
10 On Ajeg Bali, see Nakamura (2006: 309).
11 The majority of inhabitants of Bali Island are Hindu Balinese. Bali also has various religious minorities who are also original inhabitants, including Muslim Balinese, Catholic Balinese and Bali Aga, the original Balinese people who have been on the island since before the arrival of Hinduism. For a more detailed definition of the Balinese, see Nagabuchi (2007: 71–73).
12 For this epigram, see Hitchcock and I Nyoman (2007: 171–174).

Chapter 5

1 In a similar context to the public space crises caused by regional security, the increase of gated communities is also becoming an issue in today's society (Blakely and Snyder 1997). Holland, whose successes with social housing are often cited, is no exception (Aalbers 2003). The author has previously examined the rise of gated communities in Bali and explored the characteristics and possibilities of the forms of mobility they embrace (Hishiyama 2010).
2 Denpasar City (Kotamadya Denpasar) became independent from Badung Regency in 1992 to be recognized as a Special City, with the scale and authority equivalent to the other eight regencies (Kabupaten) on Bali Island. Special cities and regencies are classified as second level local governments (Daerah Tingkat II) after provinces, which are classified as first level local governments (Daerah Tingkat I). The city's police precinct includes the neighboring Badung Regency, and the integrated precinct is governed by the Polisi Kota Besar Denpasar (POLTABES Denpasar).
3 Please refer to Hishiyama (2008) for the establishment of regional security systems by neighborhood groups and their subsequent efforts to bolster the image of the tourist area in Sanur District.
4 Figures are based on interviews conducted with respective district chiefs in December 2008, June 2009 and September 2010.
5 According to an interview with Mr. M, the ex-chief of neighborhood group Pesalakan, the public's evaluation of the police's security effort, on a scale of one-to-three, used to rate worst or second worst. Please refer to the following paragraph for further details on Mr. M.
6 Descriptions of PKD are based on interviews with PKD's adviser, chief and members, Siskamling members and an ex-chief of neighborhood group Pesalakan Tuban in December 2008, June 2009, January and September 2010, respectively.
7 Siskamling is an abbreviation for Sistem Kaemanan Lingkungan and refers to a regional security system that was originally formulated in 1980 as

the centralized regime's organization terminus. It was formed by private defense organization Hansip (Pertahanan Sipil) and guardsmen from a company called Satpam, and its function included the mutual surveillance of community members (Barker 1999). However, in the case of Bali Island, the night watch patrols and groups were also called Siskamling. In this case, Siskamling was organized in units according to banjar and sometimes such patrols were conducted in traditional attire. In recent years, self-defense groups organized by neighborhood groups in emergencies such as city riots have also been referred to as Siskamling (Dwiant 1999)—it has clearly become a relatively common word for self-defense groups.

Descriptions of Siskamling are primarily based on interviews conducted with Mr. Mendera but also with PKD's adviser, chief, and a PKD member as well as a Siskamling member in December 2008, June 2009, January and September 2010, respectively. The author visited three Siskamling stations during the research period to inspect the facilities and meet the members and accompanied members during their night patrol.

8 The history of PD is still quite short. The party was established in 2001 to support the current President Susilo Bambang Yudhoyono into office, who was then the Coordinating Minister for Political, Legal and Security Affairs under the Megawati government.
9 The division of seats in congress are 14 for PDIP, 11 for GOLKAR, nine for PD and a total of six for the remaining five parties
10 Under the centralized regime, domestic security duties were mainly carried out by the armed forces. The police were positioned as the fourth force following the army, navy and air force and their power was very limited.

Chapter 6

1 This statement has profound implications today, in the wake of neoliberalism's global ascension. Assuming that the spirit of neoliberalism lies in the 'denial of public power,' it is obviously likely that governance, which has arisen in the post-'big government' institutional environment where public power has been reduced, is to become associated with neoliberalism. It also seems that government, which is transitioning to 'small government,' is under reconstruction in order to base its existence on governance as an institutional fiction. In any case, noting the affinity between governance and neoliberalism is now a key to understanding the world. Needless to say, even in the present case where a post-'development' phase is at issue, the affiliative relationship between governance and neoliberalism seems to hold the key to solving the riddle. Note that in the present case, neoliberalism is expressed in the 'form' of aspirations for a 'beautiful town' entailing intolerance towards 'foreign others.'
2 According to a man from Kintamani in his late 30s who now lives in a southern suburb of Denpasar city, in his primary school days 'shopping in town' meant going to Gajah Mada Road. He says that Gajah Mada Road was attractive in that it had all kinds of specialty shops lined up which sold everything you needed, and that not only Denpasar residents but all Balinese people longed to walk that street. However, he says that apart from hawkers making bulk purchases, ordinary people no longer satisfy their material needs and desires or sightsee in the area. Instead they go to

new malls and shopping centers by car or motorcycle. Still, Gajah Mada Road retains its function as a tourist hotspot due to its traditional market and historic townscape.

3 I hear that currently the cultural city project has not yet been abandoned, as this last mayor has become vice-governor. The project was originally developed as part of a tourism strategy, and this is where the tree-planting plan on Gajah Mada as the main street and the cleanup of Tukad Badung River came from. However, under the circumstances where the dark side of tourism itself surfaced and now has to be faced, the project eventually sympathized with Ajeg Bali that aspires for a 'beautiful town' by eliminating its seedy elements.

4 This recommendation is more or less intended to exclude KIPEM. For Balinese people, *kaki lima* is rooted in the eating habits of ordinary Javanese people and seeing an increasing number of *kaki lima* on the street means an increasing number of Javanese, particularly those of lower classes. For this reason, the appearance of *kaki lima* on the street indicates, for Balinese people, that a foreign 'lowly' culture is being embedded in the Bali community, going further than implying that it ruins the traditional townscape. In Bali Province, each of the districts and the municipality has its own regulations on *kaki lima*. Considering that KIPEM substantially forms the base of global tourism, however, the exclusion of *kaki lima* and, in turn, KIPEM, seems to include factors that may undermine the livelihoods of Balinese people.

5 I would like to point out here that even though the tree-planting plan for Gajah Mada Road had been announced as a local community initiative in connection with the cleanup plan for Tukad Badung River, it was actually based exclusively on growth and development without an underlying consideration for community sustainability rooted in its ecology and biodiversity. This seems to be closely related to the fact that its superior project, the cultural city project, has been consistently based on the growing fruit of global tourism. When we come to think of it, Denpasar city has in the meantime advocated for a compact city, but even this has always been in line with urban development policy.

6 As is well known, the Balinese community has a dual structure consisting of *banjar dinas* (neighborhood administrative units) and *banjar adat*, which, in turn, constitute a system subordinate to *desa dinas* (administrative village) and *desa adat* (customary village), respectively. This dual structure is said to have derived from the Dutch colonial government's exclusion of *adat* (custom) from the system. The power structure consisting of *desa dinas* and *banjar dinas* was originally positioned along a vertical administrative line, constituting the terminal portion of the top-down control exerted by the central government. By contrast, the structure consisting of *desa adat* and *banjar adat* has been said to have self-governing functions to handle local issues independently. However, even though *dinas* and *adat* are originally systemically separate, in terms of function the distinction between them is unclear in some respects, with some functions being shared or interpenetrative. Moreover, in recent years, particularly in urban areas, it seems that *adat* has become more like *dinas*, further blurring the distinction between them (Yoshihara (ed.) 2008). These circumstances seem to be more or less related to the communities' 'approval,' as outlined below.

7 Mr. S, the head of the *banjar*, served as head of the *desa dinas* for 10 years before taking his current post. He became close to the last mayor during his service as head of the *desa dinas*. When Mr. S left his *desa dinas* post, the last mayor told him that if he served well as head of *banjar adat*, he would definitely be given a chance, and this was why he assumed his current post. However, Mr. S claims that he does not like local politics itself, where '*janji-janji* politics' (perfunctory, irresponsible politics) prevail. He also states, 'Considering my past career, it is not absolutely impossible that I become a statesman. If I become one, I hope to play a role as a bridge between the government and the community.'

8 Excessive security was initially seen only at some hotels and restaurants, but has spread to local communities in recent years. In response to this, communities have undergone sporadic reorganization. Neighborhood watch organizations rooted in *adat* have been reorganized, and organizations directly linked to the police have been developed under the name of community policing. As for streets, many surveillance cameras have been installed.

9 Begun at the initiative of the *Bali Post* group, Ajeg Bali was a cultural-educational movement, evident in the fact that it sought to make the Balinese language a compulsory subject in primary schools. As seen in the present case, it has now expanded to include activities ranging from urban restructuring to those supporting community policing. Ajeg Bali's unique nature, which is deeply rooted in the movement's historical and cultural structure, can be seen in the fact that its reaction to post-regionalization has been expressed as the pure self-presentation of Balinese Hindu, instead of nationalism.

10 This aspect strongly resonates with the 'differentialist racism' raging in Europe that has been noted by Hideharu Saitō and others. It cribs and reverses the position of structural anthropology that respects cultural diversity and equality and emphasizes the irreducibility of differences between cultures in an attempt to *exclusively* obtain the 'right to difference' of cultures (Saito and Iwanaga 1996). This type of movement has subsequently erupted in many different parts of the world, assuming diverse forms.

11 In order to support the top-down development measures from underneath and actively promote them, the development regime extensively saw a practice where customary mutual aid, which had originally existed for the construction of personal safety nets, was provided through vertical relationships similar to the so-called 'patron-client' model. This was intended to make up for the 'poverty of the government' by mobilizing the community. However, it eventually resulted in continuous 'shared poverty' in communities, as pointed out by Geertz (1963).

12 The relationship between 'globalization and locality' has been discussed more than enough. However, as far as I know, so far there seems to be no established broadly accepted theory. Nonetheless, recent trends seem to include a tendency to understand the two concepts as interactive, instead of contrastive. In the context of this recent trend, while Ajeg Bali certainly represents an ardent reaction to globalization, it would be necessary to carefully analyze how globalization encompasses this movement and, conversely, how it incorporates globalization. The point of this analysis is to establish how linear thinking can be relativized.

13 Spontaneous town planning has often been mentioned, but it should be clearly distinguished from the emergent town planning referred to in this context. Needless to say, town planning begins with one person and another 'neighboring' each other. However, if this situation is absorbed into homogeneity, no emergent town planning will begin. What is important is that town planning secures a 'mechanism for establishing dynamic relationships from the inside through encounters and qualitative comparison with foreign things' (Yoshihara 2010b: 29). It is certain that if this mechanism is secured, emergent town planning will, unlike spontaneous forms, never be trapped in communitarian arguments.

Chapter 7

1 The entry into and concentration in certain self-employed businesses (economic niches) can also be explained by the concept of 'middleman minority,' which has been widely used among ethnicity researchers since it was proposed by Blalock (1967). For example, Van den Berghe (1981), from the perspective of its economic activity, summarizes that the middleman minority is less wealthy than the ruling class and wealthier than the original residents, plays the role of an intermediary between them, does not engage in large-scale capitalist operations due to lack of capital and resources, is characterized by a labor-intensive enterprise using family labor and adopts the core principle of kinship or ethnic nepotism for employment. These aspects of the middleman minority are applicable to subcontract sewing (*mão de obra*), *pastel* selling at the *feira livre*, hardware sales and cosmetics retailing, to be discussed in this paper.
2 However, Aldrich and Waldinger (1990) did include the characteristics of the local market (local characteristics) as they cited selective immigration, local characteristics, economic self-help organizations and ethnic networks as markers of migrant groups and called them 'mobilizable ethnic capital.'
3 The composition of the membership in 2006 shows that a majority (60%) are first generation migrants, but there are many Brazilian-born second generation (29%) and third generation (5%) members as well, whereas in 1984 almost all members were first generation migrants.
4 Annual events organized by the branch include the annual general meeting, the New Year's celebration, the seniors' day celebration, family sports and athletics meets, gateball competitions and Festival Okinawa (Shibu Sōritsu 50-shūnen Kinen Shi Henshū Iinkai (ed.) 2008: 323).
5 The geographical location (including its peripheral position) of Vila Carrão was of critical importance to early-stage urban adaptation decisions such as occupation selection and land/house purchase.
6 The narrator of this case is the eldest daughter of this family who was 15 years old when the family relocated to the City of São Paulo.
7 The entry of the Okinawan migrants to the City of São Paulo's central market was initiated by Ushi Taba, a migrant who arrived on board Kasato Maru in 1931. Many Okinawans followed him into the farm produce wholesale and retail sector (Imin Shi Kankō Iinkai (ed.) 2000: 116–117).
8 *Feirantes* selling agricultural produce bought their merchandise at the city's

central market where many Okinawan brokers and retailers worked and sold it at the *feiras*.
9 In the case of *pasteleiro*, the number of issued business licenses has not increased since the business was formally authorized in 1978. A license is sold if it is not passed on to a successor, but it affords a certain level of income security in the sense that the number of *pasteleiros* at the *feiras* is limited. There was also a mechanism for income security at another level in that the purchaser of the *pastel* license received training from the previous licensee for a certain period and inherited the predecessor's original recipes and much of his clientele.
10 The number of *pasteleiros* has remained the same and about 400 pastel sellers are still operating in the *feira livre* system. In the case of Okinawan *pasteleiros* (also applicable to *feirantes* in general), however, the business is rarely passed on from one generation to the next as a 'family business,' as shown by the case example. When there is no successor to the business within the family, the *pasteleiro* license is put on the market. Okinawan *pasteleiros* often sold their licenses to other Okinawan migrants. A certain level of income was guaranteed in this sense. There was also a mechanism for income security at another level. The number of *pasteleiros* has remained the same, and about 400 pastel sellers are still operating in the *feira livre* system. In the case of Okinawan *pasteleiros* (also applicable to *feirantes* in general), however, the business is rarely passed on from one generation to the next as a 'family business,' as shown by the case example. When there is no successor of the business within the family, the *pasteleiro* license is put on the market. Okinawan *pasteleiros* often sold their licenses to other Okinawan migrants.
11 For a detailed report on the sewing business, see Mori (1998).
12 The *patrão* refers to the client of a sewing subcontractor who places orders.
13 The most important characteristic observed in the case is that the family carried out subcontract sewing based on the division of labor among family workers and especially the fact that work hours were allocated between brothers and sisters in a flexible manner to allow them to attend higher education while being engaged in the family business. This means that their self-employed business strategy for economic ascension and stability includes another parallel economic adaptation strategy that may be called the 'white-collar technocrat strategy through higher education.' This can be observed in changes in the aforementioned occupational composition of former Oroku villagers.
14 Needless to say, the peripheral nature of Vila Carrão means that land and housing were available at affordable prices to family members who branched out or set up on their own.
15 These 500 families include migrants from mainland Japan and non-Japanese Brazilian families who also moved to and settled in Vila Carrão.
16 'Once you employed 14 or 15 local people (non-Japanese Brazilians), you could buy a house in a year.'
17 Postwar immigration to Bolivia from Okinawa Prefecture started in 1954 and many migrants settled in the Okinawan settlement under an official program up to 1964. However, a majority of them relocated to Brazil or Argentina, or returned to Okinawa or Japan for the aforementioned reasons.

According to re-settlers from Bolivia in São Paulo, family migrants (a couple with children) often chose to move to the City of São Paulo, and young single migrants tended to move to Buenos Aires in Argentina. A majority of those who came to São Paulo re-settled in Vila Carrão and its neighboring eastern districts. The number of re-settled families exceeded 300, and they formed an association called Bolivia Shimbokukai based on the shared experience of re-settlement from Bolivia. Re-settlers with a relatively large family labor force preferred to go into subcontract sewing while those with a relatively small family labor force worked as *feirantes*.

18 The number of branch member families increased rapidly from 274 at the end of the 1960s to 428 by 1975, which is comparable to the peak membership of 429 in 1984. These numbers do not include first and second generation migrants who went independent from their birth family. If this group were included, the number of families of Okinawan descent would total around 1,000.

19 'Ethnic goods' here refers to products that are linked to the *origem* of Japan and Okinawa (foods, offerings for ancestor worship rites, incense sticks, Japanese/Okinawa cuisine, travel to Japan/Okinawa, karaoke, etc.).

20 The occupational composition of the Oroku and Tabaru Association shows that the proportion of grocery shops and supermarkets was about 26% in the 1970s. The proportion of grocery shops had decreased by 1987 as they converted into supermarkets, and both categories had shrunk considerably by 1997.

21 The decline of the effectiveness of the *tanomoshi* did not occur equally to all Okinawan self-employed businesses, but 'the age of pure mutual aid ended and the *tanomoshi* was polarized between the large type of *tanomoshi* for capitalists to gather more capital and the entertainment type *tanomoshi* for the purpose of social gathering' (Ōshiro 1986: 114). A 1986 survey by the University of the Ryūkyūs shows that 88% of Okinawan-Brazilians participated in some form of *tanomoshi*, and those who do so for 'socializing' purposes exceed those who use it as a 'fundraising means' (54.8% versus 48.2%).

22 The reorganization of Brazil's sewing industry entailed the entry of Taiwanese sewing entrepreneurs who took advantage of preferential treatment for the development of northeast Brazil to establish a sewing base in the northeastern region and mass-produce jeans using cheap labor. It further led to preferential measures to compete in the domestic and export markets and the establishment of new sewing bases in the states of Goias, Parana, Santa Catarina and Para, which decreased the relative importance of the traditional sewing bases in Brás and Bom Retiro. Under these circumstances, members of Brás Hōsei Keizai Kyōkai (Okinawan Sewing industry Association) adopted countermeasures such as the closure of the manufacturing division and concentration on retail sales, but many of the underfunded businesses were unable to secure capital to pay off redundant employees or renew their office leases, and 12 to 13 of those established in Brás District were driven into bankruptcy.

23 The management of Company A is a family of re-settlers from Bolivia who set up a head office in Vila Carrão and branch offices in Liberdade District and Tsurumi Ward in Yokohama, Japan, and used this network to begin sending Okinawans to Japan as early as 1983–84. One of their motives to

treat *dekassegui* as a business was information from an acquaintance in Bolivia and a request to recruit *dekassegui* workers to Japan.

Chapter 8

1. This study was supported by Grant-in-Aid for Young Scientists (KAKENHI 21730489).
2. This article was reportedly a reprint of the original document published 30 years previously, which means that it was actually written in the early 1940s.
3. Some hold the view that the Japanese of the prewar period did not purchase real estate because they aspired to return to Japan when they saved enough money. However, Tsujimoto and Kuda (2010) question this conclusion. Purchased real estate could be sold upon leaving the country, thus 'aspirations to return to Japan' does not seem to be a convincing reason preventing the purchase of property. From the fact that the Japanese immigrants of the prewar period had limited wealth, returning to Japan probably represented an unattainable desire. People who cross borders often say they will return to their home country someday, knowing that this is an unachievable dream.
4. These references also cite the sharp rise in interest rates. In ROSCAs where fund recipients were decided according to a bidding system, the fund recipient had to pay interest. The mechanisms of bidding and interest are complicated and beyond the scope of this paper.
5. Koike, Nakamaru and Tsujimoto (2010) claim that in order to prevent defaults, besides peer selection, there must also be a rule forbidding members from receiving funds if they fail to pay their contributions prior to receiving funds.

Chapter 9

1. Much research on re-migration, or emigration of immigrants, does not distinguish between return-migration to migrants' countries of origin and onward migration to third countries (Constant and Massey 2002). In this paper, this term mostly refers to onward migration to third countries.
2. The findings reported in this paper are based on ethnographic research in Japan and the US that I conducted during 1996–1998 and supplementary research carried out on and off during 2004–2007. Personal names used throughout the text are pseudonyms.
3. I estimated the out-migration rate during 1990–2000 as follows: the number of Brazilian (Peruvian) nationals officially registered in Japan in 1990 plus the number of newly admitted migrants during the period of 1990–2000, subtracting the number of those present in Japan in 2000. I did not consider the number of deaths, Japanese-born children to these nationals or naturalizations occurring during the period, since the data were not available and these figures were estimated to be relatively negligible. Out-migration as well as in-migration include 'temporary' moves. It is difficult to distinguish between 'temporary' and 'permanent' migration; and Japan does not admit foreigners as long-term settlers (or immigrants), even though the majority of South American migrants are admitted as quasi-

settlers. Thus, the estimated out-migration rate reported here is a very rough figure.
4 According to INEI (2004), 9,775 Peruvians returned to Peru from Japan during the year, including those on short visits.

Chapter 10

1 For works on the education of immigrant children see Miyajima and Ōta (2005) and Shimizu and Shimizu (eds.) (2001). Kawakami Ikuo has also put together a collection of interviews with ten people who grew into adulthood after having left the land where they were born, entitled *I Too Was a 'Migrant Child'* (2010).
2 When she arrived in Japan, Mrs A began taking Japanese courses run by her local authority, but after the birth of her children she mastered the language through self-directed study. She then built up her Japanese speaking ability by, among other things, joining mothers' groups. There may be some individual differences in the approaches taken, but most of the wives accompanying their husbands coming to Japan to study make a point of learning Japanese before their children start school. There is also a strong trend towards migration to Japan among families in which both parents have already acquired this linguistic resource prior to migration.
3 The practice of sending children away for an early experience of study abroad before their university years, known as 'early study abroad,' began to attract attention as a new social phenomenon in Korea from the late 1990s. According to statistics published by the Korean Education Development Office, a total of 2,259 students (including 235 primary school students) undertook early study abroad in 1995. These figures have gone on to reach: 4,397 students (including 705 primary school students) in 2000; 20,400 students (including 8,148 primary school students) in 2005; and 27,349 students (including 12,531 primary school students) in 2008. The numbers of primary school students going on early study abroad in these figures surpassed the total number of middle and high school students in 2002, and by 2008 had become more than twice the number of high school students. However, the total number of students undertaking early study abroad has been falling steadily since reaching a peak in 2007, and had decreased to 20,000 students in 2010. The backdrop to this decline is the realization that the early study abroad that had been going on for more than 10 years had not necessarily led to good outcomes. Difficulties in adapting to life back in Korea once these students returned, because of the lingering influences of their time abroad, and the ill effects on families of living apart were some of the things that led to early study abroad being seen as a social problem.
4 However, owing to the fact that increasing numbers of couples were having their children in the US in order to avoid conscription, there has recently been a change in the law with the result that having been born overseas is no longer a sufficient basis for exemption from military service.
5 An ethnic community created by Korean immigrants can also be found in Tokyo's Shinjuku Ward in Japan. It is so thoroughly Korean that it is possible to live using only Korean within this community. This type of community is widely used as a resource by students to enrich their time abroad and also by entrepreneurs to expand their businesses. For a realistic

picture of ethnic communities in Japan see Katō (2010) and Kawamura (ed.) (2008). On Korean entrepreneurship and businesses within communities, see Hayashi (2004).
6 Hiratsuka Raichō, a leading member of the women's liberation movement, began the first issue (1911) of *Blue Stocking*, a literary magazine produced by women, with these words: 'She was an authentic person. Now, woman is the moon. She lives dependent on others, she shines by the light of others; she is a pale-faced moon, resembling a sick person.'

Chapter 11

1 The explanation of 'Colonia-go' in Nakai (2005: 152–153) is clearly incorrect. He 'introduces "Colonia-go" spoken by Japanese-Brazilians which is a mixture of Japanese and Portuguese as an example of an intermediate language,' and mentions some examples of 'Colonia-go' which 'is based on Portuguese incorporating Japanese vocabulary' spoken by Japanese-Brazilian *dekassegui* workers living in Japan such as (1) *É lá em* Toyota, Toyota-shi (There is in Toyota, Toyota City), and (2) *Você já mandou o papel lá pro* kenkōkai? (Have you sent your paper to the health association?).
2 By Kaigai Nikkeijin Kyōkai (The Association of Nikkei and Japanese Abroad). http://www.jadesas.or.jp/ (accessed 2011/4/1).
3 A survey conducted in Colônia Aliança (Aliança settlement) in Mirandópolis (inland rural village) and 'Fukuhaku-mura' (Fukuhaku Village) in Suzano (suburban rural village), both in the State of São Paulo, conducted by 'Burajiru nikkei shakai ni okeru gengo no sōgōteki kenkyū oyobi kiroku hozon jigyō' (The project for multidisciplinary research, recording and preservation of the language of the Japanese-Brazilian community), Gengo no sesshoku to konkō (Language contact and admixture), Intāfēsu no jinbungaku (Interface humanities), Osaka University 21st Century COE Program. See Kudō et al. (2009) for details.
4 Other characteristics of 'Colonia-go' include the use of vocabulary and grammar peculiar to the Nikkeijin community and a limited number of polite expressions. See Kudō et al. (2009) for more detailed linguistic features.
5 *Koronia manyōshū* is a collection of 'tanka' poems compiled to commemorate the 70th anniversary of Japanese immigration to Brazil to provide a full overview of 'tanka' poems composed by immigrants over time. It contains 6,634 verses published in Japanese language newspapers and magazines in Brazil before and after the Second World War and selected from public entries.
6 'Hakugo' means 'Brazilian language' that is equal to 'Burajiru-go.' Portuguese spoken in Brazil is often called 'Burajiru-go' (Brazilian language), but not 'Porutogaru-go' (Portuguese language), in the Nikkeijin community.
7 There were Portuguese language textbooks for immigrants heading for Brazil, such as *Jitsuyō Burajirugo* (Practical Brazilian language) (1934) compiled by Takumushō Takumukyoku (the Ministry of Colonial Affairs) and *Shotō Burajiru-go dokushūsho* (Teach yourself Brazilian textbook for beginners) (1932) by Nippaku Kyōkai (Japan-Brazil Association), but a majority of the immigrants only learned some greetings in Portuguese on the transport ship.
8 'Hakujin' means 'Brazilian person.'
9 Against this backdrop, since 2007 Centro Brasileiro de Língua Japonesa has

been offering an intensive Japanese language course for *dekassegui* workers to Japan called 'Sokuseijuku *(curso rápido)*' (a rapid course in Japanese).
10 Kansai Kokusai Sentā (The Japan Foundation Japanese Language Institute, Kansai) launched a new official site, 'Anime manga no Nihon go' (Japanese in *anime* and *manga*) on February 1, 2010 to serve these new needs in Japanese language education. *http://anime-manga.jp/* (accessed 2011/4/1).

Bibliography

Aalbers, M. 2003. 'The double function of the gate: Social inclusion and exclusion in gated communities and security zones.' Paper presented at the conference, *Gated Communities: Building Social Division of Safer Communities?* University of Glasgow.
Akoku Nippo. 1971. 'Yugamerareta tanomoshikō no seishin' (Distorted spirit of rotating savings and credit associations). April 24: 3.
Aldrich, H. and R. Waldinger. 1990. 'Ethnicity and entrepreneurship.' *Annual Review of Sociology*, 16: 111–135.
Andō, Z. 1966. 'Koronia ni okeru Nihongo no unmei' (The fate of Japanese in the Colonia). *Koronia Bungaku* (Colonia literature). São Paulo: Koronia Bungakukai, 2: 46.
Aneesh, A. 2006. *Virtual Migration: The Programming of Globalization*. Durham: Duke University Press.
Aoyagi, I. 1941. *Burajiru ni okeru Nihonjin Hatten-shi (jō)* (History of Japanese development in Brazil (1)). Tokyo: Burajiru ni okeru Nihonjin hatten-shi Kankō Iinkai.
Aoyagi, I. 1942. *Burajiru ni okeru Nihonjin Hatten-shi (ge)* (History of Japanese development in Brazil (2)). Tokyo: Burajiru ni okeru Nihonjin hatten-shi Kankō Iinkai.
Ardener, S. 1964. 'The comparative study of rotating credit associations.' *Journal of the Royal Anthropological Institute of Great Britain and Ireland*, 94: 201–229.
Ardener, S. and S. Burman (eds.). 1995. *Money-go-rounds: The Importance of Rotating Savings and Credit Associations for Women*. Oxford: Berg.
Aruzenchin Jiho. 1930. 'Kakuchō yori jūjitsu: Hōjin sosai kōshu gyōsha ni nozomu' (Enhancement over expansion: Request to Japanese vegetable farmers). September 27: 1.
Aruzenchin no Uchinānchu 80-nenshi Henshū Iinkai (Editorial Committee of the 80-Year History of Okinawans in Argentina) (ed.). 1994. *Aruzenchin no Uchinānchu 80-Nenshi* (Eighty-year history of Okinawans in Argentina). Centro Okinawense en la Argentina.
Asher, M.G. and A. Nandy. 2006. 'Health financing in Singapore: A case for systematic reforms.' *International Social Security Review*, 59: 75–92
Bali Post. 2000. 'Tabanan miliki "Pecalang" saka bhuana sakti.' June 16.
Bali Post. 2001. 'Tertibkan besakih, Desa Adat turunkan Pecalang.' April 18.
Bali Post. 2005. 'Bendesa pakraman bahas pilkada "Ngebug Kulkul" boleh, libatkan Pecalang juga boleh.' June 13.
Bali Post. 2006. 'Potas ikan hinas, ditangkap Pecalang laut.' June 27.
Barker, J. 1999. 'Surveillance and territoriality in Bandung.' In B. Anderson (ed.), *Figures of Criminality in Indonesia, the Philippines, and Colonial Vietnam*. New York: Cornell Southeast Asia Program Publications, 95–127.

Bauer, T. and K. Zimmerman. 1997. 'Network migration of ethnic Germans.' *International Migration Review*, 311: 143–149.
Bauman, Z. 2000. *Liquid Modernity*. Cambridge: Polity Press.
Beenstock, M. 1996. 'Failure to absorb: Remigration by immigrants into Israel.' *International Migration Review*, 30(4): 950–978.
Bhatnager, S. 2006. 'India's software industry.' In V. Chandra (ed.), *Technology, Adaption and Export: How Some Developing Countries Got IT Right*. Washington: World Bank, 95–124.
Blakely, E.J. and M.G. Snyder. 1997. *Fortress America: Gated Communities in the United States*. London: Brookings Institution.
Blalock, H.M. Jr. 1967. *Toward a Theory of Minority Group Relations*. New York: John Wiley.
Borman, E. 2004. 'Health tourism: Where health care, ethics, and the state collide.' *British Medical Journal*, 328: 60–61
Boyd, M. 1989. 'Family and personal networks in international migration: Recent developments and new agenda.' *International Migration Review*, 23(3): 638–670.
BPSB (Badan Pusat Statistik Propinsi Bali). 2000. Bali dalam Angka: Bali in Figures 2000.
BPSB (Badan Pusat Statistik Propinsi Bali). 2006. Bali dalam Angka: Bali in Figures 2006.
Brooks Jr., F.P. 1995. *The Mythical Man-month: Essays on Software Engineering*. Reading: Addison-Wesley Publishing Company, Inc.
Brubaker, R. 1998. 'Migrations of ethnic unmixing in the "New Europe."' *International Migration Review*, 32(4): 1047–1065.
Burajiru Jihōsha (ed.). 1933. *Burajiru Nenkan* (Brazil yearbook). São Paulo: Burajiru Jihōsha.
Burajiru Nikkeijin Jittai Chōsa Iinkai (ed.). 1964. *Burajiru no Nihon Imin: Kijutsu-hen* (Japanese immigrants in Brazil: Descriptive edition). Tokyo: Tokyo Daigaku Shuppankai.
Chanda, R. 2002. 'Trade in health services.' In N. Drager and C. Vieira (eds.), *Trade in Health Services: Global, Regional and Country Perspectives*. Washington DC: PAHO, 35–44.
Chee, H.L. and Barraclough, S. 2007. 'The growth of corporate health care in Malaysia.' In H.L. Chee and S. Barraclough (eds.), *Health Care in Malaysia: The Dynamics of Provision, Financing and Access*. Oxford: Routledge Malaysian Studies Series, 19–39.
Chee, H.L. 2010 'Medical tourism and the state in Malaysia and Singapore.' *Global Social Policy*, 10: 336–357
Chin, C.B.N. 1997. 'Walls of silence and late twentieth century representation of foreign female domestic worker: The case of Filipina and Indonesian female servants in Malaysia.' *International Migrant Review*, 31(2): 353–385.
Comité de Investigación y Redacción de la Historia del Inmigrante Japonés en la Argentina (ed.). 2002. *Aruzenchin Nihonjin Iminshi, 1, Senzen Hen* (History of Japanese immigrants in Argentina, 1, prewar period). Federación de Asociaciones Nikkei en la Argentina.

Constant, A. and D. Massey. 2002. 'Self-selection, earnings, and outmigration: A longitudinal study of immigrants to Germany.' Discussion Paper 672. Bonn: Institute for the Study of Labor (IZA).
Crime Control Policy Council of Japan. 2003. 'The action plan for the realization of the crime deterrent society: Aiming the revitalization of "the most safe and secure country, Japan."' Tokyo. (In Japanese.)
Cukier, J. and G. Wall. 1994. 'Informal tourism employment: Vendors in Bali, Indonesia.' *Tourism Management*, 15(6): 464–76.
Daring, D. 2003. 'Unity in uniformity: Tendencies toward militarism in Balinese ritual life.' In A.T. Thomas (ed.), *Inequality, Crisis and Social Change in Indonesia*. London: Routledge Curzon, 196–202.
DaVanzo, J. 1976. 'Differences between return and nonreturn migration: An econometric analysis.' *International Migration Review*, 101: 13–27.
DaVanzo, J. 1983. 'Repeat migration in the US: Who moves back and who moves on.' *Review of Economics and Statistics*. 65: 552–559.
Davis, M. 1990. *City of Quartz: Excavating the Future in Los Angeles*. London: Verso.
Denpost. 2009. 'Demokrat geser dominasi PDIP di tuban.' April 13.
Denpost. 2009. 'Tuban dinilai masih kalah jauh dari samigita.' January 3.
Desa Adat Tuban. 2004. Surat Perintah Desa Pekraman Tuban. No.01/DAT-PW/X/2004.
Desa Adat Tuban. 2006a. Struktur Pengurus Petugas Keamanan Desa (PKD).
Desa Adat Tuban. 2006b. Pepalihan Prajuru Pecalang Desa Pakraman Tuban Warsa 2006–2009.
Desa Pakraman Tuban. 2006. Pepalihan Prajuru Pecalang Desa Pakraman Tuban.
DeVoretz, D. and J. Ma. 2002. 'Triangular human capital flows between sending, Entrepot and the rest of the world regions.' *Canadian Studies in Population*, 291: 53–69.
Dinas Tata Kota Pemerintah Kota Denpasar. 2006. *Terms of Reference Kegiatan Sosialisasi Rencana Penataan Koridor Jl. Gajah Mada Denpasar*. Place of publication unknown.
Dwianto, Raphaella D. (1999), 'Urban riots and vigilante groups.' *Annual report of the Tohoku Society for Urbanology*, 1: 34–51. (In Japanese.)
Dwijendra, N.K.A. and N.M. Yudantini. 2007. 'Studi penggalian aspirasi pemilik toko dalam rangka penataan koridor JL. Gajah Mada kota Denpasar.' *Jurnal Permukiman Natah*, 52: 62–71.
Edin, P., R. LaLonde and O. Aslund. 2000. 'Emigration of immigrants and measures of immigrant assimilation: Evidence from Sweden.' http://ideas.repec.org/p/hhs/uunewp/2000_013.html
Ericson, R.V. and K.D. Haggerty. 1996. *Policing the Risk Society*. Toronto: University of Toronto Press.
Foucault, M. 1966. *Les Mots et les Choses*. Paris: Gallimard.
Fox, Jon. 2004. 'From national inclusion to European exclusion: State, nation and Europe in ethnic Hungarian migration to Hungary.' Working Paper. La Jolla: Center for Comparative Immigration Studies.
Gaimushō Tsūshōkyoku (International Trade Bureau, Ministry of Foreign

Affairs). 1929. 'Zaia Hōjin shakai no kinyū jōkyō' (Financial situation of the Japanese community in Argentina). *Imin Jōhō* (Immigrant information), 1(7): 67–75.
Geertz, C. 1962. The rotating credit association: A 'middle rung' in development. *Economic Development and Cultural Change*, 10: 241–263.
Geertz, C. 1963. *Agricultural Innovation: The Process of Ecological Change in Indonesia*. Berkeley: University of California Press.
Giddens, A. 1998. *The Third Way: The Renewal of Social Democracy*. Cambridge: Polity Press.
Groenendijk, K. 1997. 'Regulating ethnic immigration: The case of the Aüssiedler.' *New Community*, 23(4): 461–482.
Hakkoku Nichigo Gakkō Rengōkai (ed.). 1966. *Iku Sanga* (Many mountains and rivers). São Paulo: Hakkoku Nichigo Gakkō Rengōkai.
Handa, T. 1952. 'Burajiru ni okeru Nihongo no unmei' (The fate of Japanese in Brazil). *Jidai* (Epoch). São Paulo: Doyōkai, 15: 7–21.
Handa, T. 1970. *Imin no Seikatsu no Rekishi: Burajiru Nikkeijin ga Ayunda Michi* (History of the immigrant life: The path of the Nikkeijin in Brazil). São Paulo: Toppan Press.
Handa, T. 1980a. 'Burajiru Nikkei shakai ni okeru Nihongo no mondai (1)' (The problem of Japanese in the Nikkei community in Brazil (1)). *Gengo Seikatsu* (Language life). Tokyo: Chikuma Shobō, 346: 75–81.
Handa, T. 1980b. 'Burajiru Nikkei shakai ni okeru Nihongo no mondai (2)' (The problem of Japanese in the Nikkei community in Brazil (2)). *Gengo Seikatsu* (Language life). Tokyo: Chikuma Shobō, 347: 58–65.
Handa, T. 1980c. 'Burajiru Nikkei shakai ni okeru Nihongo no mondai (3)' (The problem of Japanese in the Nikkei community in Brazil (3)). *Gengo Seikatsu* (Language life). Tokyo: Chikuma Shobō, 348: 67–73.
Harvey, D. 2005. *A Brief History of Neoliberalism*. Oxford: Oxford University Press.
Hayashi, N. 2004. *Kankokujin Kigyōka: Nyūkamā no Kigyō Katei to Esunikku Shigen* (Korean entrepreneurs: Entrepreneurial processes of newcomers and ethnic resources). Tokyo: Nagasaki Shuppan.
Hechter, M. 1987. *Principles of Group Solidarity*. Berkeley: University of California Press.
Heeler, P. 1982. 'A model of the demand for medical and health services in Peninsular Malaysia.' *Social Science and Medicine*, 16: 267–284.
Henderson, J. 2004a. 'Healthcare tourism in Southeast Asia.' *Tourism Review International*, 7: 111–121.
Henderson, J. 2004b. 'Paradigm shifts: National tourism organisations and education and healthcare tourism. The case of Singapore.' *Tourism and Hospitality Research*, 52: 170–180.
Higa, M. 1982. 'Burajiru ni okeru Nihonjin ijūsha no gengo tekiō' (Language adaptation of Japanese immigrants in Brazil). *Raten Amerika Kenkyū* (Latin American studies). Tsukuba: Tsukuba Daigaku Raten Amerika Tokubetsu Purojekuto kenkyū soshiki, 4: 153–179.
Higa, M. 1983. '"Shakai hōgen gaku" no juritsu wo mezashite' (For the establishment of socio-dialectology). *Gendai Hōgengaku no Kadai* (The issues of contemporary dialectology). Tokyo: Meiji Shoin, 1: 51–69.

Higuchi, N. and S. Takahashi. 1998. 'Zainichi Burajiru shusshinsha no esunikku bijinesu, Kigyōka kyōkyū shisutemu no hatten to shijō no hirogari wo chūshin ni' (Ethnic businesses of the Japanese Brazilians in Japan: Focusing on the development of the entrepreneur supply system and market expansion). In Instituto Iberoamericano, Jōchi Daigaku (ed.), *Iberoamerika Kenkyū* (Iberoamerican study), 1–15.

Hishiyama, K. 2008. 'Local security in post-Suharto Bali: From inequality to equality of participation.' In M. Shima (ed.), *Status and Stratification: Cultural Forms in East and Southeast Asia*, Stratification and Inequality Series. Melbourne: Trans Pacific Press, 7: 163–79.

Hishiyama, K. 2010. 'Uneasy society in Indonesia: With special attention to the gated community and CCTV in Bali.' *Procedia—Social and Behavioral Sciences*, 2.1: 14–23.

Hitchcock, M. and I.N. Darma Putra. 2007. *Tourism, Development and Terrorism in Bali*. Aldershot: Ashgate.

Hōmu Shō Hōdō Shiryō (Ministry of Justice, Information Materials). 2009. 'Heisei nijūnen ni okeru Nihon Kigyō nado e no Shūshoku o Mokuteki toshita "Gijuku" matawa "Jinbun Chishiki/Kokusai Gyōmu" ni kakaru Zairyū Shikaku Nintei Shōmeisho Kōfu Jōtai ni tsuite' (About the exchange of documentation in 2008 for permission to reside (in Japan) for foreigners wanting to work for Japanese companies and other establishments on the basis of having special technical skills or cultural knowledge or being international civil servants).

Hosaka, M. 2005. 'Fukushi shakai kaihatsu gaku eno hōhōron-teki kōsatsu' (Methodological discussion of welfare and social development studies). In Nihon Fukushi Daigaku COE Suishin Iinkai (COE Promotion Committee, Nihon Fukushi University) (ed.), *Fukushi Shakai Kaihatsu Gaku no Kōchiku* (Construction of welfare and social development studies). Kyoto: Minerva Shobō.

Hugo, G. 1993. 'Indonesian labor migration to Malaysia.' *Southeast Asia Journal of Social Science*, 211: 36–70.

Hugo, G. 2006. 'Forced migration in Indonesia.' *Asian and Pacific Migration Journal*, 51: 53–85.

IDB (Inter Development Bank). 2005. 'Survey of remittances from Japan.' Accessed September 1, 2008 at *http://www.iadb.org/NEWS/Display/PRView. cfm?PR_Num=52_05&Language=English*.

Iguchi, Y. 2009. 'Gaikokujin seisaku no kaikaku to aratana Ajia no keizai renkei no tenbō—Nyūkan seisaku to tōgō seisaku o kibantoshite' (New policies for foreigners and the prospects for building new economic linkages to Asia). *Imin Seisaku Kenkyū*, 1: 18–29.

Imin Hachijūnen-shi Hensan Iinkai (ed.). 1991. *Burajiru Nihon Imin Hachijūnen-shi* (Eighty years of Japanese immigration to Brazil). São Paulo: Imin Hachijūnen-shi Hensan Iinkai.

Imin Shi Kankō Iinkai (ed.). 2000. *Burajiru Okinawa Ken Imin Shi: Kasato Maru Kara 90-Nen* (History of Okinawan migrants to Brazil: 90 years since the *Kasato Maru*). São Paulo: São Paulo State Government Printing Office.

INEI (Instituto Nacional de Estadística e Informática). 2004. *Encusta Nacional de Hogares*. Lima: INEI.

Iqbal, M. 2001. 'The migration of high-skilled workers from Canada to the United States: The economic basis of the brain drain.' In W. Cornelius, T. Espenshade and I. Salehyan (eds.), *The International Migration of the Highly Skilled: Demand, Supply, and Development Consequences in Sending and Receiving Countries.* La Jolla: Center for Comparative Immigration Studies, 291–323.

Ishi, A. 1997. 'Daisotsu gishi ga 3K rodosha ni nattatoki' (When university graduate engineers become laborers engaged in dirty, difficult and dangerous work). In H. Kawai and K. Uchibashi (eds.), *Shigoto no Sōzō*, 102–139. Tokyo: Iwanami Shoten.

Ishi, A. 2003. 'Transnational strategies by Japanese Brazilian migrants in the age of IT.' In R. Goodman et al. (eds.), *Global Japan: The Experience of Japan's New Immigrant and Overseas Communities.* London: Routledge Curzon.

Ishii, Y., M. Sekine and Y. Shiohara. 2009. *Ajiakei Senmonshoku Imin no Genzai–Hen-yo suru Maruchikaruchuraru–Ōsutoraria* (The present situation of professionals who migrate from Asia: Multicultural Australia in flux). Tokyo: Kei Gijuku Daigaku Shuppankai.

Ishikawa, T. (ed.). 1999. *Nikkei Imin Shiryōshū.* Nanbeihen, Bekkan (Information book about Japanese immigrants. Supplementary Volume, South America). Nihon Tosho Center.

Jan S., Y. Bian and M. Jumpa et al. 2005. 'Dual job holding by public sector health professionals in highly resource-constrained settings: Problem or solution?.' *Bulletin of the World Health Organization*, 83: 771–76.

JICA (Japan International Cooperation Agency). 1991. *Ijūchi Gaiyō: Heisei 3-Nendo Ban* (Overview of migrant settlements: 1991 edition).

JICA. 2002–2003. *Mangrove Information Center Report.*

Johnson, J.M. and M.C. Regets. 1998. *International Mobility of Scientists and Engineers to the United States: Brain Drain or Brain Circulation.* National Science Foundation, June 22, 93–316.

Joppke, C. 2005. *Selecting by Origin: Ethnic Migration in the Liberal State.* Cambridge: Harvard University Press.

Kabpaten Badung. 2001. Peraturan Daerah Kabpaten Badung Nomor 5 Tahun 2001 tentang Penyelenggaraan Pendaftaran Penduduk.

Kabpaten Badung. 2003. Peraturan Daerah Kabpaten Badung Nomor 3 Tahun 2003 tentang Perubahan Pertama Kali Perda No.5 Tahun 2001.

Kaigai Nikkeijin Kyokai. 1988. *Kaigai Nikkeijin.* 27.

Kaigai Nikkeijin Kyokai. 1989. *Kaigai Nikkeijin.* 56.

Kajita, T., K. Tanno and N. Higuchi. 2005. *Kao no Mienai Teijūka–Nikkei Burajirujin to Kokka/Shijo/Imin Nettowaaku* (Japanese-Brazilians as faceless permanent residents: The state, markets and networks among immigrants from Brazil). Nagoya: Nagoya Daigaku Shuppankai.

Kanchanachitra, C., S. Wibulpolprasert and T. Thammarangsi. 2007. 'Gender and physician mobility in Thailand.' In L. Reichenbach (ed.), *Exploring the Gender Dimensions of the Global Health Workforce.* Cambridge: Global Equity Initiative, Harvard University, 153–83.

Katō, T. 2010. *Motto Shirō!! Watashitachi no Rinjin—Nyūkamā Gaikokujin to*

Nihon Shakai (Let's learn more!! Our neighbors: Newcomers from overseas and Japanese society). Kyoto: Sekaishisōsha.

Kawakami, I. (ed.). 2010. *Watashi mo 'Idōsuru Kodomo' Datta—Kotonaru Gengo no Aida de Sodatta Kodomotachi no Raifu Sutōrī* (I too was a 'migrant child': Life stories of children brought up between different languages). Tokyo: Kuroshio Shuppan.

Kawamura, C. (ed.). 2008. *'Imin Kokka Nihon' to Tabunka Kyōseiron—Tabunka Toshi, Shinjuku no Shinsō* ('Japan, an immigrant nation' and the theory of the coexistence of multiple cultures: The underbelly of Shinjuku, a multicultural city). Tokyo: Shōshoten.

Kelling, G.L. and C.M. Coles. 1996. *Fixing Broken Windows: Restoring Order and Reducing Crime in Our Communities*. New York: Simon & Schuster.

Kelurahan Tuban. 2000. *Profil Kelurahan Tuban 2000*.

Kelurahan Tuban, 2006. Struktur Pengurus Petugas Keamanan Desa (PKD) Desa Pakraman Tuban.

Kelurahan Tuban. 2007. *Profil Kelurahan Tuban 2007*.

Kepolisian Negara Republik Indonesia. 2005. Kebijakan dan Strategi Penerapan Model Perpolisian Masyarakat dalam Penyelenggaraan Tugas Polri: Surat Keputusan Kapolri No.Pol.: Skep/737/X/2005 tanggal 13 Oktober 2005.

Kepolisian Negara Republik Indonesia Daerah Bali Kota Besar Denpasar. 2006. Pembentukan Bantuan Keamanan Desa (BANKAMDES) sebagai Wujud Nyata Peran Masyarakat dalam Menjaga Keamanan Lingkungan.

Khaw Boon Wan (Minister of Health, Singapore). 2003. 'Old dream, renewed ambition.' Speech given at the launch of Singapore Medicine, October 20, Camden Medical Centre. Accessed February 1, 2011 at *http://www.moh.gov.sg/mohcorp/print.aspx*.

Kigyō. 1972. 'Tanomoshikō' (Rotating savings and credit associations). Zaia Nikkei kigyō shinkō kyōkai (Association for the Promotion of Japanese Enterprises in Argentina). October 11, 3.

Kikumura-Yano, A. (ed.). 2002. *Amerika Tairiku Nikkeijin Hyakka Jiten* (Encyclopedia of Japanese descendants in the Americas). Tokyo: Akashi Shoten.

Kōdo Jinzai Ukeiri Suishin Kaigi (Council to Promote the Entry of Highly Skilled Workers into Japan). 2009. 'Gaikoku kōdo jinzai ukeiri seisaku no honkakuteki tenkai o' (Toward a serious forward-looking policy for receiving highly skilled professionals from abroad).

Koike, S., M. Nakamaru and M. Tsujimoto. 2010. 'Evolution of cooperation in rotating indivisible goods game.' *Journal of Theoretical Biology*, 264: 143–153.

Kompas. 2010. Edition of November 26, 2010.

Koronia Manyōshū Kankō Iinkai (ed.). 1981. *Koronia Manyōshū* (Collected poems of the Colonia). São Paulo: Koronia Manyōshū Kankō Iinkai.

Kōsei Rōdō Shō (Ministry of Welfare and Labor). 2008. 'Ichibu jōjō kigyō honsha ni okeru gaikokujin shain no katsuyō jittai ni kansuru ankeeto chōsa' (A report on the survey of firms on the upper stock market regarding the employment of foreigners in their head offices). Accessed September 19, 2009, at *http://mhlw.go.jp/houdou/2008/12/h1208-1.html*.

Kudō, M., K. Mori, I. Santō, K. Lee and Y. Nakato. 2009. *Burajiru Nikkei*

Okinawa-kei Imin Shakai ni okeru Gengo Sesshoku (Language contact in the communities of Japanese and Okinawan descendants in Brazil). Tokyo: Hitsuji Shobō.

Kurasawa, A. 2009. 'Hinzū to Isuramu no chōwa-teki kyōzon' (The harmonic coexistence of Hindu and Muslim). In A. Kurasawa and N. Yoshihara (eds.), *Kawaru Bari, Kawaranai Bari* (Changing Bali, unchanging Bali). Tokyo: Bensei Shuppan, 69–88.

Kurata, Y. 2004. 'Nihon ni okeru gaikokujin IT gijutsusha koyō no genjō' (Report on the employment situation of foreign IT specialists working in Japan). Discussion Paper no. 217 in the series *Sedaikan Rigai Chosei ni Kansuru Kenkyu* (Research papers on adjusting the interests of different generations). Tokyo: Hitotsubashi Daigaku Keizai Kenkyūjo.

La Plata Hochi. 1970. Kotoshi wa kokusei chōsa no toshi: Zaia Hōjin jissū gaisan matomaru (A census was carried out this year: Real figures of the Japanese in Argentina have been estimated). January 22, 6.

La Plata Hochi. 1970. 'Saikin no fukeiki han-ei: "Tanomoshikō" ga dōyō' (Recent economic recession provoked unrest in 'rotating savings and credit associations'). April 30.

Laclau, E. and C. Mouff. 1985. *Hegemony and Socialist Strategy: Towards a Radical Democratic Politics*. London: Verso.

Lan, P-C. 2006. *Global Cinderellas: Migrant Domestics and Newly Rich Employers in Taiwan*. Durham: Duke University Press

Lansing, J.S. 2006. *Perfect Order: Recognizing Complexity in Bali*. Cambridge: Princeton University Press.

Lingkungan Pesalakan Tuban. 2006. Registest KIPS dan STPPTS 2006.

Lyons, L. 2007. 'Dignity overdue: Women's rights activism in support of foreign domestic workers in Singapore.' *Women's Study Quarterly*, 35(3–4): 106–122.

Maeyama, T. 1972. 'Tomato to konpyūta engi' (Tomato and computer luck). *Koronia Bungaku* (Colonia literature). São Paulo: Koronia Bungakukai, 18: 112–131.

Maeyama, T. 1983. *Imin no Nihon Kaiki Undō* (The movement of migrants to return to Japan). NHK Shuppan.

Maeyama, T. 1990. 'IV. Imin-teki shōsū minzoku Nikkeijin (Burajiru)—Chūkan mainoritī no mondai' (IV. Migrated ethnic minorities: Japanese (in Brazil)—The issue of the middleman minority). In T. Ayabe (ed.) *Bunka Jinruigaku Tokushū Sekai no Shōsū Minzoku* (Cultural anthropology special series, Ethnic minorities of the world). Academia Shuppankai, 208–221.

McKenzie, E. 1994. *Privatopia: Homeowner Associations and the Rise of Residential Private Government*. London: Yale University Press.

Mangrove Information Center. 2002–3. *Solid Waste Management Survey in Desa Pemogan Denpasar City-Bali*. JICA.

Marshall, T.H. and T. Bottomore. 1950. *Citizenship and Social Class*. London: Pluto Press.

Massey, D. and F. García España. 1987. 'The social process of international migration.' *Articles. Science*, 237(4816): 733–738.

Masuda, Y. and T. Yanagida. 1999. *Peru: Taiheiyo to Andesu no Kuni* (Peru:

The nation with the Pacific and the Andes Mountains). Tokyo: Chūō Kōron Shinsha.
Matloff, N. 1998. 'Debunking the myth of a desperate software labor shortage (Testimony to the U.S. House Judiciary Committee on Immigration).' Accessed September 19, 2009 at *http://www.cs.ucdavis.edu/~matloff/itaa.real.pdf.*
Meerman, J. 1979. *Public Expenditure in Malaysia: Who Benefits and Why?* New York: Oxford University Press for the World Bank.
Michalowski, M. 1991. 'Foreign-born Canadian emigrants and their characteristics, 1981–1986.' *International Migration Review*, 251: 28–59.
Ministry of Justice (Japan). 1990. *Kokusai Jinryū*, 7.
Ministry of Justice. 1994. *Shutsunyūkoku Kanri Gyōsei no Genjō to Tōmen no Kadai* (The present situation and issues regarding the administration of immigration control). Tokyo: Ministry of Justice.
Ministry of Justice. 2000. *Dainiji Shutsunyūkoku Kanri Kihon Keikaku* (The Second Basic Immigration Control Plan).
Ministry of Justice. 2004. *Shutsunyūkoku Kanri Nenpō* (Annual report of immigration control). Tokyo: Ministry of Justice.
Ministry of Justice. 2009. 'Heisei nijūnen ni okeru nihonkigyō eno shūshoku o mokuteki toshita gijutsu matawa jinbunchishiki, kokusaigyōmu ni kakawaru zairyūshikaku ninteishōmei shokōfu jōkyō nitsuite' (The number of visas issued for engineers and specialists in humanities and international services for Japanese companies in 2008). Accessed July 1, 2011 at *http://www.moj.go.jp/PRESS/090714-2-1.pdf.*
Ministry of Labor. 1999. *Daikuji Koyō Taisaku Kihon Keikaku* (The Ninth Basic Employment Measures Plan).
Mita, C. and K. Horisaka. 1986. 'Dai 13 shō Nihon to Burajiru' (Chapter 13 Japan and Brazil). In M. Yamada (ed.). *Gaisetsu Burajiru-shi* (Brazilian history in outline). Tokyo: Yūhikaku, 261–282.
Miyajima, T. and H. Ōta (eds.). 2005. *Gaikokujin no Kodomo to Nihon no Kyōiku—Fushūgaku Mondai to Tabunka Kyōsei no Kadai* (Foreigners' children and Japanese education: The challenge of the non-attendance problem and the coexistence of multiple cultures). Tokyo: Tokyo Daigaku Shuppankai.
Moran, M. 1991. 'The frontiers of social citizenship: The case of health care entitlement.' In U. Vogel and M. Moran (eds.), *The Frontiers of Citizenship*. London: Macmillan, 32–57.
Mori, K. 1998. 'Sengo ni okeru Okinawa kei imin no esunikku shokugyō toshite no kusutūra (hōseigyō)—Midoruman mainoriti heno michi' (The sewing industry as the ethnic occupation of Okinawan imigrants into Brazil in postwar years: Paths to the middleman minority). Sanpauro Jimbun Kagaku Kenkyūjo (Centro de Estudos Nipo-Brasileiros) (ed.). *Jimbunken* (Japanese-Brazilian study. No. 1), São Paulo: SENB, 43–55.
Mori, K. 1999. 'Burajiru kara no Nikkeijin dekasegi no Jūgonen–Kanryū-gata Iju toshite no "Dekasegi"' (Fifteen years as a Japanese-Brazilian migrant worker: Circulating between residencies). *Latin American Report*, 16(2): 2–13.
Mori, K. 2006. 'Burajiru no Nihonjin to Nihongo (kyōiku)' (The Japanese and the Japanese language (education) in Brazil). *Kokubungaku Kaishaku*

to Kanshō (Japanese literature interpretation and appreciation). Tokyo: Shibundō, 71(7): 6–47.
Morokvasic, M. 1983. 'Women in migration: Beyond the reductionist outlook.' In Phizacklea (ed.), *One Way Ticket, Migration and Female Labour*. London: Routledge and Kegan Paul.
Morokvasic, M. 1984. 'Birds of passage are also women.' *International Migration Review*, 18(4): 886–907.
Murata, Akiko. 2009. 'Fukugengo jokyo ni okeru burikoraaju ga imi suru mono –Kōgakukei no futatsu no kyōdotai ni okeru jirei kara' (The meaning of bricolage in multilingual situations: Case studies of two communities in engineering science). *WEB-ban Riterashiizu*, 6(2): 1–9.
Na Ranong A., V. Na Ranong and S. Jindarak. 2009. *Thailand Medical Hub: A Research Report in Thai Bangkok*. Thailand Development Research Institute
Nagabuchi, Y. 2006. *Bari, Shūkyō, Kokka* (Bali, religion, state). Tokyo: Seidoshya.
Nagano, Y. 2008. 'Kōsaku suru esunishiti to dentō-teki seikatsu yōshiki no kaitai' (Intertwined ethnicity and the dissolution of the traditional lifestyle). In N. Yoshihara (ed.), *Gurōbal Tsūrizumu no Shinten to Chiiki Komyuniti no Hen'yō* (Advancing global tourism and the transformation of local communities). Tokyo: Ochanomizu Shobō, 289–360.
Nagano, Y. 2009. 'Esunishiti to ijūsha' (Ethnicity and migrants). In A. Kurasawa and N. Yoshihara (eds.), *Kawaru Bari, Kawaranai Bari* (Changing Bali and unchanging Bali). Tokyo: Bensei Shuppan, 146–165.
Nago Urawakai en la Argentina (ed.). 1994. *Kyū Nago-chōjin Aruzenchin Ijūshi* (History of the immigration of Nago-chōjin in Argentina). Club Nago.
Nakai, S. 2005. *Shakai Gengogaku no Shikumi* (The workings of sociolinguistics). Tokyo: Kenkyūsha.
Nakamura, K. 2006. 'Kaikaku ki Bari no chihō media' (Bali's local media in the period of reform). In T. Sugishima and K. Nakamura (eds.), *Gendai Indonesia no Chihō Shakai* (Local communities in modern Indonesia). Tokyo: NTT Shuppan, 285–315.
Nakato, Y. 2007. 'Burajiru ni okeru Nihongo kyōiku no aratana chōryū: Burajiru shakai ni hirakareta Nihongo kyōiku e' (A new current in Japanese language education in Brazil: For Japanese language education open to Brazilian society). *Okayama Daigaku Bungakubu Kiyō* (Bulletin of the faculty of letters, Okayama university). Okayama: Okayama Daigaku Bungakubu, 47: 85–98.
Naradha, ABG Satria (ed.). 2004. *Ajeg Bali: Sebuah Cita-Cita*. Denpasar: Bali Post.
Nekby, L. 2004. 'The Emigration of Immigrants, Return vs. Onward Migration: Evidence from Sweden.' Accessed at *http://ideas.repec.org/p/hhs/sunrpe/2004_0007.html*.
Nihon Imin Gojūnensai Iinkai (ed.). 1958. *Kasato Maru* (The first immigrant carrier Kasato Maru). São Paulo: Nihon Imin Gojūnensai Iinkai.
Nihongo Fukyū Sentā (ed.). 1990. *Kyōshi-yō Shidōsho 1: Kaitei 1, 2, 3, Nihongo de Hamashimashō* (Teacher's handbook 1: A revised version 1, 2, 3, let's speak Japanese). São Paulo: Nihongo Fukyū Sentā.

Nippaku Bunka Fukyūkai (ed.). 1961–4. *Nippon-go* (Japanese), vol. 1–12. São Paulo: Nippaku Bunka Fukyūkai.

Nomoto, K. 1969. 'Burajiru no Nihongo' (Japanese in Brazil). *Gengo Seikatsu* (Language life). Tokyo: Chikuma Shobō, 219: 67–75.

Nordholt, H.S. 2005. 'Bali: An open fortress.' In *Bali, Narasi Dalam Kuasaan: Politik & Kekerasan di Bali, I Ngurah Suryawan*. Yogyakarta: Ombak, xiv–xxiv.

Oshiro, T. 1986. *Nanbei no Uchinanchu Keieisha ron*. Japan.

Ōta, T. 1959. 'Burajiru hōjin no gengo seikatsu' (The language life of the Japanese in Brazil). *Gengo Seikatsu* (Language life). Tokyo: Chikuma Shobō, 97: 64–70.

Pachanee, C. and S. Wibulpolprasert. 2006. 'Incoherent policies on universal coverage of health insurance and promotion of international trade in health services in Thailand.' *Health Policy Plan*, 21: 310–318.

Pachanee, C. and S. Wibulpolprasert. 2007. 'Trade in health services in the ASEAN context.' In C. Blouin, J. Heymann and N. Drager (eds.), *Trade and Health: Seeking Common Ground*. Montreal: McGill University Press, 151–66.

Paurisuta Shinbunsha (ed.). 1958. *Koronia Gojūnen no Ayumi* (The fifty years of the Colonia). São Paulo: Paurisuta Shinbunsha.

Phua, K.H. 1991. 'Privatization and restructuring of health services in Singapore.' Institute of Policy Studies (IPS) Occasional Paper no.5, Singapore: IPS

Picard, M. 1996. *BALI: Cultural Tourism and Touristic Culture*. Singapore: Archipelago Press.

Propinsi Bali. 2001. *Peraturan Daera Propinsi Bali Nomor 3 Tahun 2001 Tentang Desa Pakraman*.

Purcal J. 1995. 'Economic growth and social engineering in health in Singapore.' In P. Cohen and J. Purcal (eds.), *Health and Development in Southeast Asia*. Canberra: Australian Development Studies Network, The Australian National University, 59–76.

Putnam, R.D. 2000. *Bowling Alone: The Collapse and Revival of American Community*. New York: Simon & Schuster.

Rabobank International Asia Pacific. 1999. *Impact of the Crisis: Immediate and Long-Term Outlook for Asian Health Care Markets*. Research Consortium of Rabobank International Asia Pacific, Asia Health Ventures, and The Economist Conferences, Singapore.

Ramos, F.A. 1992. 'Out-migration and return migration of Puerto Ricans.' In G.J. Borjas and R.B. Freeman (eds.), *Immigration and the Workforce*. Chicago: University of Chicago Press.

Reisman, D. 2006. 'Payment for health in Singapore.' *International Journal of Social Economics*, 33: 132–159.

Rudnyckyj, D. 2003. 'Technologies of servitude: Governmentality and Indonesian transnational labor migration.' Paper presented at Cornell University Southeast Asia Symposium on Transformative Moments and Movements in Southeast Asia, New York.

Saito, H. and S. Iwanaga. 1996. *Toshi no Bigaku* (Aesthetics of the city). Tokyo: Heibonsha.

Saitō, H. 1960. *Burajiru no Nihonjin* (Japanese in Brazil). Tokyo: Maruzen.

Sanpauro Jinbun Kagaku Kenkyūjo (ed.). 1989. *Burajiru ni okeru Nikkei Jinkō Chōsa Hōkokusho: 1987–1988* (Report on the survey of Japanese descendant population in Brazil: 1987–1988). São Paulo: Sanpauro Jinbun Kagaku Kenkyūjo.

São Paulo Prefecture. 2010. 'Mapa adaptado do original publicado na homepage da Prefeitura de São Paulo' (Original Map published on the homepage of São Paulo Prefecture, 2010). Accessed September 29, 2010 at *http://infocidade.prefeitura.sp.gov.br/index.php?sub=mapas&cat=3& titulo=Território&subtit= - Mapas&mpgraf=1.*

Satō, T. 1957. *Burajiru no Fūmi* (Brazilian flavor). Tokyo: Nihon Shuppan Bōeki Kabushikigaisha.

Sawa, M. and T. Minamino. 2003. 'Gurōbarizeeshonka no zainichi Indojin shakai' (Indian society in Japan in a globalizing era). In S. Akita and T. Mizushima (eds.) *Gendai Minami Ajia 6–Sekai Shisutemu to Nettowaaku* (Modern South Asia, vol. 6, The world system and networks). Tokyo: Tokyo Daigaku Shuppankai, 347–367.

Saxenian, A. 2002. 'Brain circulation: How high skilled immigration makes everyone better off.' *The Brookings Review*, 20 (10): 28–31.

Shibu Sōritsu 50-shūnen Kinen Shi Henshū Iinkai (ed.). 2008. *Sōritsu 50-Shūnen Kinen Shi* (Commemorative issue celebrating the 50th anniversary of the branch's foundation). São Paulo, 323.

Shimabukuro, S. and T. Yonemori. 1989. 'Sanpauro daitoshiken ni okeru feira to Okinawaken shusshin feirante' (The *feira* and the Okinawan *feirante* in the São Paulo metropolitan area). *Ryūkyū Daigaku Hōbungaku Bu Kiyō Shigaku Chirigaku Hen* (Annual bulletin of the Faculty of Law and Letters, the University of the Ryukyus, history and geography edition), 32: 57–103.

Shimizu, K. and M. Shimizu (eds.). 2001. *Nyūkamā to Kyōiku—Gakkō Bunka to Esunishiti no Kattō o Megutte* (Newcomers and education: On the difficulties surrounding school culture and ethnicity). Tokyo: Akashi Shoten.

Soethama, G.A. 2004. *Bali Tikam Bali*. Denpasar: Arti Foundation.

Stasiulis, D. and A.B. Bakan. 1997. 'Negotiating citizenship: The case of foreign domestic workers in Canada.' *Feminist Review*, 57: 112–139.

Sudibia, I.K. 2005. 'Kondisi sosial ekonomi pekerja migran nonpermanen asal Jawa Timur di daerah perkotaan.' *Dinamika Kebudayaan*, 7(1): 1–13.

Suryawan, I.N. 2005. *Bali, Narasi Dalam Kuasaan: Politik and Kekerasan di Bali*. Yogyakarta: Ombak.

Sutawan, N. 2006. *Transformasi Sistem Irigasi Subak*. Denpasar: Wayan Windia.

Tanno, K. 2007. *Ekkyō suru Koyō Shisutemu to Gaikokujin Rōdō* (The system for transnational employment and the foreign worker). Tokyo: Tokyo Daigaku Shuppankai).

Temasek Review. 2010. 'Two out of three doctors in Singapore are "foreign-trained."' Accessed January 12, 2010 at *http://www.temasekreview. com/2010/01/12/two-out-of-three-doctors-in-singapore-are-foreign-trained/.*

Ten, S. 2005. 'Nihon no gaikokujin kōdo jinzai dōnyū seisaku to Zainichi Chūgokujin–Chūgokujin IT gijutsusha ni taisuru jittai chōsa o chūshin ni'

(Japan's policy for bringing in highly skilled professionals and Chinese living in Japan: Some findings from a survey of Chinese IT specialists). In *Chūgokukei Ijūsha kara Mita Nihon Shakai no Shomondai* (Some of the challenges of Japanese society as seen by Chinese expats living in Japan), issued by Shakai Anzen Kenkyū Zaidan (Research Foundation for a Safe Society), 67–138.

Thränhardt, D. 1999. 'Closed doors, back doors, side doors: Japan's non-immigration policy in comparative perspective.' *Journal of Comparative Policy Analysis*, 12: 203–223.

Toyota, M. 2007. 'Medical tourism: The cases from Thailand and Singapore.' In S. Yamashita (ed.), *Cultural Studies on Tourism*. Tokyo: Shinyosha, 155–160. (In Japanese.)

Toyota, M. 2011. 'Singapore strategies on medical tourism development.' CLAIR Forum March, 33–35. (In Japanese.)

Tsuda, T. (ed.). 2009. *Ethnic Return-Migrations Around the World*. Palo Alto: Stanford University Press.

Tsuda, T. 2002. 'From ethnic affinity to alienation in the global ecumene: The ethnic encounter between the Japanese and Japanese-Brazilian return migrants.' *Diaspora*. 101: 53–91.

Tsujimoto, M. 2000. 'Imin no keizaiteki tekiō senryaku to ippan kōkan ni yoru kyōryoku kōdō: Buenosuairesu ni okeru Nikkeijin no keizaiteki kōshudan' (The economic adaptation of migrants and the cooperative behavior by generalized exchange: The rotating credit association of Japanese migrants in Buenos Aires). *Japanese Journal of Social Psychology*, 16: 50–63.

Tsujimoto, M. 2006. 'Aruzenchin ni okeru Nikkeijin no tanomoshikō: Ippan kōkan ni yoru keizaiteki tekiō senryaku' (Rotating credit associations of the Japanese in Argentina: Economic adaptation by generalized exchange). *Qualitative Research in Psychology*, 5: 165–179.

Tsujimoto, M. and A. Kuda. 2010. 'Aruzenchin Nikkeijin no seikatsu-shi' (Life history of the Japanese in Argentina). Paper presented at the 64th conference of the Tohoku Psychological Association.

Tsukazaki, Y. 2008. *Gaikokujin Senmonshoku/Gijutsushoku no Koyō Mondai–Shokugyō Kyaria no Shiten kara* (The dilemma of employing foreign specialists and technical workers: A perspective focused on their career development). Tokyo: Meiseki Shoten.

Turner, B. 1990. 'Outline of a theory of citizenship.' *Sociology*, 24(3): 189–217.

UNDP. 2009. *Human Development Report 2009, Overcoming Barriers: Human Mobility and Development*. New York: Palgrave Macmillan.

Urry, J. 2000. *Sociology Beyond Societies*. London: Routledge.

US Department of Justice. 1998. 'Japanese Latin Americans to receive compensation for internment during World War II.' Accessed September 1, 2008 at *http://www.justice.gov/opa/pr/1998/June/276.htm.html*.

Van den Berghe, P. 1981. *The Ethnic Phenomenon*. New York: Elseviar.

Vickers, A. 1989. *Bali: A Paradise Created*. Singapore: Periplus.

Vickers, A. 2003. 'Being modern in Bali after Suharto.' In T.A. Reuter (ed.), *Inequality, Crisis and Social Change in Indonesia*. London: Routledge Curzon, 17–29.

Wako, S. 1939. *Bauru Kannai no Hōjin* (Compatriots of Bauru). São Paulo: Nippaku Shinbunsha.
Watabe, I., E. Suzuki and APFS. 2007. *Zairyū Tokubetsu Kyoka to Nihon no Imin Seisaku* (Japan's immigration policy and the granting of special permission to stay in Japan). Tokyo: Meiseki Shoten.
Waters, M. 1990. *Ethnic Options: Choosing Identities in America.* Berkeley: University of California Press.
Wibowo, I. 2003. 'Neoliberalisme dan warganegara' (Neoliberalism and citizenship). In I. Wibowo (ed.), *Neoliberalisme.* Yogyakarta: Cindelaras.
Widnyani, N. and I.K. Widia. 2002. *Ajeg Bali Pecalang dan Pendidikan Budi Pekerti.* Surabaya: SIC.
Xiang, B. 2007. *Global 'Body Shopping': An Indian Labor System in the Information Technology Industry.* Princeton: Princeton University Press.
Yabiku, M. 1988. *Burajiru Okinawa Imin Shi* (A history of Okinawan migration to Brazil). São Paulo: Okinawa Kenjinkai.
Yamada, A. 2009. '"Haiteku imin" kenkyū josetsu' (An introduction to research on 'high tech immigrants'). *Hitotsubashi Hōgaku*, 8(2): 47–72.
Yamashita, A. 1993. 'Yarinaosu Nihongo ichi shian (Burajiru Nikkei Nihongo gakushūsha taishō): Hanashi kotoba wo chūshin ni' (A draft plan for relearning Japanese (for Japanese-Brazilian Japanese learners): Centering on spoken Japanese). Kōza Nihongo kyōiku (Japanese language education course). Tokyo: Waseda Daigaku Nihongo Kenkyū Kyōiku Sentā, 28: 131–141.
Yarwood, R. 2007. 'Getting just deserts? Policing, governance and rurality in Western Australia.' *Geoforum*, 38: 339–52.
Yoshihara, N. 2010a. *Fluidity of Place: Globalization and the Transformation of Urban Space.* Melbourne: Trans Pacific Press.
Yoshihara, N. 2010b. 'Gurōbaru ka to komyuniti—yuragu kyōkai to orutanatibu no kanōsei' (Globalisation and community: Swinging boundaries and potential alternatives. *Hesutia to Kurio* (Hestia and Clio), 9: 19–32.
Yoshihara, N. (ed.) 2008) *Gurōbaru Tsūrizumu no Shinten to Chiiki Komyunitī no Hen'yō* (Development of global tourism and changes in local communities). Tokyo: Ochanomizu Shobō.
Yoshihara, N. 2008. 'Aru Isuramu komyuniti' (A certain Islam community). In N. Yoshihara (ed.) *Gurōbal Tsūrizumu no Shinten to Chiiki Komyuniti no Hen'yō* (Advancing global tourism and transformation of local communities). Tokyo: Ochanomizu Shobō, 143–165.
Young, J. 1999. *The Exclusive Society: Social Exclusion, Crime and Difference in Late Modernity.* London: SAGE Publications.
Zenpaku Kyōiku Kenkyūkai (ed.) 1954. *Zenpaku Jidō Sakubun-shū* (Collected compositions of Japanese children in Brazil). São Paulo: Zenpaku Kyōiku Kenkyūkai.
Zmegac, J.C. 2005. 'Ethnically privileged migrants in their new homeland.' *Journal of Refugee Studies*, 18(2): 199–215.

Index

adaptation 123–4, 129, 132–4, 136, 160–1, 163, 178–9, 188–9, 198, 238–9
Ajeg Bali 81–2, 91, 102–3, 106–7, 116–20, 234, 236–7
articulation 106, 119

Balinese 61, 64, 67–70, 72–3, 77, 79, 82–3, 90–2, 94–5, 97, 102, 107, 115, 117–18, 234–7
banjar adat 90, 94, 114, 236–7
banjar 67–70, 81, 90, 93–4, 99, 113–15, 117, 119, 233, 235–7
batik 66–7, 69, 71–7, 80–1, 234
bilingual 205
body-shopping 8
bombing 62–3, 70, 74, 76, 81–4, 118
Brazil 6–8, 10, 14, 17, 23, 122–3, 125–8, 134–5, 138–9, 141–3, 146, 149, 150–5, 157–60, 163, 176, 179, 181–4, 187–8, 190, 211–31, 238–41, 243
bridge engineers 8

China 26, 30, 35–6, 40, 47, 230
Chinese 9, 31, 52, 76, 139–40, 157, 179, 232
circular migration 10–11, 22
see also migration
citizenship 27, 40–1, 56–7, 177–8, 180, 183–4, 233
collective action 165

collective will 119
community policing 84–90, 97, 104–5, 237
contract labor 5–6

dekassegui 7, 122, 133, 135, 157–60, 213, 229, 241, 243–4
descent 124, 126, 151, 178–83, 185, 190, 226, 229–30, 240
development 5–8, 11–12, 15, 18, 21, 24–7, 29–30, 33, 37, 43, 45, 61–2, 83, 89, 97, 105–7, 110–11, 113, 115, 117–22, 124, 132–3, 135, 139, 141, 143, 146, 152–4, 156, 158–61, 175, 177, 195, 207, 226–7, 232–3, 235, 236–7, 240, 242
domestic migrant workers 51, 232

early study abroad 204, 242
educational resources 200
enclave formation 135, 141, 143, 145–6, 153, 160
ethnic community 122, 124, 133, 159–61, 177, 189, 207, 242–3
ethnic resources 200
ethnicity 59, 85, 176–80, 184, 187, 233, 238

family network 182, 198, 203–4, 207–9

feirante 130, 132–45, 150, 152–3, 157, 160, 238–40
free-rider 165

gajah mada road 107–11, 113, 115–20, 235–6
global tourism 61, 64, 70, 83, 110–11, 117–18, 236
globalization 24, 27, 38, 91, 120, 195, 204, 230, 237
go-between 19
governance 105–7, 116, 117, 119–21, 235

hardware 130, 132–5, 141, 146, 148, 150–6, 158–60, 238
health 24–38, 43, 243
healthcare 24–31, 33–8, 43
hierarchy of states 40
highly skilled professionals 3–5, 22–3
Hindu 61, 67–71, 73, 81–3, 90–1, 93–7, 118, 233–4, 237

ID card 62–3, 66–7, 70, 76, 79–81, 233
immigrant 56, 84, 85, 89, 91, 92, 94, 95, 101, 103, 104, 105, 120, 123, 147, 163, 164, 165, 168, 176, 177, 179, 180, 181, 188, 189, 190, 195, 196, 197, 198, 203, 204, 205, 207, 208, 209, 210, 211, 212, 215, 216, 217, 218, 219, 220, 221, 222, 223, 224, 228, 229, 230, 231, 241, 242, 243
immigrant communities 212, 215, 216, 220–4 *see also* migrant communities
immigration 4, 10, 17, 22, 23, 89, 124, 126, 127, 128, 148, 158, 161, 163, 168, 178, 179, 180, 182, 183, 184, 191, 195, 207, 212, 213, 215, 216, 219, 222, 223, 226, 232, 238, 239, 243
immigration policy 4, 22–3, 178–80, 183–4, 191
immigrant workers 94, 190, 217, 219 *see also* migrant workers
indirect hire 7
Indonesia 24, 26, 29–30, 35–6, 39–42, 44–7, 50–7, 61–3, 78, 82–3, 85–6, 88–91, 101, 103–5, 107, 110, 232–3
informal training systems 124, 150
involution 135, 150, 153–4, 160

Japanese 3–8, 10–15, 17–23, 26, 87–88, 122–4, 126, 128, 133, 136–40, 146–7, 153–5, 158, 160–1, 161, 163– 4, 165–92, 196–203, 205–6, 211–31, 239–44
Japanese immigrants 122–24, 136–7, 140, 146, 163–5, 168, 177, 179–180, 211–12, 211–12, 215–22, 224, 229–31, 241
Japanese migrants *see* Japanese immigrants
Japanese in Brazil *see* Japanese-Brazilian; Nikkeijin
Japanese language education 225–230, 244
Japanese-Brazilian 6, 8, 10, 14, 17, 146, 153, 155, 160, 187, 211–12, 219, 224, 227–8, 231, 243

Javanese 66–7, 75, 79, 82, 92, 102, 234, 236

KIPEM 62, 66–7, 70, 76, 79–80, 92, 117–18, 233, 236
Korean 179, 195–209, 230, 242–3

language contact 217, 220, 230, 243
language shift 212–13
local human resources 201
local security 84, 86, 97, 99, 102
Lombok 62, 67, 77–8, 80, 82, 108, 233

Malaysia 24–30, 35, 37, 39–40, 44, 45, 48, 50–2, 77–8, 232–3
medical 24–38, 85
migrant communities 212, 215–6, 220, 221, 222–4
see also immigrant communities
middle class 26, 30–1, 34–5, 38, 52, 135, 161
migrant workers 39–40, 42–8, 50–5, 62, 77–8, 80–1, 83, 94, 190, 217, 219, 232–3
migration 1, 3–4, 6, 9–11, 17, 22–4, 39, 43–4, 54, 59, 89, 122, 124, 126–9, 138, 148, 158, 161, 163, 168, 170, 176–85, 188, 191–2, 195, 198, 207, 212–13, 215–16, 219, 222–3, 226, 232, 238–9, 241–3
migration policy 4, 22–3, 179–80, 184
military service 203, 205, 242

mother's family network 198, 209
Muslim migrants 61, 69, 71–3, 76, 81–3
mutual cooperation 163, 174

nationalism 86, 95, 97, 103–4, 223, 237
negotiated citizenship 56
newcomer Koreans 196
Nikkeijin 122–3, 179–81, 211–14, 220–9, 243

Okinawa 124–130, 132, 136, 139, 141, 146–8, 151–3, 156, 158, 161, 163, 168, 182, 220–1, 238–40
Okinawan migrant 124–9, 132–41, 143, 145, 149–51, 155, 161, 238–9

pastel 123, 130, 134–5, 137–43, 145–6, 150, 156, 160, 238–9
peer selection 173–5, 241
Pemogan village 61, 64, 66–70, 72, 76, 79, 81, 83, 233, 234
Peru 163, 176, 181–3, 186–7, 189–191, 242
Peruvian 179–92, 241–2
Philippines 24–5, 35–7, 39–40, 46–7, 50–2, 232
police 84–92, 97, 98, 103–5, 109, 141, 234–5, 237
policing 84–92, 97, 104–5, 237
post-'development' 119, 235
see also development
privatization 25, 27, 29, 31
professional 3–5, 9, 22–4, 35–6, 129, 132–5, 143, 160, 187, 190

remittance 40, 44–7, 50, 79, 232
return-migration 179, 181, 184–5, 191, 241
returning home 181, 197
risk 15, 39, 85, 111, 120
rotating savings and credit association 163

self-defense organizations 103–4
self-employed business strategy 122, 133–5, 141–3, 150, 154–5, 157–8, 160, 239
sewing niche 143, 145–6, 149
Singapore 24–33, 35–8, 40, 44–5, 48, 52
Singaporean 28–30, 35, 38
solidarity 175
South America 176, 179, 181–2, 186, 188, 191
South American 163, 176, 178–9, 182, 184, 190, 230, 241
subak 71, 75–6, 81, 234
surveillance 84–5, 105, 140, 235, 237
systemic disadvantage 43

Taiwan 26, 39, 44–5, 48, 52, 230–2
tourism 24–7, 29–31, 33–5, 37, 61–2, 64, 67, 69–70, 81–3, 94, 101, 110, 110–11, 117–18, 153, 161, 236
tourist area 64, 94, 234
tourist district 84, 92

zero-tolerance 111